# THE COVE DIARY

ANDREW CARNE

*The Cove Diary*

© Andrew Carne

Cover images: © Alison Taylor.

Published and Printed by:
Palores Publications,
11A Penryn Street, Redruth, Kernow TR15 2SP, UK.

ISBN 978-1-906845-27-8

# THE COVE DIARY

## ANDREW CARNE

Palores Publications

# CONTENTS

# Acknowledgements

THERE ARE A number of people whom I must thank for bringing this book enterprise to fruition; you may just want to throw rotten fruit at them.

First of these was the less than adoring public who demonstrated, by mistakenly opening the website page, that someone was actually reading The Diary. Then there were the contributors, either willing or else, not forgetting our, now famous, International Correspondent who was about the first to openly 'come out' as a reader. Also the Aged Parents for foolishly providing some encouragement.

Last and certainly not least the engine-room staff: my sister, Alison, for painstakingly correcting my grammar and designing the cover; Les for putting himself in the firing line for publishing (he now has a round the clock, armed protection officer); the Missus who said she wouldn't leave me on this occasion but woe betide should I produce another and, of course, the bleddy hound for providing material when all else failed.

# *Introduction*

YOU MAY BE wondering why you are even bothering to open the dust cover on this, the daily ramblings of a struggling shopkeeper buried in a rather remote corner of West Cornwall.

Well this introduction isn't going to help you. Why should it? Presumably you're old and wise enough to make up your own mind whether to part with your hard earned shillings to actually buy this book: (Hah! He has the temerity to call it a book); or perhaps you already have, at which point it's too late; or if you are particularly astute you're reading someone else's copy, possibly in a doctor or dentist's waiting room so I hope it goes well for you.

Now, if you have had a momentary loss of reason and actually purchased a copy, I can reveal that all the content has already been published for free on the Internet. Go on; feel free to give yourself a good kick in the shin. However do not despair. By having a copy in the flesh, as it were, you do not need to find a free hot spot, or a computer that your offspring is not using to order the latest mobile phone on your credit card; nor do you, having found a spare screen, have to continually scroll up and down pages, the ones on the Internet being in reverse chronological order. Lastly, of course, the volume can be used to light fires, prop the leg of a wobbly table or extract the pages to practice your expertise in origami.

There are over 365 entries, so that's a bonus for a start, as there was a bit of a stuttering start and obsessive writing didn't kick in until 30th March. Not all the entries refer to life in The Cove either: I do get out on occasion, you know. However I can assure you that each entry is deeply researched, finely tuned to respect the laws and structures of English literature (or, at least it does now after my good sister had a go at it) and firmly based on, at least the mere gossamer of truth.

I should reserve a paragraph, (no, actually a very long sentence), to thank those fine and upstanding souls who, through no fault of their own, forced themselves to read the Diaries as they appeared, almost in real time, and through emails and, in at least one case, personal visitation, to contribute to some of the themes herein. No doubt deserving of your sympathy for finding any sort of succour in the semi-literate witterings of a broken purveyor of beachside paraphernalia I can assure you that all proceeds from the sale of this book will be in no way supportive of this small band of dedicated readers. They can already afford the luxury of a web connected computer for heaven's sake.

I should also thank those poor unwitting contributors who did so through word or deed. Should you be one and hap upon a copy of this tome I sincerely trust you don't recognise yourself, as the reference is most likely to be less than complimentary. So perhaps this isn't the best time to point to the rider that any reference to persons living or otherwise is completely coincidental.

I trust that by now I have sufficiently lowered your expectations regarding the content of this edition such that the humblest scribblings of a small illiterate child would provide some entertainment. If not I must draw your attention to the small print that has inexplicably been excluded from your copy that states that refunds will not be considered.

# March

*March 16th – Tuesday* – Bunch of fishermen on the beach this morning. None had a bucket and spade so we can only surmise that they were fishing. Asked one surly chap what he was fishing for. He muttered something about a 1970's haircut and wondered off – won't be asking him again.

First student trip of the year descended upon us. About fifty teenagers piled into the shop for camera batteries and sweets. We were mindful of the locust effect but, contrary to common opinion, there are some good young 'uns out there still. Got rid of all the pasties too.

*March 18th – Thursday* – Stepping outside the comfort zone today, trip to Hayle. Now one of the benefits of such a lengthy sojourn is that Hayle is the home of some of the best shop bought pasties in the western world. Philps (probably the best) and Hampsons (a close second) beat the backside off anything west of St Ives.

Oh and actually managed to get some work done – cash & carry! Although these days its more cash for rather less carrying.

*Tuesday 17th – Wednesday* – Couple of chaps turned up this morning and started using a large blowtorch on the RNLI shop steps; a severe method of weed control perhaps? No the steps now sport a fancy yellow line denoting the edge of each step. Handy that.

*March 19th – Friday* – Fishermen getting their boats and pots ready for the new season down by the wharf first thing this morning; all that work just ahead of a week of heavy swell.

*March 20th – Saturday* – Since nothing else happened it is probably time to share a rumour concerning our local taxi man who shall, of course, remain nameless; sitting in Treen pub chatting away to a slightly unkempt stranger sharing a few short beers and tall tales. Locals looked on in awe as our local man was completely oblivious that he was cementing a friendship for life with Mr Johnny Depp.

Look out for the new Pirates' film where Johnny will be doing a passable impression of a West Penwith taxi driver.

*March 21st – Sunday* – Lifeboat exercise this morning. Impromptu meet up with the Culdrose helicopter and a meeting with the new Tamar Lifeboat for Appledore.

Not long after recovery the Lifeboat was launched again for a yacht caught up on some crab pots North of Pendeen. Appledore got there first but Sennen Cove was launched, (the first for City of London III), in case the yacht needed a tow. It didn't and Sennen Cove was recovered before 5pm.

What an exciting day!

*March 22nd – Monday* – Miserable start with The Cove full of mizzle and occasionally something heavier; but in the afternoon the sun came out with a clear blue sky.

At just about low water there was a fair few wetsuited bodies down on the beach. Had to do a double take but a view through the binoc's confirmed our first shorts only dip of the year. With a sea temp of around 9°C that's brave or downright foolhardy.

*March 23rd – Tuesday* – Rain stopped play.

Lone gannet flying west; loaded with folklore portent, that: Possibly one less gannet in the East?

*March 24th – Wednesday* – Rain again.

Couple of scaffolders turned up this morning to set up along the eastern wall of the Lifeboat Station. "Er, what time's high tide, mate?" "Put it this way, you're going to get your feet wet if you start now". Start now they did. Feisty lot those scaffolders.

A couple of hours off high water noticed that nasty rip from last year is back roughly in the same place.

Small school of dolphins playing in the surf starting in front of the chip shop and moving out towards North Rocks.

*March 25th – Thursday* – Rained again.

This was particularly poignant as it was befitting my grey mood having been kicked in the nadgers by the Government increasing cider duty unreasonably. How come, if the duty is so little currently, is it so naffing expensive at the bar? Someone's making a bob of two.

*March 30th – Tuesday* – The more astute among you will notice the lack of entries for the last few days. You will only need two words to understand the lack of other writing in this gap. It rained!

Today a bitterly raucous wind doth blow. And verily did it bloweth last night taking with it our wheelie bin that we had forgotten to tie down.

And lo did the sunshine break through and glow all around – still bleddy freezing though.

*March 31st – Wednesday* – Gusting to 67mph last night, (thanks John C. for the info).

Bit late this news but we now know that G and DJ will be taking over The Old Success Inn from May sometime. Expect Brains bitter at the bar and leek soup day in day out.

# *April*

*April 1st – Thursday* – Ah, not a half bad day today! A few more hardy souls have made it through the bad weather up country to be here. Hope they're not too upset by the prospect of a weekend of pretty awful weather.

*April 2nd – Friday* – Felt like a Saturday all day today. The only thing keeping us grounded was the price of newspapers. Better weather than advertised too other than the cold breeze blowing up the kilt.

Main man at the OS said my bottled cider was going from £3.50 to £3.70 in the very near future. For a tax rise, meaning 3p at the pump, these guys are taking the Michael. Why are they trying so hard to kill off the OS we wonder?

My mate that said, "don't care how much it costs as long as they don't stop making it", never saw this coming, I'm sure. I'm signing the pledge Monday . . . maybe.

*April 3rd – Saturday* – Grey and a little bit wet, but not as bad as advertised again; managed to keep most people away though.

The gear outside, (nets, windbreaks and balls), was just drying out nicely when it decided to piddle down just before closing. Nice!

*April 4th – Sunday* – My, my, clear blue skies, bit breezy but lots and lots of lovely faces.

Lifeboat launched for training at a reasonable hour to give the gathered flock a bit of entertainment.

Now the tale of the stray dog: old golden lab wandering around all day this end of The Cove; caused a bit of a stir, begging from customers at the café, so they called in the RSPCA – who strangely didn't want to know. Neither did the cops and the Council wasn't answering at all, apparently.

I did suggest a length of rope and a large brick would sort the problem from the end of the breakwater, but I was out voted. Eventually our local bobby came up with an out of hours' number for the Council. Their solution was for us and a neighbour to take him up to Joppa Farm, (local kennels).

Turns out the old boy was chipped so hopefully back with his owners real soon.

*April 5th – Monday* – I know this is going to get me into hot water – but heck, when it's already six inches above your head another inch isn't going to hurt.

Mums and dads with wild and errant children: no, it really isn't acceptable that your offspring throw balls at each other; scat dinosaur eggs off the shelf and pull the wings off fairy figurines.

No, they're not expressing themselves. They're turning the toy corner into a version of Gaza strip on a bad day. This is called being naughty and requires some positive parental action.

An unconvincing, "Don't do that Johnny!", isn't going to work. You know it isn't. Look, a cuff round the 'ear 'ole, (modern day equivalent, of course), doesn't turn you into Tomas de Torquemada, (head bloke, Spanish Inquisition), or, if you're squeamish, a firm escorting out of the shop isn't going to bring you Most-Awful-Parent-of-the-Century award. Honest.

What's more it will bring you our undying gratitude.

*April 6th – Tuesday* – Pretty much wet and grey all day. While still a few people around it's somewhat difficult to even make up stories about today.

*April 7th – Wednesday* – Golly Gee Willikins: sunshine!

Bit of a cold wind blowing in from the North-West but nevertheless a cracking day, spoilt only by a major disaster: the kettle broke, taking all the electrics out upstairs. Blow the electrics – no coffee. It's off to PZ for a new kettle asap.

One thing we've never seen before: Magicseaweed© has reported, "No incoming swell" for Friday, Saturday and Sunday. Watch out there'll be a lot of bored surfers around this weekend. We're getting some more beer in, prompt.

*April 8th – Thursday* – More sunshine than you can shake a stick at and hardly any breeze. What a joy to behold!

Some of the fishing fleet have gone out today. Just seen BG come back sporting some 'ansum sized pollock, line caught, of course.

Music down the OS tonight too – apparently a mix up on dates as he should have been there Friday. Nice to see they're trying to liven things up down there. Dropping the prices would work better!

*April 9th – Friday* – Bit of a chill breeze flowing through this morning, but hey that sun's still shining through so who cares, right?

Bunch of youngsters on the breakwater this afternoon clearly contemplating jumping off; all looked at each other nervously. Who would be the first? Add a girl with a camera into the mix and, hey presto, instant bravery. One of them goes in – followed after a leaden pause by the other three. Behind every great man is a female with a camera-phone and access to YouTube and three other soft ha'peths waiting to get into his shoes.

Here's a curious thing, a foreign gentlemen came to the shop to ask what time the next "white" bus was back to PZ. He'd bought a return ticket and had tried to go back on the "green" Western Greyhound that shares the same route with First Bus Group but they wouldn't honour his ticket.

Now it seems to me that things are tough enough and we could use getting as many visitors down here as possible. You wouldn't think it rocket science to get the two groups to have some sort of reciprocal agreement, now would you? They have a timetable each for the same route too.

*April 10th – Saturday* – Another cracking day with that chilly eastern breeze.

Had a chat with an end-to-ender setting off this morning; put me in mind of a couple of gals doing the same thing last week. They apparently had left three months for the job which is probably just as well. They had reached The Cove from LE and spent about an hour downing some breakfast. Hard work that first mile . . . every journey begins with just one step.

Walking back from the F&L last night across back of Esther's Field and a really clear night. The stars, indescribably beautiful. Just thought you'd like to know.

*April 11th – Sunday* – Well you could almost do the, 'Phew, what a scorcher", bit today but for that persistent cooling wind from the nor' east quarter.

Nevertheless it's a good day for budgies in The Cove. You wouldn't believe the number of cuttlefish, (or at least their pumice-like carcasses), down the bottom of the long slip and on the harbour beach.

Lifeboat out twice again this Sunday, once for training, once for real – moored rib round by Tol Pedn needed a pull back to Newlyn.

*April 12th – Monday* – That nor' easterly (gone SE for a while today) is really starting to bite a bit. Shame really with that much sunshine about – still find a sheltered spot and you should roast quite nicely.

Why is it so desperately important to have a newspaper twenty minutes before we open (8:30am since you ask)? Imagine up country you can get one at sparrow fart. Down here things are a little slower. We are, when we're open, the most westerly newsagent in the country and by the time our papers arrive the sparrow's most likely deflated.

The supermarkets in PZ get theirs a little before us if you're up for the twenty mile round trip. Even they don't open 'til 8am on Monday though.

*April 13th – Tuesday* – What on earth happened today? It just seems to have come and gone.

I can vaguely remember people coming and going in the shop, the chill wind from the morning evening out a little and a bit of sunshine going on.

Ah, that was it! Paid a few bills this morning – enough to traumatise anyone, that.

Now that her mates are out and about just around the corner, the dog thinks she can do a runner to go and see them when she wants. She's taken to sitting on her perch, just inside the doorway, where she can see everything going on. Means she's not tethered down any more, see.

Bread! There must be a sod's law of bread ordering. Brown was in vogue last week so you order more, obviously. Yep, selling more white now. The demand for bread A is inversely proportional to the amount of bread B ordered.

*April 14th – Wednesday* – Must have been an indoor event day today; quiet as the grave down in The Cove this morning. Bit of cloud and a little chilly might have had something to do with it.

Managed to forget to place both my milk and bread orders last night; luckily we are blest with suppliers who know we did mean to order and deliver anyway – mostly they're spot on too. Thanks chaps.

*April 15th – Thurdsay* – It's not only the passing of years that marks the passage of time for us.

The number of repeat customers that visit The Cove year after year are legion.

With many, it's a quick nod of recognition and some, it's a lengthy conversation on what's new in each other lives. It's very much like a snapshot in the family photo album as it's generally a whole year since we saw them last. Children particularly change so much in a year. Where once you could have given Johnny an affectionate pat on the head, now a step ladder is required if you'd care to risk it, as the head now tops a rugby player frame.

And it's surely never been a year that we last saw the Lifeboat Station's flagpole that's now been faithfully restored.

We're told that tonight the sunset should be a cracker. Icelandic volcanic dust that has stopped the nation's air traffic is likely to set off the average sun dipping to something quite spectacular, we hear.

Nice though it was, spectacular it wasn't.

*April 16th - Friday* – Another sparkly clear day again, with that knicker rattling breeze cutting in from the east.

Signs that The Cove is emptying out as families go home after the end of the Easter break; still a fair few around though.

Talking of flags and poles, (see yesterday,) we've had a few comments about ours. The poor old flags of St Piran hanging from our shop front are starting – no let's be brutally frank – have long been looking a little tattered, thin and sad. Let's face it they are over six years old and have seen a lot of action.

I have defended them against somewhat critical comments. After all the battle-scarred and crumbling flags from the Crimean War hanging in some military connected cathedrals are gazed upon with awe. I've had similar aspirations for ours, but am beginning to concede that perhaps they do need replacing.

The problem I have is this, Parrs, the flag makers, have moved up country to some god-forsaken corner of the Industrial North; somewhere beyond Launceston for heavens sake. How can we, in all honesty, fly a flag of St Piran woven in some Black Country satanic mill? I mean no offence to satanic mills and all that; nobody would really sniff at a really good quality flag of St George made in Warwickshire.

My deep search of the internet throws up no alternative so I think we'll have to bite the bullet, needs must and all that. Perhaps I can have them blessed by our friendly Cornish Bard who pops up down here once in a while. Maybe that would salve my conscience.

Now just remains what to do with the old ones; can't really just stuff them in the bin. Anyone know of any local cathedrals that are in need of some ancient flags that have flown at the forefront of battle through six summers of visitor invasions?

*April 17th – Saturday* – The last of the Easter visitors preparing to leave this morning; an army of children big and small collecting magazines and sweets for the journey ahead; no doubt a scene to be repeated many times in the coming months.

Bit more hazy today with some fluffy white clouds about and still the breeze from that eastern quarter.

The beach is really quite spectacular in sunshine like this and a fair number of people taking advantage. I imagine that it's pretty much sheltered down there.

Looks like quite a deep channel has appeared halfway between the lifeguard hut and the beach; full of water way ahead of the tide. That might cause a few issues later on in the summer if its still there.

*April 18th – Sunday* – A cracking good day for celebrations today, in fact for anything.

Someone just asked if the vintage bus was running today. Well, the first thing I thought was, if it is running they kept it pretty much clouded in secrecy, much like their timetables. The second thing I though was, gosh – you mean they have older buses than what they currently run the service with? Extraordinary!

Lifeboat was out on exercise again this morning. While last week we exercised with Penlee, this week we hosted the Penlee Mechanic. Is this the start of a foreign exchange programme we wonder?

There was a fast rubber boat out in the bay with a chap hanging off the back at the end of a piece of string; part of the preparations for the Sennen Cove Olympic 2012 wave board team, no doubt!

*April 19th – Monday* – We're all rather excited here in The Cove. You're unlikely to hear this from elsewhere as it's a bit hush, hush. However, being independent and having a laissez faire attitude to red tape, we can reveal all.

The Lifeboat, due to the fact that it can be covered by its flanking stations, has been put on standby to rescue stranded travellers on the continent. Rumour has it we could be sent as far down as Santandar and the navigators are currently working out re-fuelling stops. The boat can take on at least fifty people at a time in reasonable comfort, more at a push. Not sure the bar will be stocked as they'd like though.

I also understand that some of the larger fishing boats out of Newlyn are going to give it a go. Of course they will have to be careful of their quotas as they might have to throw some back!

*April 20th – Tuesday* – "Careful with that axe Eugene."

Avoiding the tumbleweed along Cove Road, ventured into the metropolis today. Ok call it PZ if you will but it's as exotic as it gets around here. Anyway the main purpose, other than to pick up some fancy pants for the RNLI do, was to get some timber for some shelving.

Now for those of you who know me, the words timber and shelving are seldom used in the same sentence, unless used in conversation with a professional and are then normally followed by the exclamation, – "How much?" But titter ye not. The worm has turned. Most people's mid life crisis consists of buying a Harley, leaving the wife, or failing that, kicking the dog. Now I can't ride a bike to save my life and the wife would kill me if I tried either of the other two. No this dog is having his day making stuff.

Laughter and derision cascaded off my mallard like back. I wielded tools, yes, real tools, like a saw, power drill, jig saw and even a sharpened pencil. I came shining through at the end of the day, seeing off my many detractors and leaving a perfectly stable, robust shelf albeit having had to replace the original screws that were too short. So ya-boo sucks to the lot of you.

But I digress. My sojourn to the great sprawling conurbation saw me fearlessly enter the premises of a well known builders merchants. Armed with my measurements and list of nuts, bolts and screws I flew across the shelves like someone who knew what he was doing, until I came to get the wood.

Now you have to understand that the place is filled with burly workmen, sporting wife-beater vests, tattoos and muscles like tug boats. There was at least eight staff in the shop/office and at least the same number of swarthy types in the wood yard behind. All looked capable of digging big holes with kangos, constructing whole buildings with bare hands and a big screwdriver. I felt diminished and unmanned in such company.

In fear and trepidation I joined the queue. I practiced my order, a two metre length of 2 x 1 and a three metre length of 1 x ½ etcetera, I needed to sound confident to match up to these giants of men. Then my turn came. I took a great breath and reeled out my requirements.

The big man narrowed his eyes. Had I given myself away, said the wrong thing? No. What I got was,

"Sorry mate, we're not allowed to cut wood – insurance, you know."

It was lucky Pink Floyd wrote that tune when they did. "Don't even think about picking up that axe, Eugene, my lad, until you have taken the course – manual axe handling for the slightly mentally disturbed, £200 down the job training centre – and while you're about it give the man from the Pru' a call and make sure you're covered in case you slice off your thumb or get caught for a hefty lawsuit for de-tailing the neighbour's cat."

Just wouldn't have been the same, would it?

*April 21st – Wednesday* – Bit more high level cloud today giving a kind of dull feel and the return of the chilly breeze which has really taken the edge off a bit.

However, first thing it wasn't half bad. Bread delivery came early so had some time to take the dog down the beach. It's so good to see the fishing fleet coming and going and even more particularly when one of them offers you a nice couple of ray for your tea.

The Mother-in-law loves a bit of skate and it's about the only fish the Father-in-law will eat, probably why she loves it. Me, I have fish rarely as the wife hates fish, but these boys look young and sweet and I thought," I'll have one of they".

Now the thing about ray is they take a bit of work to make ready. First you have to remove the wings from the body. First time I did this I made a real hash of it, until Big J gave me a quick lesson and thereafter it's been a synch.

But despite several words of advice, taking off the skin is still an elusive skill that I've been unable to master. For those of you that have no experience in this area let me explain. The skin is like rough sandpaper. In fact years ago that's exactly what it was used for – could have saved me a couple of quid had I known yesterday I'd have these.

Secondly the whole fish is covered in the most clingy slime ever imaginable. It doesn't wash off and even dunked in cold water for a while, is still like holding a bar of wet soap with your elbows.

And last, have you ever tried removing a sticking plaster while wearing mittens covered in olive oil? Well, let me tell you that's a piece of cake compared with trying to rip the skin off a ray wing.

Once done and cooked nicely it's a lovely bit of fish, almost worth all the effort. My mouth was already dribbling around the corners thinking about a nice little creamy Cajun sauce, bit of veg and some sweet new potatoes.

Mother-in-law telephoned last night and I thought nothing much about it until I heard, "Mum says thank you for the fish you got her."

Beans on toast tomorrow, then.

*April 22nd – Thursday* – Read in the paper yesterday a couple of likely lads have set off from Falmouth in a couple of kayaks set to go with the sun around Britain. They were in the Harbour Car Park this morning getting ready for the next leg.

Most mad cap, hair-brained, life risking and unproductive schemes of this nature tend to have a fair amount of publicity surrounding them, mainly because the loony fringes that sponsor these people need their pound of flesh.

No, the thing that struck me most about this sojourn is that it's self funded. They're doing something life-threateningly daft with their own money. Good luck lads.

Follow their progress at gonepaddling.co.uk

*April 23rd – Friday* – Still a bitter wind blowing through The Cove this morning.

Out in the bay the gannets have given way to at least a dozen terns out there. Wonderful to watch them plummet into the water. Well it must be their tern I guess.

You never see one on their own, have you noticed? It's because one good tern deserves another.

These birds are known to take drugs and there isn't one tern left unstoned.

Thankfully in the afternoon the gannets came back. I haven't got any jokes about gannets.

*April 24th – Saturday* – First overcast day for a while and still a bit of a chill wind, but change is on the way.

The weather didn't affect a perfectly nice naming ceremony for the new Lifeboat though. Everyone we've spoken to says that it was a well rounded and appropriate do and everyone thoroughly enjoyed the day. Even the four launches and recoveries in the early evening for donors' families seemed to flow smoothly.

Then after it was almost all over it rained.

*April 25th – Sunday* – After the excitement of yesterday today seems rather ordinary. Even the tumbleweed is back.

*April 26th – Monday* – Early mist today has given over to a rather pleasant day; much warmer than of late without that nasty easterly blowing in.

Nevertheless we have seen more life evenings down the OS of late than here in The Cove today.

*April 27th – Tuesday* – Another funny tumbleweedy type of day; however we did have a coach visit which does happen from time to time.

Up to last year we had suspected a conspiracy of sorts. A coach would turn up and spew out its disparate load. All, without exception, would cross to the other side of the road and walk on past on their way to Lands End – not so much as a postcard or fridge magnet would leave the shop.

Now, however, it would appear that The Cove has found favour with the coach parties. They stop and look and actually buy stuff, albeit a 15p postcard but at this time of year that's a windfall.

We suspect coach driver concessions at Lands End have ceased.

*April 28th – Wednesday* – It was on the News yesterday; they had a BBC satellite van up there recording the passing. We shall no more be distracted, bemused or simply left shaking our heads in disbelief on our way to Lands End or for that matter as we leave it.

For some they were weird totems of another age; for others a highlight of public modern art. And for some a bleddy eyesore and waste of money – although it should be said, for a change, it wasn't public money shed.

Yes, the artful carvings, which apparently took four years to create and were littered along the stables field hedge on the A30 towards Lands End have been removed. The artist and erector, Rory Te'Tigo, said it was due to him finding out his insurance didn't cover him to have them there.

It clearly took him a while to find out as the articles have been there for over four years.

*April 29th – Thursday* – This is a bit grim. There's wet stuff falling out of the sky. Even the tumbleweed hasn't been bothered to show up or, at least, roll by.

The swell's on the increase and there's mist most mornings. Must be gig weekend over on Scilly.

At last our van is empty again having been stuffed full, for the last few weeks, with the ex contents of our loft. The dusty articles have been sitting idle in our loft since we moved in over six years ago and the consensus of opinion being that if they hadn't been used for that long we, in all probability, didn't actually need them. Though the consensus was brutally extracted through hours of careful negotiation of whose was what and the level of importance of each item strongly contested.

The wife managed to get rid of a good proportion of it a couple of weeks ago at the Rosudgeon car boot – a pretty grand affair by all accounts. This still left most of the van stuffed with books, clothes and the normal weird stuff you wonder how you ever came into possession of.

Faced with the option of another crack at the car boot we opted for the apparently easy way out of taking it to a charity shop. Did I say easy way out?

Despite having telephoned ahead, the first port of call apologised for not having sufficient space to take all of the load. Unwilling to argue with a lady whose displacement between neck and midriff demanded more attention than I care to admit, I followed her direction to a second establishment that refused anything at all and the third only a couple of boxes.

Given I had to go to the cash & carry for a van load, said van needed to be emptied.

So any really needy charity shops reading this here's a tip. St Erth, (optimistically called a recycling centre), last skip on the left if you're quick.

*April 30th – Friday* – I was going to do a rather punchy satire on how teachers across the country are rushing out to buy dumbbells for their desks for much the same reason that the Government is buying Trident. But then the Daily Mail ran it as a front cover piece and that rather put me off.

Fortunately a chance meeting with my stool pigeon on the venerable Parish Council dropped something of a hot tuber in my lap or would have, had I been sitting down at the time.

It came hot on the heels of today's news that, due to the fact one of their helo's is in dry dock, British International may be flying out of Lands End Airport, (actually its official designation is airdrome but who am to split follicles on this auspicious occasion?), to better service the increased traffic for the gig race.

Someone with a much better imagination than mine had decided that The Cove would be the ideal spot for a terminus for the Isles of Scilly Steamship Company. It would slash the best part of an hour off the journey time and improve no end its carbon boot print.

For a start The Cove is unlikely to mount a sustained defence in the form of a "Friends of Sennen Cove". This, on the basis that a) there's only three men, two women and a dog who actually live here and b) they are generally pragmatic types and know a scheme with a few bob in it for them when they see it.

There also needn't be any moaning and whinging about old things being adversely affected by building works. Sure there are old things here, most of them are down the pub on Friday night, but even old things were new once. The Round House and a sizeable chunk of Tinker Tailor would have to go, but surely you can see they've had their day and a well-placed plaque, "On this spot . . ." would serve to engender the imagination of the flocking travellers as they passed by. A two hundred metre breakwater and pier running from the Harbour Car Park out across the Cowloes to dock the Scillonian III will instead one day be an historical monument for certain.

Granted the visitors in Velandreath may kick up a bit of fuss initially at the four lane road that's penned to service the new port, as it will run past their front doors. But you can hardly take into account the views of a few dozen visitors that are only here for a couple of weeks and half the year at that anyway.

The fishing fleet I hear you gasp, bum boats I retort. Some retraining would be required but what more stirring sight can you imagine than the Scillonian breaking the horizon and a flotilla of gaily decked punts rushing out to her selling nick knacks and exotic turnips over her gunnels.

Sennen Cove must rejoice in this momentous occasion and welcome the full force of the winds of change and the new era of prosperity laid out before us.

And to those few misguided detractors I can only quote that paragon of forward thinking, Lee Iaccoca, (who so lacked imagination he nicked it from Thomas Paine), "Lead, follow or get out of the way".

# May

In the news: *A lift in a Newquay hotel plummeted 80ft to the beach level. No one was hurt. Harbour authorities in Hayle have banned water sports from the estuary on the premise that they may interfere with shipping.*

*May 1st – Saturday* – The heavy rain we were promised never materialised. However little men in red shorts popped up on the beach today together with their gaily coloured flags to put on the beach. Hope they can restrain their heavy use of the colour red this year as it does so spoil the mood.

They are often seen whizzing up and down the beach on their quad bike. You'd think for a bunch of fit chaps they'd be running up and down the beach – in slow motion, of course.

*May 2nd – Sunday* – Big breeze kicking in today and it doesn't half rattle the Lifeboat Station doors.

No less than five windsurfers and two kitesurfers out in the bay, which is rare for down here. Presumably they're refugees from Hayle Towans where I understand sail sports have been banned.

Make the most of it guys. Once the thought police get wind of it they'll be down with their prohibition notices faster than a Newquay lift.

*May 3rd – Monday* – Looks like we'll have this northerly draft all week although the sun's trying hard to take the edge off a bit.

Another windsurfer out there flying in the face of authority; it could be Tiananmen square all over again. All he needs is a couple of carrier bags but I suppose the SAS, (that's the chaps against sewerage and plastic bags not the ones that shoot you), would have him then.

In this breeze the chaps fair spin across the waves. Difficult to say, but it's got to be thirty to forty knots, perhaps some knowledgeable soul can enlighten me. What gets me most, and it's the same with the kite surfers, is that they manage the same sort of speeds going into the wind. Come on, that's got to be against nature, that has.

*May 4th– Tuesday* – We, down here, are often the antithesis of what's going on in the rest of the world.

While the rest of the country's airspace was empty of all but a cloud of ash, we still had planes flying around; the rest of the country is gripped by election fever, we in contrast haven't seen a politician down here since William Pitt came down for a spot of surfing. (Go on, prove he didn't!). Even our election flyers are delivered by the postman.

No surprise then that our local watering hole, run by some faceless bureaucracy up East is still pushing out microwave mush, while the rest of the county is trading high on local produce and hand crafted meals. I know it looks good on paper, but believe us, when we say it doesn't look good on the plate and most of the visitors down here are a little more discerning than you take them for.

Still, happy news in a letter we received today: we have attracted another reader – must introduce you both someday.

So Mrs VP I think we can satisfy most of your shopping list, though a passer by had the last of our stock of St Levan lark's tongues.

## *May 5th – Wednesday –*

> *Here from the world I win release*
> *Nor scorn of men, nor footstep rude,*
> *Break in to mar the holy peace*
> *Of this great solitude.*

Our mate Lewis must have been standing on this very spot and could have been, this very day, when he wrote that. It's no wonder he started seeing fluffy white, long eared creatures with pocket watches and caterpillars smoking a hookah pipe. He'd probably have been tempted to a drag or two himself if he'd had to run a shop in Sennen Cove at the moment.

And if that were not proof enough that he was here, this should clear the matter up, "Shall the poor transport of an hour/Repay the years of sore distress." There you go, he came down by bus!

We tip our caps to you Mr Carroll.

*May 6th – Thursday* – Mr Picasso turned up yesterday to complete the painting of the front of the shop. He's been waiting for a dry spell and by some amazing shuffling of his priorities he missed it by about a week. I did tell him if he turned up it was bound to rain. I hate being right all the time.

A digger has been down the big beach today, moving rocks around ahead of the big influx, hopefully starting at the end of the month. And you thought that the big rock that appeared just where you put the last peg of your windbreak was there by nature's design. Nope, some bloke with a tractor put it there.

Now for a stream of consciousness that has absolutely nothing to do with the subsequent paragraph: self-serving, money grabbing, leeching, out of the real world, work-shy, ivory tower dwelling, lying, untrustworthy, users.

Now, it's off to watch the election results.

*May 7th – Friday* – The Lifeboat launched at quite short notice today to show support for three fund-raising kayakers paddling around the coast. They were due to spend the night here before trekking out early morning.

On arrival, some chap rolled up and wrote them out a cheque for 300 nicker. Kerrr-ching, I thank yow! Which is quite amazing on two counts: One, they've hardly started yet and two, they found someone in The Cove.

Well I think that's it for today, can't think of any other momentous event worthy of note today.

*May 8th – Saturday* – That east wind has crept back in today while we weren't looking. All I can say is my Cornish kilt is staying in the cupboard for now.

Read in the paper a couple of days ago that they've just finished the repair of the coast path up by Zennor, by putting in the old stone clapper bridges. That's roughly a geet granite slab resting on a pillar each side of the water. Clearances were so tight that they called in a couple of shire horses to drag the pillars down there. The capping stone was winched in using a 1950's tractor. All sounds like great fun.

Today the paper covered an article about the history of the St Austell brewery. The beer's still made in an 1893 mash tun and their Tribute beer was first brewed for the eclipse and was called Daylight Robbery – now, come on, you know I'm not their most ardent fan but only the most crass of commentators would draw attention to the appropriateness of the name and the pricing policy down the OS.

With the price of diesel, though, we might get a few pence off a pint if St Austell took a leaf out of the coast path team's book and delivered their brew by dray drawn by those magnificent shire horses.

*May 9th – Sunday* – All Quiet on the Western Seafront.

"Do you hear that Jenkins?"

"Sir?"

"Do you hear anything, Jenkins?"

"No, Sir, not a thing. Quiet, ain't it?"

"Yes Jenkins. Quiet. Too damn quiet for my liking."

Both listen to the wind whistling through the windbreak stand. An uncomfortable silence falls between them. Jenkins breaks first.

"What was it like in the old days, Sir?"

"Hard to say, Jenkins, seems so long ago; might have been back in the last lot. My God you should have seen them. Wave after wave of them, turn around and there was another one, out flanked and outnumbered. Didn't have to pick them off in ones and twos then, lad. No, they came to you. Queues of them back to the end of the shop they were."

"Wait! Look, over there, just passed the bus stop over there."

"I see it Sir. Just within range. I think it's a lesser spotted visitor, Sir. Shall I pot it Sir?"

"Don't be a damn fool, Jenkins. They're rarely seen on their own. Let loose at that one and a whole coach load could be round the corner. You'd just frighten them off!"

"Right, Sir."

"Steady lad, don't jump until you see the whites of their eyes, Jenkins."

"Do you think ee's heavily armed, Sir?"

"Doubt it, lad. Back in the big one in '03 they were coming at you with Louis Vuitton purses the size of handbags. These days you'd be lucky to see one with much more than a razer wallet or a pocket of loose change."

"Ok, check your equipment, Jenkins: bone china mug with seaside images, good for an opening volley, that, lad; framed print of the beach, Sennen Cove tea-towel, bags of clotted cream fudge and a dozen sticks of rock."

"What's this down your trouser leg, Jenkins? Beach parasol? Don't think you'll be needing that today, lad."

"Now don't forget, if all else fails you still have your 15p postcard strapped to your ankle. They never expect the 15p postcard."

"Ok, now's your chance, Jenkins. Remember what I taught you, keep up-wind and make sure the sun's at your back. Tally ho, Jenkins."

"Right Sir, I'm going in. Tally ho, Sir."

Some little while later . . .

"Jenkins, Jenkins, you all right lad?"

"It's all right, ir. It's just a flesh wound."

"Just take it easy, lad. Medic. MEDIC"

Sir lights a fag and slips it between Jenkins' lips.

"How did it go, lad? Did you score one for old Blighty?"

"Sorry, Sir. Did my best, Sir. She wouldn't even have a bloody postcard, Sir."

"It's all right, Jenkins. Don't try and talk. We couldn't ask any more of you. It goes like that sometimes, the swines. Shop keeping is hell."

"Jenkins."

"Yes, Sir"

"Undo the top button of your housecoat. You've earned it."

"Really, Sir? Thank you Sir."

*May 10th – Monday* – Well it turned out a bit busier today despite a still bitter wind blowing in from the NE corner.

You know it doesn't matter how well you think you have all the angles covered there's always something that will come up and bite you on the bum.

Today's nether parts nibble came from a coach load of German visitors all wanting to send Sennen's best views on a postcard back home. It's only after the 30th 'eine pound Frauline' that you realise you've run out of European airmail stamps. Whoops!

Still every cloud and all that: one of our venerated fisher-folk popped his head around the door armed with a rather splendid lobster – claws like those American baseball gloves. Shell's a bit soft which means it won't make it to market. 'Twill make it in short order to our pot, however.

Oh, how we suffer down in The Cove!

*May 11th – Tuesday* – Here's a tale of joy for you.

We have to, from time to time, replace various display stands as they become defunct or, in the case of our metal windbreak stand, rust beyond repair.

Now, I know that Cornwall Council are less than helpful when it comes to business waste disposal, but I thought I'd give them a go first, just in case things had changed under the shiny new One Council regime.

At first glance the CC website pointed me at Business Link because, "the Council works in close partnership with local support agencies". So I called Business Link who promptly told me to call the Council, but couldn't actually find the correct number but gave me a best guess.

Thus armed, I gave it a shot. The very nice lady on the end of the blower had to ask someone, but in short order told me it was nothing to do with them; they definitely couldn't help. "Not even a word of advice?" I enquired. "Talk to your commercial waste management company", they offered.

It's no wonder that so many people take the easy option and heave their rubbish off the nearest cliff.

Nice to know that our esteemed Council, whose enormously expensive re-organisation was supposed to improve service immeasurably, is so much behind local business in the county.

So, onto our contracted waste management company to whom we pay a substantial amount each year to dispose of our waste. Each year we have to complete a complicated form ensuring each party is aware of its responsibilities under the Act and that I'm aware that the company holds the relevant waste disposal licence.

So what was their advice? Well for starters they didn't want to send down their truck, as the items we have might upset the machinery; so if I wouldn't mind phoning a "man with a van" or taking it to the local tip. Well I wouldn't mind if both options weren't illegal, assuming that the man in the van didn't have a waste management licence. And if he did that would make him a waste management company and I've already got one of those although they can't take my waste away.

Write to my local MP? Last time I did that he promised his support then must have locked himself in the toilet while the voting was going on as he was written down absent according to the public whip website.

(In order to avoid a long and drawn out letter from said MP, (again, I might add), stating that he did nothing of the sort and was present and did his level best for me and the website is wrong or I read it wrong I retract the previous statement.)

The thing is if you're going to have a law that says you can't get rid of your rubbish any old how at least have some means available so that people can get rid of their rubbish without breaking that law.

At the moment it looks like I'm stuck with the items forever or must look for a dark night at the top of Pedn-men-du.

Stop Press! The woman at our waste management company, who it has to be said has tried her utmost to be helpful has come back with a solution. They can send down a flat bed truck to take away the stands. It'll just cost the odd 120 quid, oh, and can I help load the truck please?

Really can't understand why people fly-tip when such easy and cost effective solutions are available.

PS. The lobster was lovely.

*May 12th – Wednesday* – Bit of a non-descript day today little bit of sun, little bit of cloud and a couple of spots of the wet stuff here and there.

Definitely an increase in the number of our foreign friends sweeping through The Cove though. Mainly German thanks to the Rosamund Pilcher effect – Ros you lovely girl, you – but a few other nationalities too.

Got the chance to exercise a little of my schoolboy French in the afternoon. But since I haven't been a schoolboy for quite some time I suspect I may as well have been speaking Italian.

Nom de plume, mange tout!

*May 13th – Thursday* – Absolutely, stonkingly beautiful day with a big blue sky and all day sunshine. Let's hope for many more.

Now you'll love this. On the face of it not much to do with The Cove but I just had to share this with you. It was in the WMN yesterday and it's a corker.

This chap, Alex Hartley, spends some time wandering around the Arctic, as you do, noting how much ice has melted due to the fact a bunch of British politicians have been jetting all over the country telling us how good they are.

The receding ice has permitted him to discover a new island that man has not set foot on in thousands of years, if ever. He's called it Nowhere Island. Now come on. If you discovered an island you'd name it after you, wouldn't you? Unless you had a really tittersome name in which case you'd name it after your favourite dog or something.

Now Alex is a bit of an artist, which probably explains the naming issue, and he's had this blinding flash of inspiration. Why not dig up the island, put it on a barge and tout it around the south coast as an art installation. Simply brilliant.

Quite surprisingly the plan has not met with universal joy. Somewhat unbelievably the Norwegians, in whose waters the island lies, are a little reticent about letting some English bloke dig up their otherwise useless bit of gravel and take it away. I've nothing against the Norwegians but that is a little bit petty, don't you think? He has promised to put it back, you know.

At least not all involved are philistine art haters. The 2012 Cultural Olympiad Programme has dropped him a half million quid for the project, and quite right too.

So, Mr Hartley, if you're reading this highly respected online diary I have the solution. What we have to do is replace their island with one of ours. Down here in The Cove we have two islands, one of which is covered up half the time – wouldn't be missed hardly at all. What I propose is that we bag it up, lump it onto a barge and loan it to the Norwegians while you take theirs on its grand tour.

I know this fella who's a bit handy with a hammer & chisel; we'd have it bagged up in a jiffy. All you have to do, Mr Hartley, is have a little word with the 2012 Cultural Olympiad Programme and ask them to drop me down a cheque. Half a million should just about cover it.

## May 14th – Friday –

*When I meet the morning beam*
*Or lay me down at night to dream*
*I hear my bones within me say*
*"Another night, another day.*

Well this is it! This is the last day! The final time I shall write 4 in the first column of a form that asks for my age, the final time I shall write this column in the bloom of my youth.

*When shall this slough of sense be cast,*
*This dust of thoughts be laid at last,*
*The man of flesh and soul be slain*
*And the man of bone remain?*

So very depressing talking about this very day in a man's life when thoughts may turn to the morbid end of the mortal coil.

But, au contraire, my friends, actually I feel quite chipper. And why should I not be? Let's be brutally frank about it. I still have my all my own teeth, well maybe not all, those that I have are my own, well actually I do have one crown.

Most of the essential bits still operate, albeit with some assistance from modern medicine; which is something to crow about given the punishment they've received through 49 years of various forms of abuse.

Ok, there's not much in the way of hair, at least not on my head. However that started deserting me at 23 so one can hardly blame the advance of years. Ironically while the follicles on the pate diminished those elsewhere took up the slack with Odyssian tenacity.

And although the synapses now fire up like a British Leyland motor on a cold morning they do still fire up. I do suspect the wiring a little these days but mental agility was never a strong point. And anyway those that listen to my witterings don't seem to care and those that care stopped listening years ago.

So by the time you read this I will have passed into the other half of the century and taken my stunning good looks and lightning wit with me; both so hard to disprove over the internet.

So, on reflection, as I suck on my pipe and my wife rubs liniment into my back, I've ridden the last 49 years on the crest of a wave.

Another fifty? Bring it on.

*May 15th – Saturday –* Well you couldn't have had a nicer day for a birthday today ending with a lovely big blue sky.

Mr TG thoughtfully laid on a Lifeboat launch and sitting outside the station was like a mini furnace.

Now it's off up the F&L for a bit of a nosebag and perhaps a celebratory snifter or two.

Oh and thank you all for your lovely cards, kind (ahem) words and telegrams.

Next time just throw money!

*May 16th – Sunday –*

> *Shot? So quick, so clean and ending?*
> *Oh that was right, lad, that was brave.*
> *Yours was not an ill for mending,*
> *'Twas best to take it to the grave.*

Always thought that he was talking about a homosexual born in a less understanding era until I woke up this morning; now I'm sure he was talking about the morning after an excess at the F&L on a Saturday night.

Send for my revolver and a large gin & tonic!!

Actually I nicked that from a chap who's much cleverer than I, but it was so suitable and I did enjoy the joke so the first time.

And frankly that took me all my strength today.

No more 50th birthdays, pleeease.

*May 17th – Monday* – First: Happy Birthday, Sis. Always find an entry in the diary worth more than a thousand cards – cheaper too, eh?

Bright and sunshiny start to the day but decided to cloud over a bit in the afternoon. Mercury rising, definitely with that easterly breeze consigned to history, we hope.

It must be summer in the wings; basking sharks sighted off the starboard bow and one of them quite a monster.

Which leads me onto a Freedom of Information request that some bright spark decided to fire off at the Navy. "Do you chaps have any records of sea monsters?" Can just see a world-worn Commander dropping his furrowed brow into his hands in bleak despair. Once upon a time questions like that could have triggered a Ministry of Daft Questions. Let's hope times have changed.

And lastly a big welcome to G & D who, just today, took over the OS. Let's hope they can actually do something and not just preside over a Ministry of Daft Pubs.

*May 18th – Tuesday* – A bit of a more sedate day instead of a full on blazing sunshiny sort of day. The assembled crowd seemed a bit more sedate as well, not being stirred to appear until early in the afternoon. Do try and get here a little earlier if you would. Don't you know the sort of effort involved in getting a chap of my age out of bed in the morning?

It's quite surprising how quickly the concerned arms of the NHS clasped around my crumbling frame. I had two, yes two letters calling me to the medical equivalent of the MOT. The undertones of urgency in the second led me to spring, well move with purpose and intent, (carefully), to the telephone and book my appointment, which happened to be this morning.

I had been under strict instructions to cease any type of intake the previous evening and, worse, spurn my morning cup of tea lest I mar the results. So at 8am this morning I took my sallow and undernourished person to the Cape Cornwall Surgery.

Now, I can reveal their name, as you have no doubt guessed, as I have nothing bad to say about them. Having attended on several occasions I can confirm that they are a friendly bunch and seem very efficient; I rarely have to wait long.

And another very good reason to put these chaps on a pedestal is that they have very sharp instruments up there and many of them have the legal right to stab me with them.

Despite my heaping praises on these good people I have to sadly report that one of them this morning did indeed take up that right. Not only that but she felt it necessary to deprive me of quite a flagon's worth of my sanguine humours.

I shall think twice before responding to begging letters from them again.

*May 19th – Wednesday* – Yet another family birthday, this time the Dad's. Happy Birthday, Dad!

Good job we have something to celebrate. A day penned in by fog on all sides. Even hardy walkers plug away at it in the rain but the fog even sees them off. Can't be much fun walking without a view to look at and always a bit of a risk of falling off some unseen edge, I suppose.

It's fair to say that the rain kills business down here but the fog digs a hole and buries it.

Still I went out with a girl once in the fog, and mist. Oh, come on. Yes, it works better as a verbal gag but you would have laughed for Max Miller, wouldn't you?

The folks, lodging with us for a day or two, did all right though and bagged a sighting of a rare Roufus Turtle Dove in Porthgwarra. Yes, I wouldn't know one if it landed on my head either but they were pretty much convinced. So if you're a twitcher and about to get on a plane from Aberdeen on the basis of this report you can't blame me if it turns out to be a lesser spotted bustard.

Took a trip up Queens Arms, Botallack for a bit of a birthday meal and it is to be highly recommended. A pointless comparison to another more local grub house would be oh so petty and I won't do it I tell you. I won't, I won't.

Oh, go on then – it knocks spots off the OS.

*May 20th – Thursday* – A grand unveiling of The Cove this morning as the great blanket of fog pulled out to sea; its smoky fingers last seen clinging on in Gwenver and across the saddle of cape. Very poetic so it was.

Many more basking sharks out there today, from Lands End all the way round to the bay. And at 6.00pm about fifteen very optimistic surfers paddling around in what appears to be a ripple-less plate of glass, but hey, what do I know?

Spoke to our friendly electrician this morning who led me to believe that we could get cheaper 'lecky overnight if we just had a chat with our 'lecky provider. Great, I thought, then.

Thus encouraged I telephoned the number advertised on their website as "help" and, after selecting a random number from all the inappropriate options offered me, I eventually spoke to what passed for a human voice who sounded about twelve. The chap told me he was "Customer Service".

As it transpired he wasn't. He was, in fact, a foot soldier of Beelzebub destined to send poor souls telephoning an increasing number of helpdesks only to be given a further wrong number to call, each with its own complex suite of Interaction Voice Response (IVR) options. Regardless of the option you choose it will always be the wrong one.

One very promising chap made me wait 10 minutes listening to Cole Porter in the style of Shostakovich Jazz Suite played on Swanee kazoo before coming back and telling me the number he had for the next demon in line was an old one. Well thanks for that, if you guys don't have the right number what hope do I have?

He did redeem himself somewhat by actually phoning back with a number that I have yet to find, or perhaps lose, the mental capacity to try and call.

I am beginning to think that paying top dollar for electricity is but a small price to pay to avoid a long lingering death in the labyrinthine corridors of corporate customer service.

Wait for tomorrow's exciting episode which will be twice as long, have no end and will be utterly pointless but will have used up all the time you had set aside in which to do something useful.

*May 21st – Friday* – Wow, almost perfect weather! Did I say that easterly breeze was consigned to history . . . mmmm.

Almost every day we have someone come in and apologise profusely that they have to proffer a £20 note for a small purchase. Really it's not a problem: we have been highly trained and are very experienced in extracting £20 notes from visitor purses.

Frankly if you run a shop and can't handle someone slipping you a twenty then you really should be doing something else.

Took a trip up to Connor Downs, my Grandfather owned a farm and one of the original farm shops there, to get some shiny new window lettering for the shop that says we sell hot pasties. This is the next in a long line of, thus far, fruitless attempts to let people know we sell pasties.

On the way back went to the newer farm shop at the bottom of the hill in search of some particular mushrooms. It is a rather good farm shop, you really must go, and it relieved me of all my change although still without my mushrooms.

So I dropped by Lidl's to see if I could avoid a detour to one of the big supermarkets on the way home. Unfortunately they didn't have them either but on the way out I spotted some millionaire shortbread which is just the bee's nadgers.

Now here's the thing. Got to the front of the checkout and handed over the smallest currency I had, a twenty pound note. Now let me remind you, this is Lidl's, not a small shop in Sennen Cove. The tone was derisory, "A twenty for a 99p shortbread?"

You have to be joking, right? Lidl's. The man must be a closet bus driver, I thought. Let me just magic up 99p in change I haven't got. If I had 10p I would have done the old – "I've got 10p" – "That's not enough" – "I know that's why I gave you a twenty" routine but life's never like that when you need it to be.

So don't ever be shy in dropping us a £20 note. We'll take anything. At certain times of the year we'd be grateful for shirt buttons.

*May 22nd – Saturday* – I'm going to have to stop doing my Saturday diary on Saturday night. I have a really good time up the F&L and all sense and sensibility goes out the window.

Has to be said, though, they had the best band ever up there tonight – Devil's Creek. It's a blues rock band and, man, are they good. The lead guitarist chap is really in tune with his instrument. I know that sounds really heavy and serious but you should have been there, man.

That's a lot of 'man'.

Some serious news, though, boats in The Cove have been subject to some lowlife stealing fuel and generally creating havoc. Down at PK something similar happened last night. See, the fingers of reality even stretch down this far.

Anyway, you should have been here today; nearly as perfect as a day can be. Ended up with the first BBQ of the season with our neighbours and they are as nearly as perfect as neighbours can be.

Gosh, how gushing can a diary entry be? You just need to be here . . . man!

*May 23rd – Sunday* – Phew! What a scorcher as they say in the common vernacular although not so much around here.

What happens, we lay on a bit of sunshine, lovely bit of sea, Lifeboat launch and you guys never turned up.

Well, blow you lot, we're off down the beach.

*May 24th – Monday –* Another rip-corker of a day and this time real people showed up to enjoy some of it. Thank you.

For the first time in a while the day had a real holiday feeling about it. It took a while to work out what it was but I guess it's the start of seeing many more children around ahead of the main school holidays next week.

Resisting the urge to don a pair of shorts, still; first the darned things are in the attic and difficult to get to and secondly I don't want to go frightening off small children this early in the season.

Had a bit of a weird event around 7.00pm. A fine sea mist started building offshore. Within a short space of time it filled the bay and started climbing up Vellandreath. Then as quickly as it came, it just disappeared leaving the gorgeous evening to finish unhindered.

Odd place at times, Sennen Cove.

*May 25th – Tuesday –* We seem to be enjoying a bit of a mini-boom at the moment which is very nice. Shame the man on the radio tells us that a bit of shady weather is on the way. That's the end of that then.

The men at the Met Office are hedging their bets we see. One day the weekend looks ok and the next they change their minds and shove in a few rain clouds. It does none of us any good that. A poor forecast is just as bad as the actual wet stuff.

Shame we can't follow the Malaysian example where they get their pay docked for getting it wrong. Or the NE Asian example where they get shot!

*May 26th – Wednesday –* All change today; cloudy and cooler but not raining as the Met Office suggested yesterday and where have you lot all gone, then?

Forgot to tell you that our strawberries have arrived again for this year. They're local and very flavoursome. We had them last year for a very short time. What I mean is they didn't stay in the shop long and this year is no different. The first 10 punnets lasted less than an hour. He came back the next day with twice as many. He's a good lad. Raspberries next month.

You may have heard about the protest group who are trying to draw attention to the busy road that runs through their village. Their peaceful protest involved using the Pelican crossing as frequently as the mechanism would allow, passing across the road from one side to the other and back.

The other half of the village will be out next year protesting that the proposed by-pass cuts through their cricket ground/historic meadow/Celtic burial mound wherein resides a lesser spotted toad/three toed newt/rare grizzle wort.

It was with some amusement that I read today some wag had glued up the Pelican crossing button rendering it inoperable. That's the same chap busy planting rare grizzle wort on the nearby Celtic burial mound.

### *May 27th – Thursday* – Happy Birthday Rose.

Cool breezes taking the edge off a bit today but they dropped off towards the middle of the day; otherwise nice and sunny with a few folk around.

There was a mid afternoon Lifeboat launch that pulled in a few to watch. Managed to squeeze this in around preparations for a busy coming week.

Had a few language barrier problems this week taking a lady to our chilli beans when she wanted jelly beans and completely missing what a boosh was until they explained they wanted to go to Penzance on it.

Must stop listening in Cornish when these people are talking Northern.

### *May 28th – Friday* – As the last of the recent sunshine days shuffle away and the storm clouds gather the groundswell of weekend visitors files into The Cove. Just as the sun tanned visitors on their way out hide their titters and smug smiles behind cupped hands.

Has to be said the forecast for the next few days doesn't look encouraging.

Oh, heavens! Just seen the pigeon lorry up in the top field. They come here every year releasing pigeons to fly back to Northern Ireland. Quite unsurprisingly some of them decide that, having travelled here by ferry and artic' lorry, getting back on wing might be a bit of a fag.

Each year, after the race, we have the occasional incongruous sight of pigeons strutting around The Cove. Being somewhat domesticated they think nothing of popping into the shop and settling down on the newspapers. I came up into the flat once only to be confronted by one that had decided to drop in through the kitchen skylight. He was quite happy to be led, led mind you, not chased, to our front door.

Despite being tagged and registered their owners are less than interested in getting their navigationally challenged beasts back. After all what's the use of a homing pigeon that gets lost 500 yards from the lorry.

Ventured across the border to St Buryan this evening. They hold supper evenings in the Community House once a month to raise funds for one thing or another; volunteers young and old cook, wait and mind the bar.

At least seventy to eighty people, families, pensioners et al join in and for £6.50 you can't knock it. From the size of it my bit of fish must once have had a dorsal fin and teeth and the quality knocks spots off any local chippy's offering.

It is quite heart warming to see a community gather and pull together in such a way.

Don't get too gooey eyed now, they didn't chose St Buryan as the location for Straw Dogs completely by chance.

*May 29th – Saturday* – Bit of a curate's egg sort of day: good in parts. Now I do not need to tell you, dear reader, that when Mr du Maurier penned that he meant that the good was ruined by the bad. In fact parts of today were actually quite 'ansum. But as George probably had no idea that it would enter the common lexicon and propel him into immortality he couldn't have foreseen that dunces like me would misuse it.

Although the mists hung heavy and the breeze blew fell chill there were moments of brightness and there were moments of Sennen Cove busyness going on that brought a little cheer to the shopkeeper heart.

So with fingers crossed we'll hang out for another Met Office cock-up tomorrow.

*May 30th – Sunday* – Well that gave us something to do today. Busy for the first time this year and wasn't it just lovely. The rain threw a googly to the Met Office and it stayed off until early afternoon giving everyone a chance at the beach.

For once our ordering was near the mark although we could have had a few more pasties. Not bad though despite the mash up with the forecasts.

Lifeboat went out again this morning. The Sunday morning launch is becoming a bit of a fixture now and we had quite an audience this morning. Focuses the mind a bit – don't want any cock-ups in front of a crowd, though what they think of our Head Launcher in his Brokeback Mountain costume is another matter.

Afternoon fell apart a bit as the rain started getting heavier, but we still had our five minutes to closing rush.

Sorry to go on so about the weather. It becomes a central focus for us as it is the main driver for business and on the forecast rests our bread, pasty, milk, newspapers and fruit & veg orders. You'll have, no doubt, a guts full of the weather entries in the diary come October.

Tomorrow's forecast is pants by the way which probably means a nice sunny day.

*May 31st – Monday* – Golly gee wilikins as my old mentor used to say, it's the end of May already.

As I said yesterday the weather forecast was pants. I mean the forecast was pants, not the weather which is, I guess, what I guessed yesterday.

The main thing that strikes us is that there are so many nice people around and I mean that most sincerely folks, to misquote the original host of the original Britain's got the Xfactor.

Sure there are a few quirky ones around. Like the lady a couple of days back who had me take down four different brands of cigarette before she chose the first one she asked for. And I hope she doesn't mind me mentioning it because I really didn't mind at all and we had a good laugh about it especially when she came in today and did the same thing again.

Not many people get to go to work, meet lots of nice people and have a laugh at the same time in a place that's, well, Sennen Cove really.

# June

*June 1st – Tuesday* – The thick cloud that hung over the bay after the early rain slipped away like a big duvet being pulled off by some huge unseen hand. Lots of poetic things happen here if you let them. Trouble is the big hand put it back several times before it went completely.

After that, turned out to be a rather nice day with sunny spells, quite a bit of blue sky and all the good things in life. What a good ripping yarn of a day.

What could possibly top this, I thought. Then G from the OS phoned and told me that the price of my beer had dropped by a whole quid!! This appears to be a phenomenal coup and may light the way to seeing the place return to some semblance of its former glory. Let's very much hope so. At least I'll be able to fall over cheaper.

Ended up on the Harbour Beach after closing; lots of joyous people enjoying the first sunshiny evening for a few days, the odd BBQ and all that sort of good thing. Several of the local youngsters waiting on the breakwater to be pummelled off by the breaking waves coming over the top: quite spectacular.

*June 2nd – Wednesday* – What a rip spinning whirlwind of a day.

Started out with the first Lifeboat shout in a long while. A becalmed yacht with engine problems somewhere north west of Brisons at 6:30am ish this morning followed by a lengthy tow back to Newlyn in the mist.

The bay was also beset with mist for a good proportion of the day and we were beset by numerous enquiries as to when the mist would lift. Lift it did shortly before the Lifeboat was able to approach the long slip for recovery at around 1:30pm.

All together something of a stonkingly good day, most of which we were mobbed by happy shoppers who decided that just because we sold few pasties yesterday they would make up for it today when we had less of them.

Collapsed in a heap just shortly before reaching the bed.

*June 3rd – Thursday* – We do rather hope that summer is a bit like this. Have to say we've rather enjoyed ourselves this week despite the fact it's been really hard work. All our customers have been exceedingly pleasant and I really mean all.

We started out with a bit of déjà vu, (aren't you just impressed with Microsoft? All I did was type in 'déjà vu' and it automatically put in those foreign type accents and whatever the opposite is, breve possibly, – don't know if html will cope as well, but you should have jolly well been here when I was drafting this piece in MS Word).

Think I better start again.

Started off the same as it did the day before with a Lifeboat shout, this time for a trimaran, (see, I had to check the spelling of trimaran, having never had to write that before . . . it just doesn't look right). The boat was actually making headway with sails at three knots which seems a bit slow in the winds we had, so something must have been wrong.

Lifeboat was recovered at about 2:15pm with yours truly in charge of the dry end without a hint of Brokeback Mountain in sight.

Weather did us proud again and it looks like it will last until the weekend.

So when all you happy souls go home this weekend, a very big thank you from us for being so, well, happy really.

*June 4th – Friday* – Blazing hot from first thing this morning; gosh we must have been good boys and girls to deserve all this.

Not quite as busy today but we expected that with many families heading for home.

Diversification is probably too small a word for this man. He's from a farm, well he's a farmer really, just outside Sennen, well closer to Crows an Wra actually, and is best known for his excellent organic pork. We have been talking for a little while about doing some of his exotic leaves like rocket, spicy leaf mixtures, lemon balm and so forth which one can only imagine luxuriates in the bi-product from the other side of his business. We would have liked to start earlier this week but you can't hurry a good lollo rosso, now can you? Specially one with its feet in porcine excrement.

We took a few bunches of this and that and, frankly, at the end of the busy week we didn't expect to do very well with them. Imagine my surprise when by the end of the day, a few hours later, all the rocket had gone as had a couple of spicy leaf mixtures. Best not mention the porker element, eh?

Forecast has us lost in fog this evening and as I write, at midnight o'clock, best we can manage is a pathetic haze. Still there's always tomorrow.

*June 5th – Saturday* – You can tell things have got a bit quieter. I managed to read the paper today for the first time in a week. Between that and watching a tour boat allow its passengers to dive in and swim around the basking sharks I had a whale of a time if you'll allow me the quite obvious literary combination.

There wasn't a great deal of interest in the paper to share with you. They stuffed it with a nice big property section just after the bit that said house sales are down 9pc on last year, which was quite smart.

No, it wasn't until I reached the classified section that things took a turn for the bizarre. The first section is dedicated to pets and the first twenty or so are puppies for sale. Nothing unusual there I hear you say.

Now read "Miniature Labradoodle F2 Back" and tell me there's nothing unusual about a 500 word advertisement in a small ads column. No I didn't count every word, just the lines and assumed average 5 words per line, for those of you thinking I've too much time on my hands and a poor imagination.

And it wasn't just the length that had me enthralled; the content too was just plain odd. We learn that dad is pra CLEAR whatever that means and he can be SEEN (sic). The pups are kept in the kitchen and experience the "hustle and bustle" of daily life and the children play with them too. The other dogs stay outside the pen watching and listening to all going on around them, so we are told. I don't think they missed one facet of the puppies' or their lives in that advertisement and if anyone can tell me what a F2B means I'm sure I will be a much better person for knowing.

We also learn that the typesetter, (if such a thing exists anymore), got bored and cut off the last words in mid flow.

If you're interested the pups are on sale for £850 most of which will pay for the advertising bill.

*June 6th – Sunday* – Rather a nice day, especially given the forecast – again. So it turned out to be somewhat busy and by the end of the day we had even less on our shelves than the little we had in the morning. Bleddy lovely!

Basking sharks returned for an evening meal again, this time undisturbed by tour boats plopping their passengers into the water.

Instead we had a few gannets plopping into the water. Bit more natural that.

Forgot to mention yesterday, had a national supermarket home delivery van park outside the shop. Not only did the chap have the temerity to park the flaming thing there, he actually came into the shop to ask directions to his delivery. Well, you can image the shortness of the shrift he got after which I asked him to politely carry the message to the recipient of his poor value, low quality fare that far better and local produce was available a short walk from their door: the philistines.

Oh, had to look after the shop on me own this afternoon while the wife went to Morrisons this afternoon. She must be from Philistinia too – different part though.

*June 7th – Monday* – It hasn't been all bad today. The constant rain did its best to dampen our spirits and pretty much succeeded in damping our shirts and trousers too. It's not often I have to retrieve the gear from outside wearing oilers and a sou'wester.

On the up side another reader came out of the closet. Bert, of course is not his real name, but we won't compromise our readers' safety by outing them in public. So your secret is safe with us, Ted.

Rather a smart rib tied up to the western buoy tonight. Understand that there may have been a bit of a problem with the trailer. Wonder if it will still be there in the morning? Lifeboat will have to do a rather smart starboard turn if we have to launch.

*June 8th – Tuesday* – Well just how different can a day be? White fluffy clouds and long spells of bright sunshine just to spite the weather forecasters, Lawd bless 'em all.

Now, how shall I put this – very carefully, I suspect. Ah yes, this is a fabricated story and all the names have been changed to protect the embarrassed.

So just imagine if . . .

We had a bit of a Lifeboat shout that was cancelled almost as soon as it started; transpired that one of our illustrious fishing fleet had found herself in a bit of bother, engine failure and almost onto Cowloe. Fortunately the big rib, (just like the one described yesterday), was out in the bay and tossed her a tow at the crucial moment.

The inshore Lifeboat (ILB) launched shortly after and advised Falmouth that it was launching "on exercise". To which Falmouth dryly responded "would that be an exercise to assist in the recovery of Rosie Buddie with your second coxswain on board?"

To rub a bit of salt into the wounds the rib, (complete with top notch hi-fi on board), was playing the Bond music as it steamed in to assist.

One for the family album that, Phil.

Well just imagine. 'Course it never actually happened.

*June 9th – Wednesday* – Oh dear I can see myself getting into more trouble today. I suppose I could just ignore it and pretend it never happened, but I may be suppressing my civic duty. I mean I have heard that the organisation of which I can only allude is resurgent in parts of Europe.

What began this train of concern was a visit by two gentlemen from a large Western European country. Possibly father and son, purportedly walking all round Cornwall for pleasure.

It was the elder gentleman's attire that set off my suspicions. Shall we just say it was a rather Germanic take on the Boy Scout uniform? I discounted him being an extra from the last act of the Sound of Music as Metamorphosis is playing at the Minack, I checked. But given his age he could have just been reliving his particular type of youth.

It was when the map came out I spotted the obvious ruse, the one about asking where the nearest campsite was. I imagined it was only a matter of time before those questions about quiet coves and decent landing points would come up. I feigned an urgent Lifeboat exercise and gracefully retired.

Daresay he's back on his way to Brazil by now.

We have some excitement down here in The Cove, I can tell you.

*June 10th – Thursday* – I have to thank Mr & Mrs R for their email. I welcome all emails in response to Diary entries, though you must understand you will be vilified in public in response.

So, ok, I forgot we have an Austrian in The Cove and I am duly cowed and apologetic especially if said Austrian and spouse are clad in full dirndl, truly scary. But clearly my suspicious have been confirmed. You see, just because you're paranoid doesn't mean that they're not watching you already. And by the way, "Hunderl", had me going for a bit – call me picky but I'm more used to Hundewelpe. (See, thought this was just any old diary but I can do international interaction too.)

Now, I tell you those terrorists have a lot to answer for.

Had to trek up to Cornwall Farmers as we have a bit of a weed problem, they have most things up there. I took a long time looking through the weed killers they had on the shelf. Then I had to go out and get my glasses as the details on the back are written in a type font not visible to the human eye.

For a product whose main purpose is to cause widespread devastation they are, according to the small print, remarkably good for the environment. They will have your weeds drop dead in a fizzling black morass in days short. Two days later the same scorched earth will be sprouting forth award winning carrots – whether you wanted them or not.

In the face of such confusion I sought advice from the bloke at the counter. To ensure my intent was clear, I requested the agricultural equivalent of napalm. There was the briefest of pauses while the poor chap envisioned me laying waste to vast swathes of West Cornwall. 'Twas then he suggested he talk to their agronomist.

Now imagine going into Been&Queued and asking the same question. "Agromist? Third aisle down. Gardening section, mate."

That's the thing about going to the right place. It's something called service; a foreign concept to many, I know. And here I could detour for hours about a pet subject I've spent years cultivating. But cultivation was the last thing on my mind at this juncture.

Cornwall Farmer's agronomist was a font, nay a geyser, of knowledge on the subject of fluids of mass destruction. He waxed lyrical about all sorts of phosphates, nitrates, dioxides and systemic action chemicals. However, did I have a licence?

Er, no. I have a ten by ten plot I wish to extinguish all life in. Ah well in that case your only recourse is an off the shelf product that will have your weed-free award wining carrots blossoming in no time. Thanks buh!

Bloody terrorists. You know, you can't get a decent weed killer for love nor money these days. Not without a licence anyhow.

Closer to home we had a nice big basker no more than fifty yards off circling around. Shame the sea's whipped up a bit or we would have seen a lot more of it.

*June 11th – Friday* – Not at all a bad day today; sun shining, wind dropped a bit and the Missus at Royal Cornwall all day. Basking sharks back in and close to the shore again today.

Got a little sidetracked yesterday so sorry about that. Still can't wait to see the barren wasteland my pseudo napalm has created, but I won't get up there today.

Day started in cracking form, which is more than I can say for yours truly. A raucous night at the F&L fair near did for me, preceded by a somewhat first class tea at The Beach. Now I have to say that it was a tea that the words 'stonkingly good' were created for. I can only assume that the food writers who gave it a triple A rating grossly underestimated their report. Especially as the boss, who spent the evening getting his hands dirty, (probably a poor choice of metaphor), in the kitchen, offers you a Hennessy XO as a parting gesture. Thanks Mr D.

Now for a disturbing report in the WMN yesterday; thinking about it I should have reported this as soon as I saw it because obviously time is of the essence. A dastardly act of genocide is about to be perpetrated on this holy land. And what's worse is that it is endorsed by a member of our Royal Family albeit that it is his holy land that it's happening in.

The act of which I write is to 'introduce' the red squirrel to the Lizard Peninsula. That in itself sounds like a noble cause, doesn't it? Well read on and discover the awful cost that this patriation will incur.

Now I've nothing against the red squirrel per se, (don't you just hate it when people who don't know what they're talking about drop in the odd Latin phrase?). I sure it's a very pretty beast and keeps the growth of nuts down to a manageable level. Might even bring a few more punters into the county spending their English shillings, very welcome, I'm sure.

Here's the thing: Mr Red is a bit of a wimp all said and done; any competition at all and he's history. So in order to house these furry friends in the comfort that they demand, all the grey squirrels are going to have to go. Call me a cynic if you will but I doubt somehow that each and every grey squirrel on The Lizard is going to be offered a compensation package and a re-housing offer. I think it far more likely they will be recipients of a lead invitation from Messers Holland & Holland and Mr Purdy.

Have we learned nothing from history? In 1620 we sent a bunch of unimaginatively dressed chaps over to the New World, eventually nearly wiped out their inhabitants and look how that turned out. (Look if I'm going to upset nations I may as well not show bias and do them all).

47

So this goes out to all grey squirrels on The Lizard: get out of there!

Will there have to be a plaque down on Lizard soon? A simple inscription: "Go tell the squirrels, stranger passing by, that here, obedient to their laws, we lie". Or should all decent people stand up and cry foul. Stand up and be counted for grey squirrels everywhere. It could be your grey squirrel next.

*June 12th – Saturday* – An auspicious start today, our very own MBE in The Cove, but on the evidence lately it probably stands for My Boat Expired. He's in good company with Graham Nash of CSNY fame, John Kale, Bert Williams (Robert Green only has another sixty years of shame to wait, then) and closer to home Lady Mary Holborow and not forgetting Gitty Ankers.

Wind continues to blow and this time from the north west. By the feel of things it's come direct from Greenland and hasn't bothered warming up on the way. Still the sun shines and it all looks pretty darned fab.

Dot and Ernie who are knocking on the door of octogenaria arrived last night and bought their usual 30 lbs of shopping this morning to hump cheerfully up the hill. For two people slightly higher than the shop counter, this seemed too much of a tall order this time so we took them up the hill in the van.

Late news: The England team are rueing having an Italian as their manager. I understand that Rooney is likely to wake up with Robert Green's head on his pillow.

*June 13th – Sunday* – Mostly not a bad day with a fleeting spell of low cloud and rain just after lunch that cleared through pretty quickly.

Mr S had a fair bit of ribbing over his MBE at this morning's Lifeboat exercise, of course; penned in as a medical exercise with two doctors on board – sufficient to certify the crew if necessary. The exercise was sidetracked a little by a round Britain rower with an anchor tangled in some fishing gear over by Wolf Rock.

By the time they got back tide was so low we had to recover the inshore Lifeboat off the big beach. Gave me a bit of a chance to flash the blue light on the tractor – I told you its all excitement down here.

The World Cup is causing some disruption even this far away

from reality. For the England matches the newspaper men have agreed a 30 minute delay in cut off time with the unions. The impact of this translates into an hour and a half delay in getting our morning newspapers and on a Sunday that is somewhat irksome. This will be much worse when they start running into extra time and penalty shoot-outs in the next rounds, (all supposing England are able to pull up their collective socks).

Yup, I thought you'd be interested!

*June 14th – Monday* – Spoilt for choice on the subject matter front. But first the weather report for the day, as I'm sure you're all dying to know. Overcast and very windy, again from the nor' west so a mite chilly most of the day. Sun broke through in the afternoon that made it look better even if it was just as bleddy cold.

Just to say, a bit of a freak squall came through at around 10pm last night; howling wind and heavy downpour. Understand it had trees down further up – got no trees this end to knock down.

Now, as subject matter you can have water charges spread across the UK, health lobby shenanigans or number of red and white flags in Cornwall. Come on lets have a show of hands. Ok, that looks about even – I'll just have to do all three. Hang onto your hats a minute.

Now it's been long known that you chaps up country get your $H_2O$ at a smidgeon of the cost of what we pay down here. Ok, the quality's not so good but you are getting a darned good deal. Then you come down here on holiday and drink all ours and piddle in our toilets for free – well almost – and swim in our nice clean sea all of which is courtesy of our phenomenally high water rates. Oh, and perhaps our cats are fatter than yours too.

So the nice men in the Government have decided that everybody else is going to get an increase and we wholesome chaps down here will get a 10% reduction. Except Newquay where they don't drink water and apparently prefer to piddle on the pavement. What ho and jolly good show too.

Over to you, then, on that one.

Now this health lobby lot. I tell you if they directed half their energy at kicking out bright ideas aimed at the economy the recession would have been a distant memory by now.

Let me first refresh your memory when pubs were relatively cheap and the bloke behind the counter would tap you on the shoulder and send you home if you got too fuddled. Then some chaps in a smart office decided it would be a cracking idea to let people drink all day. Of course they wouldn't get drunk because they'd choose different times to drink – no one would drink all day. The bloke down the pub laughed his head off at that one.

Then when it started to look a little like everyone was drinking all day the men in the office put 26% on the drinks in the pub in a couple of years, now that would slow 'em down, wouldn't it? Except they told the supermarkets they had a free hand to basically give it away. The bloke down the pub, who couldn't afford to drink in one any more was shaking his head and burying his face in his hands by this time.

The supermarkets, who didn't have a chap behind the counter to tap you on the shoulder and send you home when you got too bladdered, dropped their prices some more, rubbing their collective hands with glee.

Now, oh yes, that health lobby. Their next bright idea is to close down the number of outlets selling booze. Um, might be a bit too late fellas, 4,000 pubs have closed in the last two years. And good luck with telling Morrisons they can't sell beer any more.

And finally, someone mentioned they hadn't seen so many flags of St George in Cornwall before. Well there is a perfectly good explanation. Some chap from the Cornish National Party or somesuch, (sorry, I'm not taking the mick – I really can't remember), decided to issue a statement to all visiting English that went roughly, "Don't fly your St George flags down here. You might upset some of us".

You can just see the bloke down the pub slapping his hand against his forehead, can't you?

*June 15th – Tuesday* – Today is a red letter day. Well actually June 11th was the red letter day but I utterly failed to notice its significance.

I had a communiqué from MM advising me that I had lost a day somewhere. I recognised the name, but just how important that email was just flew over my head. It wasn't until I checked today and, yes, I can tell you that the Sennen Cove Diary has made it; has reached a pinnacle of literary distribution. While you all thought it was a minor piece of childish rantings, written unknowingly for the bemusement of its intellectual following I always knew it had far greater potential.

Sennen Cove Diary has gone international!

My name is Sennen Cove Diary, king of kings:
Look on my works, ye Mighty, and despair!

And talking of travellers from an antique land I have always wondered why Columbus was given such reverence. Surely it would have been more momentous for him to have missed the Americas – it's bleddy huge. Be that as it may MM hails from a place that is South Carolina and it looks lovely from a satellite, which is probably the closest I'll ever get.

So thank you MM, this page will be forever in your debt.

How I missed this I'll never know. One of our customers came in and reported that there were over thirty dolphins in the bay yesterday evening. Basking sharks had been enjoying the bay all day so I guess it was the dolphins' turn.

Newspaper reports that Lion's Mane Jellyfish have been spotted all the way up the north coast from Lands End to Gwithian. Our local friendly naturalist, (not to be confused with our friendly naturist), said that a diver spotted some around Lands End this morning. Strangely these horrors prefer cooler waters. More evidence for the global warming conspiracy theorists, perhaps?

Swimming type people need to be aware that these critters give a nasty sting and lacerations. He's asked that he be informed if any turn up on the beach as they're looking for samples. If they're that dangerous best you jump in and find them yourself, me 'ansum.

Pass the heavy rubber gloves, buh!

And then to round off the day a little ILB shout to assist that big rib (no Bond music this time, eh?). Looked like it might be taking on water but can't have been that bad. She motored off round the corner to Newlyn to get herself checked over. It had Mr MBE on board – soon be calling 'ee Jonah I think.

*June 16th – Wednesday* – Today we're going to have some blue sky; the opening line of a cracking, if overplayed, song. It also happens to be true of today, though that cool breeze just doesn't want to let go.

Business picked up a tad in the sparkling looking weather. Amazing how a little sunshine lubricates the wallet. Long may it continue – the sunshine and the business.

Went off to town and celebrated with a first class curry at Baba's only to note that they've stopped their 25% off, early diner's discount. Best we have a good day tomorrow as well then – watch your change, happy shoppers.

51

Well that's it really. No fantastic stories, no rascalish quips, not a basking shark, lion mane jellyfish or pod of dolphins in sight. I think our international status has overawed me a little.

Goodnight.

*June 17th – Thursday* – Yet another blindingly good day; even the nor' easterly dropped out a bit towards the end of the afternoon.

Basking sharks back in again this morning. This one was huge and milling about by the inner channel markers. Shame the water was so choppy else we would have seen the whole shape.

Funny how some people can ask you a question and no matter how authoritative you sound or however concrete your conviction your answer will never really be, well, right.

"What's that big light patch out there?"

"There's a big area of sand out there and the dark bit is weed and rock. When the sun's at a certain angle . . ."

"Is it algae or something?"

"No, it's sand."

"There's not much sand on the beach. Is it being drawn out into the water making it murky?"

"No, I think you'll find it's the light on the sand."

"Those rocks on the beach weren't there last time I was here. Could it be . . .?"

"Lion's Mane jellyfish, Sir. Hundreds of the blighters. Wouldn't go out there if I was you."

Well you do your best, don't you?

Oh, talking of the Lion's Mane jellyfish. The MCA issued a statement saying that the report of 200+ of the creatures was "overblown and exaggerated" in the national press. I can see their point. Two years ago *The Sun* offered us grainy snaps of a basking shark dorsal fin and told us there were Great Whites in the bay.

Still the diver was there and the MCA wasn't but there's many a slip twixt the waters of Lands End and Wapping with a dodgy mobile link and lip. And half a dozen wouldn't really cut the mustard, although possibly more accurate.

The MCA did offer some advice. If you see a Lion's Mane either at sea or on a boat (sic), take a picture and report it to mcsuk.org but don't touch it.

Too right, fitting the long lens on my camera as I write.

*June 18th – Friday* – For all of you who are complaining about our soothing nor' easterly spare a thought for our international correspondent in SC, (that's what us international publications call South Carolina – read 'em and weep you lesser journals). I'm told that despite company pith helmet and tropical whites, MM is suffering in 90 degrees (in old money) and high humidity with not a draft. Turn down the spare bed MM, we're on our way.

The giant basking shark is still stalking the deep blue quite close into shore and attracting a lot of attention along with a few of its mates. New lines in the shop are beckoning. To wit stuffed toy basking sharks, basking shark mugs, basking shark tooth brushes and that old favourite stuffed basking shark head mounted on a plaque. I best get cracking. These opportunities don't last forever. Basking shark fin soup anyone?

Bit of a weather front upset the apple cart in the afternoon and we are now covered in cloud. Nothing like a bit of gloom to set the scene for England's latest attempt at kicking an imitation inflated pigskin around. Algerians playing football? Whoever heard of such a thing?

Come on you bloooos!

*June 19th – Saturday* – Oh dear. Fortunately I missed most of it but I understand that the footie was a bit of a disappointment; over-inflated egos kicking around an under-inflated ball. Still never mind Wimbledon starts soon.

Lifeboat exercise this morning for a change; what am I going to write about tomorrow for heaven's sake? Struggled a bit to get a crew out of the lame, lazy, dead and dying and we know it would have been different for a shout. But people do have to work and since most are employed in some way in the service industry here, Saturday is a big change over day and hence busy. The same excuse, of course, doesn't hold true for those out on the tear last night and still glued to their gruesome pits this morning. See I managed one sentence in there that was serious and sincere.

Baskers are back, of course, followed by an entourage of board bound surfers who don't have any waves to catch. Flat as a pancake out there today.

Weather's been odd today. Warm, certainly, but trying very hard to be foggy and looking like rain, although there was no chance of it actually doing so. Brighter later on with lots of blue sky coming through; bit of a perfect day as those leaving don't mind doing so with the weather a bit dodgy and those coming in seeing the start of some good stuff.

Lastly, (and I know it's tomorrow but you'll be reading this tomorrow and tomorrow's entry would be too late), Happy Father's Day to my Dad. I know he's an ardent supporter of the Diary, (though no funds have yet been forthcoming), so it's an ideal platform for my greeting.

Of course there will be the small-minded who may hurtfully suggest that I'm just being cheap, avoiding the cost of card and stamp. But my Dad and I understand and resist the commercial pressures thrust upon us, where weaker souls capitulate. Isn't that right, Dad?

And nothing generates a bit of loving care more than the clattering in the back of your brain reminding you that these acts of random kindness will one day translate into one's inheritance – if the old sod hasn't spent it all by then!

*June 20th – Sunday* – So no exercise launch and I've already done the Father's Day bit cos by the time you read this it would all be a bit passé. I could tell you that although a few clouds passed through in the morning the day has been spectacular.

Fortunately our Sennen village correspondent fished out, (that's a clever pun if you read on), a bit of news that I missed. I haven't been paying too much attention to the newspapers or television news recently because it seems overrun with football stories. While I can appreciate there's a bit of skill in there and can watch the occasional game I'm not what you'd call a fanatic.

Now I did catch the main news that Mr Sarkozy made a visit to the UK to mark the 70th anniversary of Mr de Gaulle spurring on his countrymen to resist the Nazi occupation. Clearly a brave thing to do from the relative safety of a BBC studio in London but it did earn him a death sentence in his absence. Apparently he, Sarkozy not de Gaulle, had a spot of lunch with Mr Cameron and the news carried a detailed list of what was on the menu. Top of the list was a Cornish sea bass.

You may not be aware that these days there is a growing preference among discerning consumers that fish on the table should be line caught. Eager to appease this burgeoning crowd, and to stick one to the Frenchies, our Cornish fishermen have taken to the old methods with some aplomb, (many have always caught fish this way). There are a few punts out of The Cove that you will see with a long pole poking out each side of the boat. Attached to this is a line with a rubber eel on the end and the craft will slowly traverse its selected patch targeting the sea bass in a method known as trolling. Mackerel and pollock are also fished for using this and similar methods: Very environment friendly and very sustainable.

Furthermore quite recently a system of tagging had been introduced. Should Mr Cameron and Mr Sarkozy have wanted to they could have identified where the fish was caught and the fisherman who caught it.

If they'd caught the real significance of it, perhaps they could have sorted out the ridiculous quota system that sees millions of fish dumped dead back into the Channel.

Gosh, you could be reading a script from the Discovery Channel today.

A bit of upset down at the OS on Friday, I think. I got this second hand so read with caution. A woman, no less, set about the doors and the lounge window in a bit of a destructive spree. She was somewhat the worse for drink so she must have been blessed with a few shillings if she got drunk in there. It was a bit extreme but I guess its one way of getting the bar maid to stop texting her boyfriend and notice you've been waiting for a drink for twenty minutes.

*June 21st – Monday* – I love the smell of sun lotion in the morning; it smells like victory.

Probably the best day of the year so far, but that's it. It's all over. The longest day has come and gone, all those Celts, Pagans and Druids can put their frocks away for another three months and get an early night and a lay in. Nights start drawing in from tomorrow and before you know it will be Christmas again.

But, not so fast there, while June 21st may be the astronomical solstice it doesn't 'zackly coincide with the traditional festivals. Midsummer is yet around the corner according to many and Penzance today will host Golowan; centred around the nearest Friday to the Feast of St John on June 24th. All this culminates in Mazey Day on Saturday when there will be much cavorting, making merry and partaking in strong liquor. Not a Cove thing at all where the abstemiousness of the old Methodist ways still hold sway, em, now and again.

The Diary's terrier-like investigative journalism seems to have deserted us of late. We seemed to have looked the wrong way for some of the things going on around here. On Friday there was a very large tent going up in Trevedra Farm. No one knew anything about it though I asked all the usual suspects. It took a visitor to tell me that it was some sort of BMX bike event and, after all that organisation, it was only for the one day.

We were a little less culpable for the second. We had a security chap in the shop today who told us that Top Gear was filming up at Lands End tonight. Further investigation revealed that is was last night. So if security for the event couldn't get the day right how were we supposed to know?

No doubt the Celts, Pagans and Druids were up at Chapel Carn Brea this evening trying not to set their frocks on fire or was that last night for the dawn? Either way we missed that too.

*June 22nd - Tuesday* – Absolute blinder of a day again; not sure how much more of this lovely weather we can take. It's just not British for heaven's sake. Even the leathery old Cornishmen are seeking shelter.

Been keeping half an ear out for the budget; no extra tax on cider, yippee, no extra tax on fags, yippee, No extra tax on petrol/diesel, yippee; until January when 2.5% will go on absolutely everything. They also look like they are going to freeze children and houses for someone's benefit. Well at least that's what it sounded like.

Yaa boo sucks to Natural England. Now it's not like me to plough into a respected national body, especially one that can stand up and support Open Farm Sunday when serious weight is being shoved behind closing them down to the public because eating pig manure makes children ill. But they have been very rude to people in the West Country, suggesting, by inference, that we're all a bit loopy, toys in the attic and prone to fantasy and delusion.

Yes we have a new hero, here in the West, Toni Bunnell, a Dr no less, who's either Italian, or a woman or both. It is important news for hundreds of us that we aren't going mad, at least as far as seeing things that don't exist or, rather, do now. Toni, our new friend, has confirmed in a study commissioned by University of Hull that strange critters stalk various parts of the country including big cats in the West. The Beast of Bodmin Moor is real!

By the report's reckoning there are 50,000 ring-neck parakeets, worryingly 13,000 yellow tailed scorpions and 10,000 Chinese water deer. Brilliantly, because it lets me do a joke, there are 10 Brazilian aardvarks in Cumbria. Please don't worry though 'cos aardvark never did anyone any harm.

Naturally you wouldn't find any aardvark in Cornwall.

Come on, who'd of thought you would have had a news story that let me get that one in?

*June 23rd – Wednesday* – A few white fluffy things out there today and a bit of haze but still jolly warm and lovely; a bit of a swell developing so that may keep the surfers happy. But not even a swingeing budget or an England football game could ruin a day like today.

Absolutely nothing momentous happened today and the papers were just full of budget unpickings. So things being as they are I'm just going to witter on for a few lines and then we'll call it a day. If you don't want to be bored senseless or have a sudden urge to watch some grass grow or watch a re-run of England vs Algeria my best advice is to go and do so.

Had a visit from the local constabulary this morning, two of them with big smiles, which was worrying cos as you know most bobbies are never happier than when they're nicking someone. As it goes business in that regard must be slow because they asked if we had anything to report or moan about.

We scratched our heads for a minute or two and the best we could think of was one woman complaining we'd run out of *Daily Mail*s at three in the afternoon and a chap telling us he could get his bottled water cheaper in Belgium.

I'd always fancied something a bit more heinous resulting in my final moments of freedom where I could shout through a broken window, "You'll never take me alive, copper" or, "It's a fair cop guv, but society's to blame". Somehow crimes against holiday makers wouldn't quite cut it so we kept schtum.

They did try and prompt us a bit but the best they could come up with was had we noticed any parking infringements, which was odd since the police can't do anything about that since decriminal-isation of the parking laws.

Both parties smiled and agreed The Cove wasn't the hotbed of vice it once was. They took down our particulars and left.

Now, if they'd sent that very nice lady sergeant who was here a couple of weeks back I would have fessed up to the great train robbery until she worked out I was only three – if, of course, she'd even heard of it.

*June 24th – Thursday –* Ooh it all looked a bit dodgy there for a minute or two this morning. But, no, the sun came back in spades: It's another corker.

Taking advantage of the weather and to some degree the lack of swell we witness a gig race meeting in The Cove tonight. Several gigs from the local area attending, I understand organised by St Agnes, racing around the bay trying to avoid the Lifeboat that's out there on exercise.

It was definitely a pretty evening watching the gigs kick up a healthy speed across the dappled waters of the bay. I understand that it is cracking cardio-vascular exercise but I'm afraid me, cardio and half-zware shag have an understanding of distant respect and I'm happy just to watch.

After a text-book recovery of both boats we retired to the wreckage of the OS to watch the sun set beautifully at almost the extremity of its northern dip.

Kind of warms the cockles, that image, doesn't it? As if your cockles need warming in this weather.

Good night boys and girls.

*June 25th – Friday –* You never think it will happen to you, do you?

You never hear of it from the likes of Tesainissons. Those big multiples cover it up; they have the resources to do so. I'm just going to have to put my hands up and admit it. I am the victim of a guerrilla shopper.

I thought I was safe. There I was knee deep in milk and bread at 7:30 in the morning and there he was. "Are you open yet?"

Call me naïve if you will but I find that a shop front with blinds down, door shut and a big CLOSED sign on the door all rather indicative of a shop that isn't open.

Now we've had trainee guerrillas before but, by and large, it's been an emergency to which we are happy to respond: my child is ill and I need Calpol; I've hurt my knee and I need plasters; I'm gasping and I need sixteen cans of beer. You know the sort of thing we mean, real emergencies.

What did this bold gangster want? Biscuits, bleddy biscuits. I feel violated.

Nice little report in the paper today. Two canoeists paddling out to Scilly, as you do when you have a canoe and a bit of time on your hands, get a bit bored and start looking around at the wildlife. At first they thought it was a basker and paddled across to have a closer look; turned out to be a Leatherback turtle a little off course; even managed to get a fairly cloudy picture of the beast.

Now it's off to my curry and cards night so don't expect any great works of literary might in tomorrow's piece.

Lastly a query has arisen from yesterday's entry. Half-zware shag I'm asked? It's a term applied to tobacco, specifically by the Dutch, meaning half cut or half rubbed, a bit finer than rough shag. "I have to give up this rough shag" isn't a reference to a ruffian wishing to depart his somewhat unrefined close acquaintance.

Oh and lastly welcome home to me Mum who's been a bit poorly in hospital, bless her. Better now.

*June 26th – Saturday* – A right stonking good summer day down in The Cove. Plenty of folk around enjoying the sunshine and many more in the water that has now reached a steaming 17 degrees, according to Magic Seaweed© (that plug's got to be worth twenty quid surely).

In the early evening our own, internationally renowned, water skier took to the waves putting on a display fit for the Olympics. This roughly translates as one of the local wide boys has strapped a plank of wood to his feet and has allowed himself to be dragged across the water, at speed, by a bunch of more sensible wide boys in a rubber boat with a big engine on the back.

Fortunately several of us are highly trained in First Aid and can spot the early onset of post-immersion respiratory syndrome, (used to be called secondary drowning until some over paid quango got involved). Unfortunately none of us know what to do about it. Fortunately for the bloke on the end of the string he is blissfully unaware of this.

However, no time to consider his fate, time to dash off to the F&L where no band is playing on the expectation that the England football team could actually play football and would come out top of their group, hence would be playing tonight. Down to the fact they are a bunch of over paid playboys who occasionally play football they scraped through second in the group and are now playing Sunday afternoon.

The upshot of all this is footballery is that there is no band and no £1 a pint during the game as compensation. What a double whammy.

*June 27th – Sunday* – Well that sun just can't help itself from pouring down on us again. And blow me a few waves for the surfers to enjoy courtesy of a geet low pressure system hanging off the west coast of Ireland. The big beastie is set to take the edge off this lovely weather next week so enjoy it while ye may.

From around 2pm you could see the tumbleweed gathering at the end of The Cove ready to roll down Cove Road when the footie kicks off.

After seven years of running a shop by the sea we've decided that we might try and sell a bit of fish. Can you imagine the innovative powerhouse we have here that comes up with such momentous decisions? From tomorrow, or today as you're reading it, we will have a wide range of fish available for ordering and next day delivery. We'd love to sell some Sennen Cove fish but that's a bit more fraught, not knowing what's coming in and when it might but there is some potential there and we will be investigating.

Now finally, what can I say? Deutschland Deutschland uber alles perhaps.

*June 28th – Monday* – Miss Cornwall? You probably do if you're not here and there again if you were between 18 and 24 you could be Miss Cornwall. Miss Cornwall wasn't and now she isn't: Stripped of her assets in some ceremony that probably resembled that cult 60s cowboy series, Branded, if you can remember back that far. The bit where the buttons are ripped from the tunic are probably favourite until the snapping of the sabre comes to mind. Ooh, very symbolic!

Some sharp-eyed sleuth in the beauty pageant organiser's office noticed something amiss with our latest trophy winner. Pulling out the erstwhile queen's previous applications, which were legion, she noticed Miss Cornwall had been 22 for three years running which still didn't come close to her true age of 27.

Now your average beauty contest judge is probably some notable from the locality: The mayor, bank manager, the local priest. You couldn't fault any of these for missing in their subjects a few added years, except maybe the priest.

Excuse me for being a tad picky here but you'd have thought that a Miss Region contest judge would be top of his game, expert in the female form, aware of every nuance of the feminine character and particularly being able to nail a young lady's age down to within something closer than five years.

Worse still, when the organiser eventually tracked down the impostor she was found living in Plymouth, that's Devon by the way. She wasn't even Cornish. That's like having a Welsh woman as Prime Minister of Australia, for heaven's sake. This is outrageous and something needs to be done. I demand that we get to the bottom of our beauty queens. A vigorous probe is required.

Which brings me on to a complete surprise; sitting in the 'on this day' column was a bit of a revelation. A national treasure, it seems, was lost this day in 1984. I always thought that it was a bit of a tasteless rag and a bit fruity at that. It may well have been as I never did read it but whatever it was *Tit Bits* managed to be it for 104 years. Wish I'd read it now.

*June 29th – Tuesday* – My personal genealogist tells me I should beware of casting aspersions on certain Welsh/Australian Prime Ministers. I understand that there is a Gillard lurking in my family closet but, fortunately, as yet there is no concrete evidence that we are connected. I have nothing against the Welsh, thankfully, so let's just keep it that way.

Well it was only a matter of time. Anyone listen to Radio Cornwall today? One of the lead stories was about a certain ex-Miss Cornwall and boy, did they make a meal of it.

I'm not sure whether I should be affronted or delighted. And, all right, I nicked the story from the *WMN* but it was only a tiny little piece; any sensible reader would have missed it. It took a daring, cut and thrust, Diary such as this to broach the matter to a wider audience, (international, remember).

It's almost scary that this publication has accumulated so much influence and power in such a short space of time. No more than a few months and we're guiding the regional media. Another few weeks and we'll have the readership of the nation and then perhaps Europe; translators across the Continent hanging on my every word and working out how to do *bleddy geet tus* in Croat. Delegations from Asia, Africa and the Americas queuing at my door – the power, the power . . .

FX: [Echoing, manic laughter fading into distance]

*June 30th – Wednesday* – Can't believe we've reached the end of the month already. Doesn't time just whiz by while you're having a ball?

I managed to get out on a little sojourn today, beyond the boundary of the known world. Turning left at the top of the hill you do feel a little queasy inside. I can image Scott, Magellan,

Armstrong all feeling the same as they stepped into the unknown. Did you know there's a road with two lanes each way the other side of Penzance? And beyond that? Well, my map says, "there be dragons".

I got back to quite a serious do. Someone had a fall off Pedn-men-du and coastguard and helo were in attendance. I know I've said it before but to watch the pilot manoeuvre so close to the cliff is really quite awe inspiring. No news yet of the condition of the climber but they were scooped off to Treliske in a bit of a hurry.

It's been a bit of a hot and clammy day for the end of June and we expect rain tomorrow. Once again there may be a bit of delay while June gets filed off to archive and brilliant July comes to the fore.

# July

## July 1st – Thursday –

> *Buckets of rain,*
> *Buckets of tears,*
> *Got all them buckets*
> *Coming out of my ears.*

Mr Zimmerman sure had today's weather pegged!

It's amazing how quickly you forget. At least two weeks of glorious sunshine and good weather then all of a sudden you spend a whole day in a damp, drizzly cloud and it seems like it's been like this forever.

Watched the rain band approach on the rain radar and it fair sped in from the Atlantic. Thought, "That'll be ok, a few hours and it'll be gone". Nope. Sped in, arrived then stayed put for the whole day.

As usual on days like this absolutely nothing happened. No interesting customers to have a bit of fun with; no silly behaviour out on the water and you couldn't see any shenanigans in the sky even if they were happening.

Then, towards the evening, as if it couldn't get any worse, it did.

Happy July everyone.

## July 2nd – Friday – Diary: New Musical Cove Express edition.

We took the afternoon, our man next door and I, and went out beyond the far distant horizon and tasted Eden. Now before you lot get all biblical on me we're talking the Eden Project here which, each year, puts on a series of blasting concerts that they call The Eden Sessions.

Your venerable and creaking jotter has been going for the past three years so, unwilling to break the habit, I went for the fourth. And for a chap that doesn't much like going further than the top of the hill the allure of the Sessions must be pretty special, you'd think.

Well, you'd be absolutely right.

For a start the venue is completely stunning. Way down at the bottom of an old china clay pit converted into a lush and verdant garden and home to the frogspawn like blisters of the biomes courtesy of Mr Tim Smit. The acoustics work brilliantly and the natural? confines restrict audiences to a mere 6,000: Very cosy.

My last three years have ranged from near drowning in rain to very overcast and threatening. Tonight however was resplendent in glittering sunshine, short skirts and bosomy ladies. Naturally I averted my eyes – several times. Oh, and there were a few bands playing too!

Our musical delight started with, on a side stage, a band called Silent Movie Project who were neither of the former but made a good fist of the latter. They even brought a healthy gathering of, not teeny, but boppers nevertheless all the way from Sheffield; a fact that we won't hold against them as long as they go back.

The main acts, Mumford and Sons and The Doves attracted a very mixed crowd, old 'uns and young 'uns and we even saw a few from down our own way.

Into the press of the main arena the stage fair exploded with the energy of Mumford and Sons playing their own special eclectic blend of London-Irish folk music with a mix of guitars, mandolins, banjo, trumpet and heaven knows what else. And boy did those chaps know how to handle their instruments. From toe tapping, body hopping jigs to soft ballads evoking the rolling foothills of, well, Streatham really.

The Doves required an hour to set up so we decided to wander to prevent the onset of DVT, if you can get that from standing up in one place for too long. The place was heaving and we were treated to the spectacle of one of Eden's eco-cycle demonstrations. Queue to get beer tokens, (tokens, literally), queue to get the beer, queue for the toilets, queue for beer tokens . . . etc. Clearly, had they properly studied the habits of the female of the species, they would have made the plastic cubicles big enough for two and halved the queue.

The Doves appeared and took Eden by storm. It's hard to describe their moogy-electro mix over-laid with tones of heavy bass and cutting rhythm guitar so I won't. All I can say that as I write my ears are still bleeding and my chest still throbbing to the beat of the big bass drum.

What a fantastic night. You should have been there.

*July 3rd – Saturday* – Off to a cracking start this morning with customers flooding the shop from the off. Signs of school children too as our Scottish friends descend upon us with their funny banknotes; (all fully acceptable in The Old Boathouse along with Groats, Sheckles and Denarii.)

Saw our first fish sale go out the door today, a nice big pollock. Already several Cove crabs have gone to deserving local mouths. We would be chuffed to pieces if this were a success. The local fish, especially nice and fresh are a wonder on the taste buds and we really want to spread the love, er, man.

Well as if I hadn't learnt my lesson from last night it seems likely that I'll do it all over again tonight with another band up at the F&L. They Fell from the Sky, which is a name that doesn't quite inspire a whole lot of confidence but we shall see.

Of course spending so much time on keeping the Diary up to date I have totally ignored the What's On page. Be aware, be very aware that the Ashley Moffatt memorial Surf Rodeo is on tomorrow, that'll be today by the time you read this and you'll probably have missed it, sorry. The day seems to go from strength to strength each year, almost certainly due to the dedicated souls who run it, which is more than a fitting tribute to the chap.

Naturally I've only ever viewed it from afar as work does rather stop me donning my wetsuit and joining in. No, really. But I'll do my best to join the thronging crowd down at the OS, (putting aside my misgivings and taking out a second mortgage for one night), where Pondlife will be playing their collective hearts out.

A full report will be here tomorrow if I have any idea of what went on.

Be there or be very disappointed.

PS. Oh, and the band, They Fell from the Sky. Yes, they probably did.

*July 4th – Sunday* – What a grey day.

It's not often you get a story handed to you on a plate. Today being a hopeless, pale shadow of a day makes it all the more welcome.

Radio Janner is a bit like today on a Sunday and so we flick the switch and tune into one of the crass and mindless commercial stations that litter the airwaves. Normally it's just a bit of background noise spattered with advertisements that generally go in one ear and out the other.

Until . . . a ten second burst! Did I just hear that right? Surely not. An elaborate and expensive hoax, perhaps. An immediate investigation was required.

It's not something I can tell you about; you will have to go there yourself. What I can alert you to is that you will be moved to tears, so have the Kleenex handy. Some, I'm sure, will have the decency to be moved to tears for the poignant sentiments expressed but most, I fear, like me will be near wetting themselves with mirth. Go there now, you can come back here when you've collected yourself. Go there now to the World Wide Web page of dearestpets.com.

Finished? Are you now collected? Careful those salty drops don't get into the works of the keyboard, now.

Come on. I mean however much you adored your little Tiddles, Butch or Rover and, Lord knows I loath our dog, (sorry, did I say loath. You know I meant love), but nothing, nothing in this world would move me to share my fondest memories of the damned animal with the bored and restless anorak-coated trawlers of the internet, (of which I'm probably one – without the anorak, of course).

And, incidentally, there are no Rovers, Butches or Tiddles returned on the site's search engine. The owners of thus named animals are far too reserved and sensible to subscribe to such piffle, no doubt.

And another 'and', why is there not a dearesthusband.com, dearestmother.com or dearestpartnerofthesamesex.com where you can leave a dedication to humans of that description? (In the name of heavens! I've just checked and the first two come up trumps but not as dedication sites, thankfully, as my point would be lying in tatters on the ground.) Do we really honour our pets more than our fellow human kind?

Alright, perhaps there might be a case for a well meaning website provider to offer a service to distraught recently bereaved pet owners to allow them to express their grief openly. Such an act or worthiness should have me cowed with embarrassment by pouring such ridicule and derision upon the charitable souls.

Nope, these boys are charging £15 a pop for a three year listing or £25 for a lifetime. So anyway this Cornwall based site can ride through my scorn and ridicule, laughing all the way to the bank. No, my scorn and ridicule has already turned to bitterness and jealousy. Why didn't I think of it first?

In the great words of WC Fields, "My advice to you is to drink heavily"; kindly guidance that I can heartily recommend having been an exponent for most of my life.

I'm off now to raise a glass or two to the chap whose untimely demise prompted a day each year of fun and jollity; a memorial far more poignant than a page on the www.

Though it seemed right to end on the last sentence I did promise you a report on said evening of jollity.

The joint was jumping all night. Rarely, in recent times, has the OS been more full of revellers. The band were awesome, the dance floor packed and the company convivial beyond doubt. I should, in all honesty, mention the service but words fail me. Just let it be said that it was a cracking, though expensive, evening and fun and joy was had by all.

*July 5th – Monday* – Picture of increasing sunshine today only for the forecast to tell us that it's all disappearing again tomorrow. Still enjoy it while we can.

There was a bit of excitement up the hill yesterday; didn't mention it, as I was not in command of the full facts, not that that's ever bothered me before. The investigation is now complete so here's the story.

A local lad coming down the hill found himself victim to a few rogue rocks falling from the hill above. Unable to avoid the avalanche, a rock passed under the car and rock and metal made contact in a fairly robust manner.

Waiting until he reached the end of The Cove to check the underside he noticed a small but insignificant oil leak from the area of the sump. Judging this to require some attention in the medium term he did a smart about turn and headed back up the hill.

Had you been following him you would have realised the reason the leak was small and insignificant at the bottom of the hill is that all the oil was in the middle of the hill; just before you spun out.

You would then have witnessed our unfortunate local lad making his way back up the hill until the point when the engine seized.

Our Lifeboat mechanic, who was heading up the hill shortly after and suddenly found he had no traction stopped to assist. He spent the next few hours pulling people out of trouble in his sizeable 4x4 until the local sheriffs arrived some two hours later.

The council have since covered the area with Sennen beach and currently there is no problem. Rain tomorrow might be interesting though.

*July 6th – Tuesday* – Well a bit of an England football team performance from the Met Office for today: lovely sunshine for most of the day; clouded over a bit in the evening. Let's hope they've got it wrong for tomorrow too.

Had a nice little order for Cove crab and lobster. Unfortunately when you're staying in a holiday let you don't always have the right facilities or equipment. Kind soul that my Missus is, lent our crab pot out and yours truly had to provide the cooking instructions. Fanny and Johnny, eat your heart out.

When we first started this addition to our already fearsome portfolio we thought about cooking the beasts as well. In this world gone mad I felt it best to check up on some of the industry best practice. It took a while trawling the internet, looking in the obvious places such as the venerable Food Standards Agency and Environmental Health – not a sausage, well, several sausage references but no crabs. Eventually tucked in the bowels of the Seafish website there was a mighty tome amongst its pages. I mean, who has the time, let alone the inclination, to write a document twice the size of War & Peace about the pit falls and do's and don'ts of cooking shellfish. Allow me to summarise the advice to a little shop run by two people: don't do it.

The amount of regulation, constraint, certification and compliance would make an EU Health and Safety chap squirm with inadequacy. Anyone would think we were making nuclear weapons. All we wanted to do was cook a flaming crab for heaven's sake.

(Oops, that's torn it. If you have a website don't use words like nuclear, weapon, bomb or chemical. Little crawlers on the Internet set off alarm bells in some shady office of the Ministry of Doom. There's some chap in MI5 going to be reading the Sennen Cove Diary from now on and wondering what the heck's going on down here.)

The day got rounded off nicely with a Lifeboat shout just after tea; this time another yacht with engine failure, two sick puppies on board and no chance of raising a sail. The 46 feet yacht is co-owned by the CEO of Hiscox, (Bermuda), the reinsurance firm. No shortage of expense, then, except maybe on engine maintenance.

Lifeboat made its best speed with yacht in tow to make it back for 1.20am with just enough water for short slip recovery carried out in a text-book operation by stalwart specialists know as The Shore Crew; shame then that the amateurs on board find it so difficult throwing a bit of rope.

*July 7th – Wednesday* – Overcast but largely dry; late turnout of folks around The Cove making us quite busy in the afternoon.

Had to do a run into town for some MDF to cover a gap behind the till where some slat wall was. It's a long story but involves my late-found skill of cutting up bits of wood and nailing them together, a form of construction that has parallels to carpentry but without the finesse and with bigger screws.

Anyway, I turned up at the national building supplies firm not long ago described. (Oh no, don't say I'm going to have to start indexing these entries for cross-referencing.) You may think I'm a glutton for punishment but it's roughly the only one so I don't have much of a choice.

However this time I was almost impressed. MDF isn't exactly the ideal eye-pleasing surface for a shop but my knowledge of available finishes isn't what you'd call broad. Then there was this swarthy builder type chap who actually asked what I was after and even asked what I wanted it for.

"How about a bit of this?" he offered, which was precisely the right thing. "It is for another customer but he's been is hospital for three weeks so why don't you have this bit and we'll order another."

Cue clouds parting, a big light and echoey voices singing hallelujah as the great god of Common Sense defeats his sworn enemies of Jobsworthiness and Aintmyjobmate.

I could have hugged him but I know that sort of thing is a tad taboo in builders' yards and can end up making your nose bleed. But, you know it couldn't finish there.

"I'll just go and ask me boss."

Now you just know that when management gets involved all evidence of common sense disappears rapidly into the red taped haze of bureaucracy. And sure enough the chap's simple request went through at least three levels of hierarchy, stone wall stares of outrage at his sheer temerity and much sucking of air through teeth.

You could see his frustration bleeding through his pores as Paperwork and The System reared up in front of him. He stood his ground and saw both those foes vanquished and emerged, at length, victorious. My hero.

Wait for next week's exciting episode as Swarthy Builder looks for a new job having been fired for innovation and using his brain.

Now off to launch the Lifeboat, on exercise, this time, with the coastguard in a stunning display of inter-service co-operation.

*July 8th – Thursday* – Not exactly wall to wall sunshine but not a half decent day to be getting on with and a lot of visitors thought so too. All rounded off with a sunset to write home about lighting up the mist hanging over Gwenver.

Quite a large swell running and we were lucky to get the lobster ordered yesterday. See the lengths our tough and dedicated fishermen go to just to satisfy our customers.

We are definitely on the outskirts of the main season now with more and more families turning up. The hours in the shop are flying by and you suddenly find out that all those things you were going to do today you'll have to do tomorrow instead.

The quirky things that happen that would be the focus of this page in a day are now becoming commonplace. Take for example the lady buying a skim board today. Now these things are the preserve of the young or the hard of thinking or both and this lady resembled neither. It's hardly circumspect to plainly state, "You're going to break your neck if you try skimming, luvver", plus I'm trying to sell it. So it took a little while to elicit that what she really wanted was an old-fashioned plywood body board.

After some consideration she felt determined to try using the skim board as an alternative body board. I did contemplate warning the lifeguards but I think it will be much more fun to let them witness for themselves a rough approximation of St Piran arriving on Sennen beach riding what, at a distance, looks like a slim millstone.

(And if you don't know your story of how St Piran arrived here you should be ashamed of yourself.)

*July 9th – Friday* – I don't know about you but I'm getting pretty miffed at The Met Office's inability to forecast anything remotely resembling the actual weather for the day. A poor forecast is as bad as having bad weather; people will decide to go to undercover attractions or St Ives. Fortunately some of our visitors aren't so easily fooled and after a dead quiet start, business picked up in the afternoon.

Now here's a sad tale of bureaucracy gone mad and governmental micro control; I was reminded of it because someone dropped off a bag full of dud batteries today.

Now why, I hear you ask, should I accept such a useless donation?

Well first, I had begger all else to write about and it was a bit of a godsend when it happened. And secondly I am required to do so by statute.

Since February this year anyone who sells more than 32kg of batteries in a year is compelled to provide a collection point. Not only for batteries that we have sold but also any portable appliance batteries. I am also required to advertise the fact that I am a collection point, no doubt on a sign x by y centimetres and in a font no smaller than p point.

I first investigated this at the beginning of the year. There are seven appointed main collection companies across the country and they are required to collect the batteries from us, at no charge. However the one I spoke to, the nearest, in Bristol, would only collect once we had filled three 25kg bags. Sometime shortly before the end of time for us I imagine.

To try and shorten this timescale a little I suggested to the two other battery sellers in Sennen that we pool our collections. I felt it probably best to check with the Environment Agency just to make sure this was inside the rules and blow me, it was, or rather wasn't covered and therefore a distinct possibility.

However. You knew there would be a however, didn't you? The nice lady at the EA very cleverly deduced that one, or more, of us would have to take our collected batteries to one of the other syndicate shops. In which case, of course, the transporter would need the appropriate licence for carrying mixed waste. If, on the other hand, we have separated out the nickel cadmium batteries we would need a hazardous waste carrier's licence.

Clearly nicad batteries are not hazardous when mixed with other batteries! There was some chap in a sweaty office in London twiddling his thumbs when this directive fell on his desk. He was no doubt delighted. Now, how can I make this five minute job last all year and involve all me mates? Ah yes!

Mr Cameron, when you get your MI5 report on the Sennen Cove Diary, there's this bloke in London that needs to go top of your cost cutting list. He's the one with the OBE for services to recycling and dropping unemployment by ten per cent.

And lastly police have caught a prolific underwear thief. No, really it was on the radio news. He was apparently the scourge of ladies' drawers until they got to the bottom of it and made a bust.

71

*July 10th – Saturday –* Don't think you can get away with that, Met Office. It was only this morning you changed your forecast to something close to today's weather. Please, sticking your head out of the window on the day and penning in some weather features does not constitute a forecast.

Still, lovely signs of business abounded despite the blanket of white cloud and, yes, we do know that it's going to rain tonight perfectly timed with me falling out of the F&L on my way home. That'll just teach me to go out and enjoy myself, won't it?

It was a day when a plague fell upon all those rich sorts in Truro as all the cash points stopped working. Now they know how it is to have the nearest free cash point five miles away. Down here you need to plan ahead if you want to have a few shillings in your pocket. And we do so love you to have shillings in your pocket.

It was only recently that Bank of Ireland generously donated a free cash point to be installed outside the Post Office in St Just. Here in The Cove we have nothing of the sort. The OS having removed theirs last year as it was often unserviceable or just unserviced when it wasn't robbing you of £1.75. In Sennen there is one in the Post Office shop and also in the F&L that will happily relieve you of a similar amount of your hard earned every time you look at it. They also don't accept foreign cards.

How then are we so derided over our paltry 60p cash back charge? You just don't know how good you got it and how we suffer for our art in The Old Boathouse Stores. Honest, guv!

*July 11th – Sunday –* What a lovely bit of day we had today. Warm and dry with our cosy little cloud cover, bit like being under a duvet.

I hope you will have noticed that the Diary has now caught up with the real date, you naughty people. Even my Dad let me blunder on with July 4th before letting me know today. It is a bit embarrassing as being a diary it's probably quite an important feature.

Our fish business came into its own over the weekend with multiple orders taken. It is a mystery why we haven't done this sooner and it really is quite good fun. We've even produced a leaflet on how to cook and dress your own crab so there really is no excuse now. So get on down here and have yourself a nice big crab and stop paying those ridiculous prices for your crab sandwiches.

The Lifeboat launched for Penberth Lifeboat Day this afternoon. Lord & Lady Banham open their garden in support of the RNLI each year and the Lifeboat slips around there to show some appreciation. It gives Mr G a chance to show off the boat's capabilities in an enclosed space and he really does an astounding performance, which, if you are on the boat, is a hair-raising experience, (or would be if I had any).

It all went a bit quiet at last knockings today, I can't imagine why. Some sort of sporting event I believe. What I do know is the flaming papers will be ultra-late tomorrow morning, probably with the ink drying on the pages.

*July 12th – Monday* – Listening to the 7:30am weather forecast for the week was a depressing affair. After every, "brightening up later" or, "rain clearing" statement came, "except in the far West and Isles of Scilly". It was enough to make me want to go to the end of the breakwater and toss myself off.

However a glimmer of hope brightened my heavy heart. I read in the papers that the BBC has signed the Met Office for another 5 year contract for their base data. Here come the blue skies.

Had a pensioners' coach trip turn up this morning, bless 'em. They'd all come from the blistering heat of Kent to be here. I think they were a bit confused that sunny Cornwall wasn't. Still, it was a few 15p postcards out the door.

You really can't help some people no matter how hard you try. I know the bus timetable is a wonderment to many and no surprise. We have done our best to simplify the comings and goings out of The Cove but it still leaves many reaching for the car keys.

One little old lady, graced with the bewilderment that only comes with great age, requested some assistance with the bus timetable. We had already been floored by her not knowing what time of day she wanted to leave or which destination she was interested in. Only a complete idiot would have persisted in responding to such a plea for help so she ended up talking to me.

In retrospect her just leaving on a bus, any bus, was probably the best solution. It is so hard to impart key information to someone who insists on talking when they should be listening. It ended with writing down the times of all the departing buses while she whittled on and pressing it, black spot like, into her cold and clammy palm.

If you see a little old lady on the tour bus looking as if she's been round a couple of times and utterly confused and in need of assistance, get off at the next stop.

*July 13th – Tuesday* – Oh dear, dear readers. It has been brought to my attention that in yesterday's sermon I may have upset the sensibility of some of you. Merely the suggestion that your humble Diarist may have contemplated a self-inflicted act against the person by propelling myself from the end of the breakwater clearly had some of you reaching for the Kleenex. Let's be brutally frank, I would have been a tad upset myself.

So let me give you my assurance that I have no such plans at present and that the near future, at least, of the Diary is vouchsafed. This in itself may have many of you heading for the end of the breakwater yourselves.

So Mr A, I hope that has cleared up the little mess I made for you yesterday.

Now, I'm sure you will all be bored to death if I went on again about how today was forecast to be rainy, and that I only ordered a rainy day's worth of bread and pasties, and how it turned out to be really sunny and warm, and we ran out of pasties and bread. So I won't.

Instead I shall wax lyrical a bit on how much we're learning about selling fish. Some of these lessons have been somewhat costly but by the time everyone's gone home we'll be experts just in time to forget it all before next year.

For example, when we order a kilogram of gurnard fillet we are charged for three kilograms of gurnard fillet because that's how much whole fish is required to produce the singe kilogram. So if you're talking about line-caught sea bass at £21.50 a kilo the exponential increase in price can be, well, a bit of a slap in the face with a wet fish.

Hopefully we are a little wiser now. Next year I can see a little vertical integration taking shape, (Miss Belfast, my school Economics teacher, if you're reading this please note that I was paying attention in class and not just besotted with your chest).

All aboard the Jolly Old Boathouse trawler.

*July 14th – Wednesday* – They do say, on a windy night, if you put one ear to the ground, you can hear the wind whistling in the other ear 'ole.

Yes, me hearties, there be a storm gathering in the South West likely to bring all sorts of doom and gloom upon us for tomorrow. For once I am with the Met Office, although I'm not sure the severity is quite as glower as they predict. So hang onto your tent pegs, we're in for a rough ride.

A vessel no stranger to a few big waves is the Feasible. Originally a 1912 steam drifter, lovingly restored in 2002, she was making her way to Newlyn for a refit. Unfortunately she started taking on water west of the Brisons on Tuesday night and Sennen Cove Lifeboat launched to tow her in. The full story is on the Sennen Cove website and, particularly her history is well worth a read.

For those of you with a mind to make something of those sorts of connections seaman Halliday was washed overboard and drowned in January 1936. He'd already been washed overboard once and back on board again. On the same day of the tow a soldier named Halliday was buried in Liverpool.

*July 15th – Thursday* – There's 'ell up in Truro this morning. Mrs Palm and presumably some of her close relations, have applied to open a shop of dubious character in the City. It is unfortunate that the premises available are squeezed between a school outfitters and a sweet shop. Some of the city elders and caring mothers are up in arms.

Meanwhile another group of city elders were visiting, against their will presumably, a lap dancing club on a fact finding mission, you understand. Happily they didn't have to fork out of their own pockets; these places are expensive for heaven's sake, (so I've heard). No, this was tax-payer funded and I'm so glad my hard earned went to such a worthy cause.

We have often thought about using the Old Boathouse stores for another purpose during the winter months and the way things are going this could be the year. Naturally we would respect the ambience of The Cove so we were thinking something along the lines of a series of tableaux à la Mrs Henderson's Windmill Theatre of the 1930s.

The ladies of the Chy Byghan retirement home have already expressed an interest as has the Wednesday Lunch Club although one or two are concerned that they wouldn't be able to remain still for more than a couple of minutes at a time. I think we might have to do something with the heating as well.

So, come November, city elders, you are cordially invited to see how exotic and heritage can be melded into a tasteful, cultural experience; on the tax-payer, of course!

And the best news of the day concerns our esteemed and committed parliamentary representative for this neck of the woods. A man who will stand up and be counted with passion and dedication for a cause he believes in. Never will you see this man falter in his fight for justice and would rather fall on his own sword than yield to the perpetrators of wrong.

So you will have no doubt that he set his lance at the proposed VAT rise and nailed his colours to the mast, caring not a jot for a mixed metaphor or two. He raised questions in parliament and faced up to the goliaths pushing through this heinous act.

Though battered and blasted by those giants and ultimately failing to turn their minds did he falter? Did he yield? Did he cease from mental fight and did his sword sleep in his hand?

Well, yes actually. Last seen heading for the queue marked the ayes to the right. But let's give the boy a little credit, he also voted for the nays.

*July 16th – Friday* – Thought we'd skipped straight through to November there for a while yesterday. The sea was wild, the wind high and the rain it pelted down.

It hadn't escaped my notice that it was indeed St Swithan's day yesterday. I felt it might have been a bit obvious and perhaps even a bad omen to bring it to the fore on the day itself. He must have been a bit of a smart lad, Swithan. He would have known that by the 20th century or so his name would have disappeared into oblivion much like Casimir of Poland, who was clearly expecting the canonisation of a whole raft of other Casimirs and Denis, patron saint of fire engines.

Engineering his immortalisation must have been some trick. Ok, getting buried in some grim and damp place was the easy bit. Orchestrating seven weeks of precipitation after some misguided monks tried to move your mortal remains took a bit of pulling off, I have to admit. And one thing's for sure: he didn't work for the Met Office else it would have been Swithan who? by now.

Much more clement day today with a few lost souls wandering around just so pleased it wasn't raining anymore.

F&L are putting on a bit of a summer party tonight with BBQ and surf band which I'm contemplating attending purely on a fact finding mission, you understand. Dress is summer party wear. In the end discretion got the better of me; couldn't find my galoshes and overcoat either.

*July 17th – Saturday* – Blue sky and sunshine – a total beach day.

A new influx of visitors, which is always refreshing and plenty of wetsuits, body boards and beach goods going out the door. Three nice big fat lobsters delivered on a same day service. That's what you call going the extra mile.

I sometimes just wonder if people really appreciate just what a fantastic shop The Old Boathouse is. You just don't know how much we suffer to bring the people of the world great goods and perfect service. Working night and day, fingers worked to the bone, shoulders up against that wheel and noses rubbed raw on the grindstone.

Feeling sorry for us yet? Ready to throw your accolades in this direction – or just money? Nope, didn't think so.

Well, blow you lot anyway. It's off to the F&L for definite tonight. Devil's Creek are playing and you don't miss them if you can help it.

All you're going to get tomorrow is a jaded old shopkeeper giving a raggedy, half attentive service and probably the wrong change. Yup, back to normal tomorrow.

A footnote on the night's performance. They say that blues guitar players are born not made. Okay perhaps I made that up but this boy can sure play blues guitar like it was an extension to his body. His voice is gritty and resonant. Their version of Red House probably had Hendrix wishing he'd paid more attention in class. Why these boys, and Guy in particular, have not had greater media attention is a mystery. But, selfishly, I'm glad 'cos I can still see them at the F&L and not fork out £80 plus, (of which they're worth every penny), to see them in the far distance of a major music venue.

*July 18th – Sunday* – Rather a half decent day again, and again completely at odds with the forecast. Consequently the day took a little while to kick off until people realised they'd been duped.
I'm going to start a campaign to have the calendar date stay the same forever; it is such a bore having to change the Diary header everyday. Thanks to J&D for pointing this out this time.

Lifeboat shout last night at around 1.00am. This was for a man-over-board, actually a woman, about fifty miles out. Yachts returning from the Cork weekend lost a team member over the side. She was in the water for two hours before a fishing boat spotted her and the Chivenor helo picked her up. She is recovering in Treliske.

This was amazing in itself and the woman is one lucky little bunny, that's for sure. However the real story here is the woman's fortitude. Initially it was reported she was in the water without any lifejacket or buoyancy aid. The truth emerged that the lifejacket she was wearing was attached to the boat by a safety line. Having fallen off, with the speed of the yacht, the line was dragging her under and against the boat. In a fabulous moment of clarity she reasoned to remove the jacket and her wellies and use her waterproofs as a buoyancy aid.

In a heavy swell and in such a moment of trauma how many of us would have had the presence of mind to act so calmly?

*July 19th – Monday* – First, Happy Birthday to my Father-In-Law; he's unlikely to read this as he doesn't have a computer but it's the thought that counts, I'm told.

I must have some masochist in me from somewhere. It could have come through my mother's side although she was a nurse so that probably makes her a sadist. Perhaps she was a carrier. Her father ran his own business, so he must have been a masochist, although I think he would have been bamboozled in today's risk and blame averse environment. He was in haulage.

Perhaps I should explain that I haven't been piercing parts of my body or walking over hot coals although it's starting to look attractive by comparison. No, I've been trying to elicit some simple information from my utility company.

To cut to the chase, I applied for a direct debit over the telephone a few months ago despite having resisted their wily attempts for some years. Call me impulsive if you will, but I have that wild streak in me. I think it came from a distant uncle who used to take his clothes off at cricket matches. Never belong to club that would have you as a member he used to say then stride off with a big cigar in his mouth and a strangely bent gait.

But I digress.

I had parted with the salient details that allowed the young lady to plunder my bank account for large sums of hard earned.

Two months later and still no plundering; something's amiss.

My masochistic gene gave me a little nudge. I telephoned them.

Rather cleverly they have a telephone system that you tell your account number to. This is so the agent has your details before they answer the telephone.

It works like this. You speak your account number to an electronic voice. It says it doesn't understand you. You key in your account number. It repeats it back. The operator answers the telephone.

"Hello, can I have your account number please?"

"I told your telephone system and it repeated to me. Didn't it tell you?"

"No, it doesn't work."

I don't know how many departments 'lectric 4 You has but I think I spoke to most of them. Eventually someone admitted that they had an outsourced unit selling the direct debit offer. They use a different computer system, their own probably, and pass the customer details back to 'leccy 4 You by spreadsheet. How quaint!

"So what happened to my direct debit, then?"

"Er, we lost the spreadsheet."

"Um, it had my bank details on it."

"Oh!"

"Quite. Oh."

I have a masochistic urge to send them a letter. I can only blame the parents.

*July 20th – Tuesday* – Like the old 1970's film, The Fog, is back. It's a terrible, terrible thing . . . the movie, that is, although the mist is pretty bad too. It has been with us all day and despite the forecaster's promise that it would clear from the west in the early afternoon.

As appears to be the standard the beach was red flagged. The lifeguards want to be able to see people drown and not just hear them.

The hiatus did give us a chance to take on board the shipping order we need in preparation for next week. This is when we hope all hell will break loose and we'll be inundated with customers. All the same we'd prefer to be busy non-stop and just collapse in a heap in September.

Mist cleared early evening and, yes, the bay is still there and everyone came out of the woodwork as if materialising out of thin air.

Strange days like these we can do with having few and far between, thank you.

*July 21st – Wednesday –* Well that's it. I suppose it had to come at some point. The grubby signs of modern civilisation have ever been edging in this direction and now, it seems, they have arrived. But even inevitable, they are still unwelcome visitors.

Yes, the dark shadow of crime has fallen over this little preserved corner of the world.

It would have started so well too. The sun broke through this morning and it all went off like a rocket. Had to make an emergency run to our store to pick up more stock. Yippee customers at last.

Did that sound enthusiastic and genuine? Good, I'm so glad because I don't want to burden you with the aching sorrow that pervades my once joyful heart.

Forecast for the weekend looks pretty good and there's more than an even chance they're right for a change. So pack your bags and get on down here sharpish. Oh, and don't forget your shillings!

Of course you would need fewer of them but for the senseless criminal acts these low forms of life perpetrate against us.

It's also beginning to look like the season's started. The beach is crammed but mainly because the tide is in, people enjoying their al fresco meals, even outdoors, and youngsters tomb-stoning off the breakwater. The latter is perfectly safe, by the way. Unless you do it at low tide when it will hurt rather as there's no water in the harbour.

Our master criminal perhaps should try it, the swine.

I spent all today hoping that whosoever it was would come in and own up. He was desperate, destitute, his children were sick and needed sustenance; Russian mafia had his family held hostage and he did it under duress; he'd been hypnotised by aliens and had no notion of what he was up to. And of course, worse still it could have been a her.

Sadly I waited in vain. Some begger filched a litre of skimmed milk sometime between 6.00am delivery time and 7.00am when I got downstairs. Skimmed for God's sake! Who steals skimmed milk? Not even a bleddy blue tit would steal skimmed milk! It is a deed most foul that will go down in the annals of criminal history as one of the great unsolved mysteries of our time. At least in Sennen Cove.

*July 22nd – Thursday* – The molten sunshine was bouncing off the paving stones this morning but had mainly ceased by the time we opened. Looking at the rain radar, kindly provided by the Met Office as a reality check against their daily guesses, we're in for a bit more.

But, blow me, it stayed largely dry, though a little overcast at times with a cool northerly breeze. Once people had worked out what pants the forecast was they started turning up in numbers in the afternoon.

Fish, crab and lobster orders seem to be turning over nicely, though there seems to be a scarcity of mackerel. I understand from our expert fishermen that they begger off to St Ives on a rainy day, just like everyone else.

Managed to ruin someone's day by letting her use our tape measure to fit a pair of ladies shorts; unfortunately the numbers on the tape exceeded her expectations. I'm not sure I helped by telling her I'd see if we had an extra large in the shorts she was after.

You do have to weigh up all the factors before joshing with a customer thus. For example are her arms longer than the width of the counter and is she carrying something that would serve as a makeshift cudgel? I think I did all right. At least the swelling on my left ear is easing a little.

*July 23rd – Friday* – A spankingly good day full of sun, swimsuits, buckets and spades and plenty of smiles; I think you have the picture. And the best t-shirt caption this year, "Hug me, I'm organic". I didn't, incidentally, no matter what anyone says.

Our big pots for cooking crab turned up today. The grand plan is to lend these out with crab orders as most of the holiday lets won't have pans big enough. Watch the crab sales dry up now.

Went to our store after closing to do a spot of restocking, heck, we just can't stop when we get going. We have to be a bit choosy as to what goes in the store as it isn't mouse proof. As if to prove the point I uncovered a small nest amongst our boxes.

Now you're either going to be pragmatic with me or hate me forever. So if you're a big softy where small animals are concerned, look away now.

I'm afraid the nest had to go. As I turned it out in the field I noticed the tiniest of creatures, barely alive I'd suggest. With a little more investigation there was a larger model, no bigger than the first joint of my thumb, which was a little more lively, the beast, not the thumb joint. I consulted our local expert who reckoned from my detailed description that it was a common shrew that I'd evicted.

Come on, they're wild animals and they're now out in the wild. I could have done worse and squished them, now couldn't I? No actually I couldn't; they looked ever so sweet and I felt really guilty afterwards.

Anyway, hopefully the stock is safe for another little while so I guess you could call that a shrewd move!

*July 24th – Saturday* – Well, this is the day we thought we'd be buried in customers throwing their hard earned shillings in our direction. Busy though it was it didn't quite come up to expectations.

Of course not helped by this week's occupants of the holiday let two doors down, begins with a Sanderling, (you know who you are) calling in their groceries from an overpriced, poor quality, purveyor from PZ. Shopping local to these people presumably means not going to Fortnums.

Rubbing salt into the wound again, (see June 6th – hey, cross indexation really rocks), the driver had to ask directions from us. Obviously I was very adult about it and politely instructed him. Wonder how long he spent looking around St Just?

Weather was another factor with low cloud all day but warm and mainly dry; would have put off the less hardened visitor. But then the mist descended.

Goodnight Vienna . . . er Sennen Cove.

*July 25th – Sunday* – Lifeboat Flag Day and what a jolly day it was too. The sun it did shine nearly all day after a bit of a dodgy start. The visitors, verily did they flock to our shores and mightily did they maketh merry.

One very merry sole arrived outside our shop in his silver Saxo automotive transport. He was in such haste to acquire some early morning beverage of the merry making type he did quite forget how to navigate, mounting the pavement so close to the shop that had the bleddy hound been there she would have been very thin by now. He also scat his wing mirror on our wheelie bin.

The Missus took great delight, therefore, in advising the lanky youth that Mr Cameron's willingness to reduce the open all hours drinking policy this country, in error, has adopted had come early to The Cove; we can't sell alcohol before 10.00am on a Sunday.

Mr Plod, if you're reading and have an interest, we have his index number.

Other hapless vehicular visitors to this end of The Cove include a preponderance of happy caravaners. Happy, that is until they discover, for the larger part, that they cannot progress further because of the awkward corner around Tinker Taylor and the Roundhouse.

The reason for their demise is that there is a caravan park half way to St Just that insists on calling itself Sennen Cove Caravan Park. If you're heading there it is quite reasonable to suggest, but clearly quiet wrong, that you would follow the signs to Sennen Cove.

Yesterday, in front of an audience of Lifeboatmen blessed with the most wicked sense of humour, one such caravan driver arrived. Seeing the possible difficulty ahead he despatched his missus to scout out the way ahead. In a decision that will have, no doubt, led to some good natured banter around the campfire that evening she gave her hubby the OK to proceed.

Now the clever thing about the corner at Tinker Taylor is that getting in is easy. It is the getting back again that is the interesting part. There is a nasty granite post right on the corner, its purpose is to protect the corner of the house from caravaners and other larger vehicles and does its job exceeding well. As a right hand car driver it's almost impossible to see.

Our brave Lifeboatmen, alerted to the impending entertainment, each found a comfy viewing angle.

To give the chap his due he did an admirable job. It did take him a while, though, causing traffic to back up in both directions. He received a hearty congratulation from the gathered crew.

We have seen a double decker bus do it once. He had lost reverse gear and had no choice. It did rather involve more brute force than finesse but still managed to get back through with only minor scrapes from the granite post and the metal fender at the top of Tinker Taylor's roof.

What an exciting day.

*July 26th – Monday* – Had a few moments today so decided to dust off my 1936 edition of Boys Own Book of Fib Telling. What an interesting read it was too. Sure it can be applied even in today's complex world.

Well I'm sure you expected me to lay into the huge bonuses handed out to those lovely chaps at the Met Office for doing such a fab job. Their forecasts have been so faultless that you and I have given them a few extra shillings in their back pocket this month. But I'll hear nothing of it. I'm sure they deserve every penny.

Instead I'll enlighten you to two other things that happened today and neither of them very pleasant.

First our friend, he of the impaired driving skills, came back. Not that I knew it at the time as the Missus served him yesterday. You just have one of the 'uh, oh' moments when certain people walk in and he was one of them. Armed with two cans of strong lager he wanted pay by card then he didn't, then he did, then he wanted small change, then a note. Oh yes, a right bright spark this one.

Needless to say any shrift he receives on his next visit will not be lengthy.

The second bad thing was that our perfectly pleasant sunshiny day turned increasingly to cloud. It started high then came lower and lower until our heads were in it. Can't see a bleddy thing now.

> *Shopkeeper, never chase the sun.*
> *Laugh yourself, and turn away.*
> *Mask your hunger; let it seem*
> *Small matter if he come or stay;*
> *But when he nestles in your hand at last,*
> *Close up your fingers tight and hold him fast.*

With a little apology to Robert Graves whose birthday it was today.

Sorry GBS, just didn't have the time, Happy Birthday to you too.

*July 27th – Tuesday* – Not the most blessed July day The Cove has ever seen but as I pointed out to a few customers it's warm and it's dry and as Mr Steinman would have us believe, "two out of three ain't bad". Then in the early afternoon it turned to one out of three, which was.

Received a package in the post today from  obviously well heeled and avid fans, okay it was my parents; a mousetrap and a humane one at that apropos of my rodent problem in the store. I shall treasure it always.

The following may sound ungrateful, so please do not misunderstand me; I would hate to dissuade other keen readers from sending me gifts, say, piles of unwanted ten pound notes, just for example.

Allow me to expand upon the logical process my mind is following here. Your average mouse finds his way into my store, sniffs some tasty morsel secreted down this tube, which rather worryingly closes behind him. Well things ain't so bad, tasty morsel to eat, nice snug tube to sleep in, safe from predators. Then in the morning he is transported and released back to the same field he came from the previous night.

The point is this: if I were a mouse, had free food, safe lodgings and a free trip home what would I do?

"Hey, Mickey! Here a minute. You'll never guess what happened to me last night?"

"You're kidding, right? No way! Hey Minnie, get the kids, we're going on a trip."

No offence, Mum, Dad, but I think I might require a less mouse friendly solution.

*July 28th – Wednesday* – My mouse problem seems to have taken on a life of its own. I've been inundated with an email which shows just how desperately popular this subject has been. Thank you MM, but a 'no vacancy' sign just won't cut it, though I'm sure it works fine in the polite society of South Carolina. These are Cornish mice, a rough lot, and therefore know that 'no vacancy' during July and August simply means you can squeeze a few more in if the price is right.

Despite a dodgy forecast the weather turned out to be pretty fair today and all in all pretty busy too. Low cloud didn't plague us until late in the afternoon then everything disappeared. Which is amazing as it was Culdrose Air Day today and it usually tips down.

They usually send something down this way and this year it was a couple of bi-planes of the wing walking display. (Why I specified bi-planes I don't know. Wing walking on a mono plane would be quiet a feat.) Anyway the wing walkers obviously didn't fancy the long haul and got off somewhere en route.

Had to trip out to St Just on a covert mission this evening, no, please don't ask, it was covert. Anyway it'll be all over the press tomorrow: secrets ain't what they used to be. Anyway, as they say around here, the mist was as thick as a bag, which is going to force my hand into revealing a pet hate.

Now you'd think in failing light and visibility down below fifty yards, headlights would be a no-brainer. Well it is, so what does that make those people driving with parking lights or no lights at all? Invisible, mainly. They're called 'parking' lights for a reason. My guess is that these are the same people who drive around in perfect conditions with their fog lights on.

And on a lighter note, TL tells me another reader has come out of the closet, though what he was doing in there I really have no idea. It occurs to me we ought to have a reader's Christmas bash this year. The three of us will have a right good time.

*July 29th – Thursday* – Hardly anything could ruin a perfectly good day like today: the sun splitting the hedges from the off, endless lines of happy customers and a couple of happy shopkeepers.

I'm sure you all have an inkling that we have miles of beautiful countryside down here, (for those of you who live in conurbations and are unfamiliar, that's the greenish dry bit opposite the bluish wet bit). Too many miles for those of you who reach Launceston and think, "Ah, Cornwall, we're nearly there"!

There are certain sets of people, who, despite being washed out year after year enjoy setting up little tents when away. These people are called campers or, as we like to put it, hopeless optimists. For this purpose kindly, (spelt enterprising in Cornish), landowners have set aside plots of land complete with services such as running water, (from a tap, as opposed to through your tent), showers and other facilities. It works very well, so I'm told, giving the camper a sense of oneness with nature, (mainly the beetles, ants, funny smells, etc.), in greenish pleasant surroundings.

Why then would anyone wish to pitch their tents in a parking bay in the Harbour Car Park? I don't believe they even had a ticket.

A chap turned up this morning sporting a t-shirt with the logo, 'BBC Documentary, Making Mike Stay'. This could not pass without comment, so I commented. The chap said he was Mike and was intending to move to Australia. The documentary was about a group of people making him walk around the coastline of Britain from Dover with the aim of making him stay.

I think his mates want him to go; I can't think of anything more likely to compel me to begger off than being frogmarched around the coast with a camera stuck in my face.

Paradoxically I don't think he wants to go. First it would be a very short documentary if he decided in Brighton that he'd had enough and secondly he was a bit reticent to leave The Cove. Three hours, he was, having his brekky across the road.

Still awake? Heck, you think this is a long one. I've already had to defer one of the stories until tomorrow.

But finally if you want to know the time, ask a policeman, but please, not in Sennen Cove.

Our local bobby often comes and shows a presence outside the local tea kiosk for an hour or two, (maybe a small exaggeration, Superintendent). It is a well-known crime hotspot, obviously, and a handy place to park to deter would be illicit dog-walkers and insurgent bird spotters.

They are, of course, not just there in a crime-stopping role. In the matter of a few minutes our knowledgeable peelers had directed disoriented visitors to the toilets, Lands End, the beach, a good place to have cream teas and informed them of the local cinema showing times.

With Tourist Information centres due to close all over the county it is good to know that the cost saving measure isn't going to leave our visitors in the dark.

Unfortunately I didn't witness this selfless act of community spirit; the police car wasn't there as long as usual.

*July 30th – Friday* – First, a very big welcome to TC for coming out and joining us, welcome brother and share the love. [FX: heavy boots running into distance.] Only kidding TC we have yet to reach full evangelical status.

Your suggestion of a Christmas club weekly subscription is an excellent idea. Just send a tenner a week to the address on the website and I'll keep it safe, well, until we fold just before the holidays.

Low cloud clearing just before lunchtime. Warm and dry until late afternoon when that horrid little weather front came through. But even then not half as bad as the picture the forecast painted.

Got a call from a young lad representing the electricity board, who had read my letter of last week and wanted to acknowledge they'd got it. Of course had I known in advance it was them calling I would have asked him to key his telephone number into the key pad, got him to wait ten minutes then asked him to repeat it.

Anyway, this is the letter that suggested they were somewhat negligent in losing my bank details on a piece of paper passed between a third party, that did some work for them, and one of their departments, (see July 19th). Please, you must try harder to keep up. I also regretted losing the discount I would have had by now had they not lost it.

The young man was very polite and offered a discount that I would have had as compensation for not applying the direct debit earlier. The amount was small, compared to the electricity bill, enough to buy half a dozen pints at the F&L or half of soda and lime and the OS. Fair's fair: I accepted. Oh and would I still like him to pursue the small matter of losing my bank details? Nice try 'lecky man, too right I would me 'ansum. I'm hanging on for one of those out of court settlements that pays off the mortgage.

The OS, despite its shortcomings, was always going to be the place to be tonight. The Mosquitoes were playing and just about anyone of note was there getting on down.

They play hard and fast, a Mexican group from Hayle, a town that has far more than its fair share of Mexican connections, tipped a sombrero to a Latino beat and had even the most timid on the dance floor. G assures me that they're for real and from Hayle's famous Mexican quarter. Still I'm not so sure, as none of them had a droopy moustache. Nevertheless the illusion works so well.

The lead singer's boundless energy was clearly infectious. Their ability to carry impossible songs into the mainstream is the stuff of legend. If you listen hard, lyrics like, "We're hairio, we're scario, we give you malario", from their title track just slip into place alongside the dance crazy beat. Even the, (slightly) slower Angelo – "Angelo, he was the baddest on the peddalo." failed to get the jumping floorboards to stop vibrating.

What a white hot night it was.

*July 31st – Saturday* – Groggy start but brighter later: That's me not the weather although the weather was doing something similar.

We appear to have a new transatlantic reader, I think. Welcome DH and sorry MM you are no longer alone that side of the pond but we still love you, honest.

Busy in parts today but not a patch on previous years. We hope that this isn't becoming a pattern for the rest of the summer holidays.

Mr Supermarket home delivery driver dropped in again. He's really taking the mickey now, though he did have the decency to be wearing an embarrassed smile as he came over the threshold. He wasn't falling for the St Just ruse again so I sent him to St Levan.

Familiar faces are starting to appear for the normal first two weeks of August fling. Our friends from Northampton way pitched up early with hounds in tow. The dogs are currently ensconced in our flat with our hound looking a little nose out of joint. And, of course the two young offspring are in attendance.

We have been cultivating these two from an early age to appreciate the Dickensian art of child labour. Not that we're sending them up chimneys, how cruel would that be? No, we have coached them to cry pitifully outside the shop and lure innocent and caring adults into the clutches of the expert sales team within. The little minxes are well looked after, naturally, with a pat on the head and always the promise of sweeties in abundance if they turn up again tomorrow. Ah, the innocence of youth.

Not sure I'll be making it up the F&L tonight having over trained slightly last night. No doubt I'll feel as right as ninepence come time to go and end up regretting it all tomorrow. Ah, the hardships one has to endure.

# August

*August 1st – Sunday –* Welcome to August.

Met office played a blinder today. They changed the forecast first thing from grey and miserable all day to sunny spells from mid morning. It rained all day. What a classic!

Here at The Old Boathouse we're always keen to help customers out with their queries, no matter how bizarre or difficult. As a case in point a lady asked me today if I was into athletics. I told her that, though once my frame mimicked that of the late Johnny Weismuller, a tragic injury had cut short my dazzling career in sport. The doctors also told me I'd never play the piano again which was a relief since I'd never been able to play it before either.

Since then I had concentrated on the slightly less taxing pastimes of drinking heavily, eating and sleeping it off. Sadly the Weismuller physique hasn't endured such a sedate lifestyle, which is now more Oliver Hardy without the moustache.

At which point the lady interrupted and said what she really meant was had I heard how Jessica Ennis or some chap did in the Heptathlon, which I hadn't.

I'm very grateful to some news feeds coming in from different directions.

First to the South East seaboard of the USA where, jealous of our recent over-hyped jelly fish attack here in The Cove, they have organised one of their own. Luckily our hardened reporter has a pool to retire to in such events but even that is not free from the dangers of the natural world. Agkistrodon piscivorus lives on a diet of fish and frogs but has been known to indulge in a little carrion and has been also known to frequent our reporter's pool. It is related, (distantly), to our Cornish viper and is commonly known as a Water Moccasin or Cotton Mouth over there. Venomous, its bite can make you very poorly or occasionally dead – so please be careful MM, The Diary can't afford to lose you.

And our second input, I've deduced from references to racing pigeons and black pudding, (no pulling the wool over our eyes, TC), comes from up t'north and is very concerned that the increasing readership will put an unbearable strain on my resources.

Aye, 'appen like as not, lad, go to the foot of our stairs, ba Christmas t'Diary will be writing its sen, (and for the benefit of

90

those readers listening in English: By Yuletide the Sennen Cove Diary will be entirely written by contribution).

*August 2nd – Monday* – A day not even the most super of superlatives could adequately describe. We were mobbed from the off today and don't mind admitting we were overcome on occasions. The weather hung in there like a Trojan with just enough cloud to get people off the beach and into the shop. Don't you just love it when a plan comes together?

Well almost - ran out of pasties before lunch despite having ordered many more than normal. That's the irksome thing about days like this: no matter how hard you try and prepare it's never quite enough.

Now as the great bird of speed drops one in the eye of the sands of time and the sun starts to tinge the cloud with ribbons of red and orange, it's time to restock and prepare for a slightly less full on day tomorrow if the forecast is to be believed.

Feeling sorry for us yet? About as sorry as I'll be, thinking of all you lovely chaps toiling away when I have my feet up in November I expect.

*August 3rd – Tuesday* – Not quite the rip sizzler we would have liked as a follow on to yesterday. However the mizzle and low cloud cleared away and left a half good afternoon with even some bits of blue towards the end.

Several businesses in The Cove should be mindful that today is a bit of a red letter day. Without the momentous occasion that occurred in 1829 we would be seeing visitors perplexed, trying to make do with makeshift bowls or trying to balance their creamy frozen deserts on a napkin, perhaps.

Oddly, the first usage of this essential food item was seen at a musical concert and, rather specifically, one that was playing Rossini's William Tell. Yes, it was in the newspaper today that on August 3rd 1829 the first cornet was used.

We should be mindful too about the chap who pointed out that the Granchester clock time was set at ten to three and more famously that some corner of a foreign field would forever be England. And he should know since he wound up buried in one, dying not from enemy ballistics but from an unsanitary mosquito: how the irony must have stung. Yes, for the benefit and edification of our readers we give you Mr Rupert Brooke, whose birthday it was today in 1887. Have heart, though, it wasn't all bad for the fellow. Allegedly he had a bit of a frolic with Virginia Wolfe, skinny dipping in Cambridge, which must have been interesting.

Doomed though it may be, I feel duty bound to attempt to add a little culture throughout these pages from time to time. It is merely for your edification and to add a little colour to your fraught and hectic lives. I doubt very much that it works but it does so pad out an otherwise abrupt entry.

And lastly, a very Merry Birthday to me dear old Mum, (well it's tomorrow, actually but I'm always a day behind or in front or something), who's still a little poorly and at the mercy of a crumbling NHS, which seems to be more crumbly up there than it is down here.

So as the strains of the last post of reality echo across The Cove, played on the ice cream cornet of nature, it's time to say goodnight and enter our own particular land of dreams.

*August 4th – Wednesday* – Well, after a right dodgy start the sun broke through and gave in to some lovely blue skies. Unfortunately the wind picked up from the north and made it rather chilly.

This does not seem to have mattered one iota to the army of beach visitors camped out across Whitesands. Our windbreak supplies seem to have taken a little battering too. Whoopee!

A few years ago now I did a well walk. Stop tittering in the back, there, I've had enough rise taken out of me by the Missus, thank you. It involved following a chap around St Just looking into holes in the ground. The chap is Rory Te'Tigo, he of the Lands End roadside statues fame, and very knowledgeable he was too. Knowledgeable, possibly, but blessed with common sense, no.

He's doing it again this year and probably on his own. I imagine he spent a good deal of time knocking up his schedule, brushing up on his well history and printing a nice big yellow sign that he touted around the locality. The dates are nicely spaced and in high season too and the walk includes a cream tea at Boscaswell House Hotel so should attract a decent crowd.

Well, no actually, not a soul will turn up. Unfortunately he omitted to mention where to gather for this edifying event or even, if you managed to guess, you wouldn't have a clue what time, he left that off too.

Fish, crab and lobster really took off today; we could hardly fit them all in the refrigerator. We had to break up a boundary dispute between two crabs that was about to turn a bit nasty.

We were lucky too as the sea state took a turn for the worse and all fishing was cancelled. Our man Big J really pulled out all the stops to get us our lobsters. What a very good man his is too.

Look out for big prices on line caught in the next few days.

*August 5th – Thursday* – Another dink blusher of a day and did the folk go mad, mad, mad. Yes they did. However by sixish you could see the mackerel sky herald the promised front bringing in the wet stuff and some dank weather. You just knew it couldn't last.

An even bigger fish day, the biggest so far of the new venture; there were so many crabs we had to set up a soup kitchen to keep them all happy. It was the endless cups of iced tea that really did us in. Bleddy fussy these Newlyn crabs, the Sennen boys just sit there and take what you throw at them. Hardy sorts.

Couldn't tell you much of what happened today; it all went by in such a rush. I can tell you by the end of the day the shelves were empty and my bones had started to creak a little.

The Missus, bless her, went lame first thing with some sort of foreign bug. Gave her a few minutes off to recoup her strength then pressed her back into action again. You know, I must have a benevolent streak in me somewhere. Can't imagine where it came from but I must get it fixed some time.

And lastly a small matter needs to be cleared up. A reader, who shall remain nameless for his own security, is confused that there appears to be two personas involved in the production of The Diary, the Diarist and Shop Keeper.

Well Mr X, never heard of Bruce Wayne and Batman, Clark Kent and Superman, John Prescott and Harriet Harman, (well have you ever seen them together?) Clearly you are sworn to secrecy from this moment forth and take this dangerous knowledge to the grave.

Please eat this diary entry after reading.

*August 6th – Friday* – Misty grey start to the day with a little mizzle to add to the unpleasantness; dried out later but still a good amount of cloud around.

Spent the first half of the day below stairs in the scullery, cooking crab for the upstairs lot; daresay I'll get the scrapings from the table if I behave well enough. Ended the day with a crab picking party with the girls. Surprised they didn't start singing,

'You'll never walk alone'. But that was a clam bake so it probably wouldn't have worked anyway.

I did tell you yesterday that the Sennen crustaceans are a tough bunch. The lobsters were in the freezer at about -25 for a good hour and three quarters. When I got them to the pot they were still making a bid for freedom. Had to give them another hour before they eventually went under. Cooked up lovely though – gosh how we slum it down here.

Another bit of nastiness last night in The Cove. Some kids thought it a great giggle to set fire to the toilet rolls in Mr Shannon's car park toilet and the wheelie bins as well for good measure. I'm sure the Fire Brigade thought it highly amusing too.

Well that's the end of one of the most boring and monotonous Diary entries for a while. Of course you may disagree, that it's been a while, that is. However I make a solemn promise that I won't mention fish, crab or lobsters in the next entry.

Got a nice bit of butterfly leg of lamb coming tomorrow.

*August 7th – Saturday* – I hake to carp on about the weather but it was amazing how quickly the grey clouds shot away this morning leaving us with clear blue skies just before opening. Nice to see a few sun breams at last; it's about time we hal a but of good fortune.

A little bit out of range this but interesting nevertheless. A couple of dedicated soles, from Dover possibly, have reinvigorated a watermill out at Zennor and are now producing flour available from their plaice and at local farmers markets. They are using traditional method of high milling involving grinding the wheat twice for finer flour. The chap leading it was big in fashion in the 70s and still keeps a mean mullet and a few colourful crevettes.

It is amazing what you can achieve if you put your mind and a bit of hard work to it. A big success like this and the world's your oyster.

Our friends staying up the back here had a bit of a shock yesterday. No sooner had they opened the door to let a bit of air through than a sparrow hawk flew in. The chap's a keen amateur photographer so what was the first thing he reached for? Yup, a towel to throw over it. Had I missed such a photo opportunity I think I would have been inclined to clam up about it.

So as the last of the sun's ray wings over us, it's a case of rallying the spirit to force some enjoyment at the F&L. Another

Cornish rock band and at least they know how to tuna guitar, maybe a bass guitar at that. I think they play some local take on rock ballads so it's likely we'll hear a bit of Bon an Chovey. I'm sure the evening will be brill.

Ah well, cod is in his heaven or perhaps that's just an old monk tail. Either way a day to warm the cockles of your heart.

Sorry, had to be done.

*August 8th – Sunday* – Summer visited The Cove today in all its glory and all things were joyous.

The Lifeboat had an exercise launch to show off a bit, taking our revered Head Launcher on a jolly. Pity the poor chap who had to look after a very vocal Tyson who isn't too keen going on board with his Dad; the dog never stopped barking until the boat came back.

We spent the whole day flying and running out of things again which is so frustrating and something we can do very little about. Even now, late in the evening, we have a team of young slaves re-stocking shelves. And before you lot go all reformist on me we're only reviving the old traditions where children used to work in the mines for a pittance. It's good for tourism.

That reminds me, I need to go down and put some bread and water under the door lest those chaps from 'save the oppressed' get a bee in their bonnet about me.

Only a short one today as I'm completely cazzoodled.

*August 9th – Monday* – This is a very biblical type of land down here. For every good day we have we are visited upon by pestilence and plague tenfold. Today's plague was low cloud and mizzle to start the day and low cloud thence onwards. Although teasingly some blue sky made an appearance shortly before it started raining frogs.

Tomorrow we are to be beset by locusts and every first born shall have boils on their bums. But I think that's more to do with what they ate in St Ives, Flambards or wherever they went on their grey day today.

A note to any Parish Councillor listening in to this broadcast: some investment in wet weather activities in The Cove would not go amiss. I'm thinking a waterslide off Ped-men-du, perhaps, convert the funicular at Carn North to one of those fast vertical lifts that make people spill their milkshakes over themselves and a covered awning over the length of Cove Road under which bumper cars could be deployed.

For good measure we could all wear bright red uniforms, say hi de hi a lot and have a baby with the best boil on its bum contest.

And isn't it true that when you're trying to break yourself of a habit or a fixation there are reminders everywhere. Today sees the birthday in 1593 of Izaak Walton, he of The Compleat Angler fame; bleddy fish again. Though how he managed to write a book when he couldn't even spell the title is beyond me.

Of course it wasn't a big seller until Waterstones opened in 1982.

*August 10th – Tuesday* – A morning of gloom and wet, drying out in the afternoon and breaking through to unneeded sunshine by the evening. Damnit!

A good day for delivering sofas, you'd think. Well not if you're Does Furniture Sometimes, according to one of our roving reporters. Said company decide to send an eight tonne truck to the narrow country lanes of Cornwall from some foreign part.

Having scraped in with the lorry largely in one piece they decide the slope before them a little too Eiger like and run for their flat land of multi-lane highways.

Furniture to Suit Everyone, unless you live in a slightly awkward place on a hill.

But for a misguided act of philanthropy in 1842 we would have been spared today's torture.

We had a dark and menacing visitation today. Two small children and their mother, we thought, but no. This was Beelzebub and Astaroth on an earthly rampage set to pour terror into the hearts of unsuspecting shopkeepers.

The signs were clear, such as grimacing and smarting at the sounds of 'please' and 'thank you' and removing delicate ornaments from the shelves and smashing them heartily on the floor. When confronted they force their compliant mother to deny they were ever there while they laugh and cavort.

We prayed to the great god Arkwright to look down and smite these outcasts of Hades but the great man stayed his hand. It took all our restraint to do the same.

You would have thought the father of the British police force would have known better, wouldn't you? Peel, on one of his off days presumably, introduced an Act of Parliament that opened the door to devil children and mothers attendant to their offspring's every whim.

If not for the Mines Act the little beggars would still be labouring hard underground and leaving good, (possibly), shop-keepers to their honest, (in the most part), living.

*August 11th – Wednesday* – Slowly chugged into a bit better weather today, although the cloud looked rather menacing at times. Word on the street is good for a few more days, (although I daresay the rider 'except in the far west' still applies).

Busy night for Falmouth coastguard and particularly Rescue 193, the helo out of Culdrose; they attended four shouts without refuelling. This included a suspected stroke at Minack and a chap working on the jack up rig at Lizard Lifeboat Station. The latter sounded a bit heroic as one of his work mates had to swim out to the rig to assist. We got to know most of the crew when they were in The Cove working on our Lifeboat Station so we hope the chap is ok and makes a full recovery.

They also airlifted an injured party off an Irish Ferry in the Traffic Separation System (TSS) between Lands End and Scilly and helped locate some clever soul climbing at nightfall on the cliffs up north somewhere.

Gosh, there's a rarity: a Diary entry played with a straight bat. Well almost . . .

If you see a bright light in the sky tonight chances are you're living in the vicinity of a friend of ours who's birthday it is today. That Bikini Isle type glow will be her lighting up the candles on her cake as she's fifty today, (well tomorrow, but you know by now what I mean).

I know she won't mind me mentioning that she's fifty years old as she's not at all sensitive in that way.

Happy 50th VGB.

*August 12th – Thursday* – Another grey start, middle and end to a day hailed as being nice and sunshiny. At least it's dry.

But ah, the glorious 12th – unless you're a grouse at which point you'd be justified at feeling a little aggrieved.

Had our first no show for ordered fish yesterday. He even gave us a contact number that didn't exist, so it was deliberate. Highly amusing, I'm sure. You do realise innocent, sentient beings gave up their life for you, don't you.

Spring tides at the moment, which means there's no water in the harbour at low water. Boats generally have to be in or kept out until flood time. This, of course has no meaning to the brave or hard of thinking. One of our local lads rowed with powerful intent towards the harbour entrance, cutting through the water with grace and ease. Doesn't work so well on top of a bunch of weed, does it, lad. Don't worry; I won't mention your name, Elliot. Oops.

Here's an old favourite to share with you. If I've told you before you will get only the slightest inkling of how we feel when we hear it again.

We sell stamps, in abundance, and we sell them off a big sheet of a hundred. The first year we were here we sold books and the world and his wife only wanted one or two so we responded and sold them individually from then on. So here's the conversation:

Customer: I'll have a book of stamps please.

Us: We don't sell books; we sell stamps individually.

Customer: Oh, I see.

Us: So how many stamps would you like?

Customer: Oh, I'll just have a book, then.

Us: Aaaaargh.

The inshore Lifeboat went out on exercise tonight and almost immediately was diverted to a shout. A mature kayaker returning from a trip round to Penberth was caught out by the ferocity of the tides at Lands End and un-kayaked. He was extremely fortunate that someone spotted him from LE point and called in the emergency. He was in the water about ten minutes before the ILB got there. The boy Elliot redeemed himself with some professional radio work – luckily he wasn't driving.

And lastly, I would have done a few lines of Southey, a poet laureate, born today in 1774 as seems to be the tradition of these pages. But I'm not sure verses about young children playing football with exhumed skulls is what this Diary is all about.

Perhaps if he'd taken a leaf out of his mates' books and written about daffodils or old seamen he might have been in with a chance.

Strange lot these Bristolians.

*August 13th – Friday* – Another disappointing day although it did have its moments and the sun eventually broke through in the afternoon. The group sitting outside Breakers Café during a bit of wind and rain enjoying their breakfast under a compact umbrella didn't seem to care much, though. That's what you call determination.

It is not commonly appreciated how much stress we in the service industry are subjected to, (alright, some people in the service industry), especially during the busy periods.

A steward on an internal US airline obviously had one moaning Minnie too many. A woman had given the poor chap a tirade of abuse over baggage that she hadn't been allowed to take on board, according to an eyewitness. It was clearly the final straw.

At the end of the flight he commandeered the intercom and thanked everyone who had been supportive of his role in the past. Grabbing a couple of beers from the trolley, he fired off the emergency evacuation slide and did a grand exit: goodbye and thanks for all the fish.

He's up before the beak on several charges but is gaining Facebook support climbing at 1,000 additions a day.

So, happy travellers, be very, very nice to us. Throwing money often helps.

Lifeboat shout mid afternoon to a stranded yacht with failed steering off Wolf Rock. A tow back to Newlyn and recovery at around 9.00pm just rounded off the day.

*August 14th – Saturday* – Had a quick look at the Met Office forecast for today, this morning; wall to wall sunshine for the weekend. That probably explains why it's raining then. To be fair it did brighten up later but that chilly northerly wind just keeps coming.

Well, here we are again. Yes, the last changeover for the two weekers happened today and they're all in and nicely snuggled down. Familiar faces and a few new ones slipped into the mix and very welcome their wallets are too.

The weatherman was a little cagey this morning on the radio, so lets just hope he's wrong and we have some decent weather to throw at these good people.

And talking of time it doesn't take much looking back in history to discover things haven't changed much. Take for example Cologne Cathedral that was finished today in 1880 after 632 years of work. That's almost as long as they've been working on the Camborne by-pass and that looks no closer to being finished.

Then at last knockings we get:

"Can you recommend a good locals pub around here?"

"Yep, F&L, packed with the beggers."

"No, no that's full of tourists."

Couple of seconds to pick myself up off the floor.

"Ah, right, you're looking for a pub in West Penwith in the middle of August that only has locals in it, like you read in the Boys' Own book of 1892 "Best Locals Only Pubs in West Cornwall."

Believe you have a long search on your hands, me 'ansum.

So as the rubber gloved hand of our consciousness examines the passage of time it's time to say goodnight.

*August 15th – Sunday* – The sun certainly had his hat on today along with shades, shorts and Hawaiian shirt. Little bit of a northerly rush but, apparently, down on the beach it was blazing.

Very much a full on day for us and even needed a trip to the store to get more stuff. Once again couldn't tell you much about what happened elsewhere as it all went zooming by.

We do know we had an ambulance down after the First Responder and paramedics had both attended. A young girl is all we know but have no further detail yet. Information tends to take a while to filter from one end of The Cove to the other.

On top of it all had another Lifeboat shout, this time to a 26 feet boat off Tol Pedn with a seized engine. The boat went out around 1:30pm and returned about half four after a tow into Newlyn.

There now follows a short advertising feature on behalf of The Beach restaurant:

With visitors staying with us, and after a day like today, tripped down to The Beach restaurant for some of their excellent and very reasonable priced pizzas to bring home. When I got there discovered that they don't do them Sunday nights as they have their barbeque going. Oh my word, blow the guests and the Missus, I nearly stayed and had one: Trevaskis Farm beef burgers, monk fish kebabs, marinated chicken, mackerel etcetera.

I dribbled all the way home.

Spent the evening putting things back on shelves, well the Missus did, ready for them to disappear again tomorrow, hopefully.

*August 16th – Monday* – Early mist on the hills cleared to a rather hazy day but with blue skies and plenty of warm sunshine. None of this gives the slightest hint of the impending doom we are facing and like certain governments we have sexed up the current forecast so as not to alarm our visitors.

I'll either end up earning a small fortune on the lecture circuit or, knowing my luck, more likely wind up in a wood somewhere drowned in a convenient vat of cider having inexplicably tripped over my own bootlaces, which inadvertently I'd tied together, allegedly.

She's still around, I'm glad to report. Mrs Angry from Weybridge dropped in to tell me that I really ought to employ some traffic wardens in The Cove. Her coach had been delayed further up by cars parked either side of the road, a restriction in the flow of customers that, no doubt, would see the ruin of my business before the end of the week.

She has a point. It is not so much parking than a case of 'stop driving somewhere random' with these people.

Here's an interesting pastime: sweeping the evening beach with a metal detector. I'm sure it has its moments and occasionally might pay dividends. I'm not sure this particular couple will win many friends. They were running their little plates on a stick in between family groups sitting on the beach.

"Oh look, I found a watch."

"I know, it's mine, I just put it there."

"Ah well finders keepers."

And today television celebrities in The Cove. Frankly they could have done a jig in front of me and I still wouldn't have known who they were. One or the other or both were in Eastenders or some such, which explains my ignorance.

They came in the shop, I can only assume, to wonder at the birthplace of The Sennen Cove Diary. I made myself scarce; I prefer a low profile.

*August 17th – Tuesday* – I fear the wheels of reality are falling off and that the whiff of doom hangs heavy in the air.

I must explain the portents that have led me to this conclusion.

First, I very nearly overslept this morning. And when I managed, manfully, to pull my considerable presence from my pit to face the day, the day stared back with gloomy visage and misty rain.

Secondly one of my first customers felt it acceptable to maintain a mobile telephone conversation while approaching the counter for service. He clearly felt it sufficient to gesticulate his requirements rather than use the accepted method of polite speech. This doesn't generally work, as in such circumstances I respond by reading a newspaper or going off and doing something mundane until the subliminal message gets through. It irked me nevertheless.

The third was a completely pointless trip to Penzance. I have studiously avoided such a sojourn during August for over seven years and having been unpleasantly reminded why, I shall avoid it in future as well. The constant whining in my ear 'ole to acquire some must-have mobile telephony machine must have weakened my resolve; I shall wear earplugs from hence forth.

And not least amongst these is that my chair has sheered a bolt. This is not just any bolt or, for that matter, any chair. The bolt appears to be a crucial one, a lynch pin if you will, that not only holds the arm on but also maintains the stability of the backrest. This renders the chair uncomfortable and somewhat precarious to perch upon. While I will try hard to pretend that this matter is but a trifle, you must understand, dear reader, that this is the chair upon which my weary frame reposes to pen this very page.

I tell you that along with the fragile fabric of the universe my bottom hangs in the balance.

*August 18th – Wednesday* – Met Office gave out a sunshiny sort of day so naturally we had a bit of rain, but very little. So they were almost right. Well done. To be brutally fair the nice bits were very nice.

We've had a little more slave labour staying with us for the last few days. It's not quite so much fun as they're bigger and older than the last lot and don't fit up chimneys any more. They managed to clear our big grocery delivery between them yesterday, which takes some doing.

We must have worn them out, though, as they haven't moved off the sofa today, watching trashy daytime television. Bless 'em.

It really is quiet frightening the weight of responsibility we carry on our shoulders. The information that we proffer needs to be accurate, fair and honest, well as close to honest as still makes us a bob or two. What tackle is best? Where can I fish from? How long does it take to get to Lands End? Where's the nearest cashpoint? Where's the nearest cashpoint? Where's the nearest cashpoint? Where's the nearest cashpoint?

I'm having a sign made up tout de suite.

So as the Ghengis Khan of life topples off his horse of time and into the dung heap of eternity I must close and head to my bed.

*August 19th – Thursday* – We waited in the ops room, Nobby and me. Waiting was the worst part. You knew they were coming;

you could see them on the radar screen. They had come before but whether we weren't a big enough target or just by luck, they passed us by.

This time was different. This time we knew we'd cop it.

There were people on the street and you just wanted to go out and shout at them, "Incoming! Get out of here. Go and find shelter." But it was hopeless. It would just cause panic. We couldn't warn them. Just watch, we had to tell ourselves. T-shirts and shorts mainly, poor beggers. Nothing to protect them from what was coming.

I always thought we were lucky but there's nothing lucky about being the ones left behind. Those not caught out in the open when it came would be down the pub by teatime exchanging tales of how they got away with it – this time.

The first few waves went north of us and up the Bristol Channel.

"Looks like the North Coast is going to get it. Maybe we'll be lucky again," mumbled Nobby quietly, not expecting an answer. He knew.

We watched the radar screen as the first few smaller waves headed north while the main force was gathered behind, slowly, inexorably moving in towards us. The blue bits, the out-riders, softening up the target. Behind that the greens and yellows: The heavy stuff. That could really ruin your day. A bit of pink in there, targeted, you had to find some deep shelter then. Thankfully no reds: We grinned mirthlessly at that.

"Best get ready, Nobby."

I called it in early. No point struggling to get covered after it starts. We'd both seen plenty of those 'give it another five minutes' heroes and we didn't want to be one of them.

Nobby grinned, that toothless grin of his, and tossed me my Sou' Wester and oil skins.

"Bleddy rain," he muttered as we headed for the shelters. Then barely, audibly, "The horror. The horror."

Win him an Oscar, that voice of his, one day, I thought.

*August 20th – Friday* – It took folk a little while to discover that The Cove was under the cloud today and therefore quite warm and clammy as opposed to on top of the hill that was in the cloud and cold and damp. It was a bit like being in a tent all day. Word on the street is that something similar is on the cards for tomorrow too.

Adolphe Pegond: a name that will go down.

Actually the event itself was a bit of a 'so what' moment in history. However he started a fashion that is still followed today. Ninety-seven years ago today he was recorded as the first person to jump out of a perfectly good aeroplane and parachute to the ground.

We have several people in The Cove from time to time that attempt similar operations by jumping off The Cove Hill. They don't seem to be terribly good at it as it takes forever for them to come down. They could be up there today and no one would ever know.

The good news is my replacement chair arrived today. The bad news is I haven't had the time to put it together yet. I'm sure the resulting bottom ache is reflected in my prose; I've found it extremely difficult to string two sentences together today.

So as the parachutist of life jumps out of the aeroplane of eternity and the rip cord of fate comes off in his hand, its time to give up and go home.

*August 21st – Saturday* – Still plenty of that mist around on the hills but again The Cove sat under it. There were even some bright spells but not too many characters around to witness it, it being change over day an' all.

A few people have been in this year looking for those old-style plywood surfboards. My guess was they weren't made any more and a couple of the enquirers were willing to try and use a plywood skim board as an alternative. Feedback was that it didn't cut the mustard.

Well, imagine my surprise when a couple walked in today sporting a plywood surfboard each. One of them was in metallic silver and carried an Apple Computer trade mark. Now unless Steve Jobs was really ahead of his time and patented his well known icon in the 1950's these were new boards. (Sometimes I wonder what I'm doing here, you know. Having a razor sharp intellect like that is a bit scary, what.)

My enquiries uncovered that they are indeed crafted today, albeit in Devon. Their website is keen to point out they are designed in Cornwall so it's not all bad.

So hold onto your hats boys and girls, next year in The Old Boathouse Stores we're going retro. They'll sell like hot potatoes – possibly.

And now for a message to the end to ender doing 900 miles for some charity or other. He's been up and down Cove Road all day in his van with two bikes strapped to the top.

"You're cheating!"

Another reader opened their soul in the shop and admitted their guilty secret today. I gave her absolution and she passed on her way. Don't think she was cured though.

So it's off to the F&L again for another mind bending, ear twisting blues session. Oh what a sorry life I lead.

*August 22nd – Sunday* – Woke to the first sunshiny day for a while. Yesterday Met Office website looked good for all day and by this morning was suggesting some late rain. Little by little we started hearing rumours of something big coming in from the south west including possible gale force winds; naturally nothing on the Met Office website until quite late when they issued a weather warning.

As if to acknowledge this upset to our three days of sun the Lifeboat launched at around 10.00am to aid a beam trawler 28 miles north of Pendeen. That just left the inshore boat to take care of the Cape swimmers on their annual bash at swimming from Cape to Brisons – oh, and back again.

The Cape swim is always some spectacle. Lots of little dots near the horizon milling about. I'm sure it looks much more interesting from Cape to be fair.

Some bright sparks telephoned 999 when the Cape Swim organisers let off a couple of flares for the end of the race. The inshore Lifeboat had just got back in the harbour when it was tasked to investigate. It had just got back again when the ALB, just passing Cape with its tow, radioed in for a pasty delivery.

We were inundated by a bus load of Chinese people late in the day. These were the same crew that had taken about a million photos of themselves with the hound. We're going to have to start charging, LE signpost style, to protect our investment.

Anyway, I digress. The crew of Chinese people were wondering why our trusty bus service had not seen fit to provide the last open top tour bus to St Ives, having waited thirty minutes beyond its scheduled arrival time. I tried to explain that the fleet had been converted from horse-drawn omnibuses some years ago and was prone to failure.

105

Sure enough when I telephoned our slightly more reliable taxi service they explained that the bus had indeed gone lame and as a consequence all the taxies, (one actually) was a tad busy.

We tried Penzance but they couldn't help either. Luckily a Good Samaritan with people carrier offered to take them to St Just and catch another bus from there. I think they're probably still waiting.

Thinking an international incident had narrowly been avoided a small family came in bedraggled from the storm with a similar story. They were headed for Kelynack camp site.

Since The Old Boathouse Stores bus service was headed that way anyway we dropped them off en route.

A busy day to be sure and the rain held off until late in the afternoon which was decent of it.

Recovered the Lifeboat at 10.00pm.

*August 23rd – Monday* – We started out grey and overcast and as the day progressed the sun broke out and so did the wind. By the end of the afternoon the sea had been beaten into a frenzy. Amazingly the lifeguards managed to keep the beach open for swimmers albeit a limited stretch in front of the hut, but jolly good on them for doing so.

There was a host of gulls bunched up on the water just below the chip shop. With every big wave that came in they took off in order before settling again managing a pretty good attempt at a Mexican wave. Damned clever Sennen gulls.

Seems to be an awful lot of people taking a bit of notice of Cornwall these days. *The Times* on Saturday ran a full page feature about the number of A-listers who holiday in the county.

Now Mr Depp we know all about, being best mates with our local cabbie, who still doesn't have a clue who he is. *The Times* had him down as frequenting Bryher, (Mr Depp, not our cabbie), but we know better: that he is rather keen on Treen. What we didn't have a clue about was who else is a Treen advocate.

They had him down as ABC, which was rather confusing as I thought it might have been Martin Fry, (ex-lead singer of the band ABC. Not for one moment suggesting you are uncultured, dear reader, but merely you are probably too youthful and spry to remember 1980's soul bands).

But I digress. No, the man they referred to is no other than God's own envoy on Earth, unless you're not C of E, in which case he's just some bloke in a funny hat and robe who happens to be rather well known as the Archbishop of Canterbury. Which brings me to an even greater point, that ABC is not a TLA of Archbishop of Canterbury, unless you expand TLA to be Two Letter Acronym, which of course isn't the accepted extrapolation, which is why it took me a few minutes to work out who they meant and led me to incorrectly infer the aforementioned lead singer.

So, I'm very glad we cleared that up.

The other A-listers, clearly with no imagination, descend on the posher bits around Padstow where, I'm sure, they are most welcome, though a couple whose names elude me now, holiday in St Mawes.

Sennen was mentioned in the report, but for not having any A-list visitors but was noted for having a couple of authors!

So good people, pack your bags and head on down to Sennen where the closest you'll get to A-list is the fading menu on the OS wall and as for celebrity, well, need I say more?

*August 24th – Tuesday* – A blustery day as Pooh would say; or as a Sennen shopkeeper would say, a Pooh day. Actually it brightened up and became sunny and very, very busy.

I signed up to one of those Number Ten petitions some while ago. I just had an email reminding me. It was to do with duty on alcohol so it must have been when the last lot were in around April last year. My interest being purely professional, you understand.

Now the real reason for the Government hosting these petitions is that when the big jack boot eventually comes stamping, they know who to pull out of their houses and put up against the wall. Conversely, of course, come the revolution the modern day Robespierre will look at the list and say, "You're oall rite, me 'ansum, let's go piddle in their swimming pools together."

Anyway, I digress. The petition to which I refer closed in June and attracted just five thousand signatures. Seeing the concerted opposition they were up against the new Government decided on a conciliatory response which, roughly translated, says, "We make a lot of dosh from duty on ale so tough luck." Well worth putting my head above the parapet for, I'm sure.

We've had a helo overflying several times today, filming at quite low levels. If that's *OK* magazine again I shall get really upset. I've already told them once.

Lastly we had a Lifeboat shout at around 2:30pm. It was one of, if not the fastest launch at five minutes from page to hitting the water. It was cancelled immediately as we heard that lifeguards had recovered the casualty over at Porthcurno.

I only have scant and hearsay information on the outcome and this is no place for it anyhow. Terry will, no doubt have a full report on the Sennen Cove website by morning.

*August 25th – Wednesday* – You'd have had to be completely useless to have got the forecast wrong for today. So I was somewhat surprised when it rained and then it rained some more. Rumour has it we had it easy down here in The Cove. With the wind coming in variously from the south east and south west it was pretty wild on top and down the other coast.

We have a drain at the back of the shop that, from time to time, floods and water comes into the store room. Unchecked it will traverse the shop floor and puddle by the newspapers. They don't make buildings like that any more! When this happens there's only one thing for it: get down and dirty with a hand down the drain and clear out the gunk.

Now the wise and astute would suggest that only a complete fool would wait until it rained before cleaning out the blocked pipe. This is presumably why I found myself this morning armed with rubber gloves and overalls kneeling in the pouring rain with my arm down the drain. Knowing that the process is effective for a while is little comfort when you're soaked to your knickers with an arm covered in foul smelling sludge.

And that's a pretty fair analogy of where this business will be if we have any more days like today.

Spare a penny for an old shopkeeper, mate?

*August 26th – Thursday* – Got out of bed this morning and tripped over the bleddy hound. This was partly because the bleddy hound has started sleeping in altogether different places throughout the night and partly because daylight, aided and abetted by the weather being pants, hadn't crept into the room yet.

Yes, shades of autumn are beginning to slink into Cove land. The days are only just longer than the nights, which means a beer festival starts up at the F&L tomorrow, (or tonight as you're reading this). I understand that the marquee is already set up and the beers are quietly settling down.

The Cornish have a certain reputation for being somewhat parochial over other people's liqueur. So naturally a vicious guard animal has been employed to protect the beers overnight. He has brought his dog too: a formidable coupling. (I've been asked to write that. A would be thief would probably use said guard as a doormat while the dog would rather be chasing wildlife more its size. It's a small Jack Russell.)

Still if any beer is left, it should be a cracking good three days of responsible drinking; after which all our visitors will have gone home leaving us to enjoy our responsible hangovers.

Still, today was altogether better than yesterday, and let's face it, it couldn't have got any worse. The predicted mammoth swell never materialised today and many enthusiastic surfers will have hit the pub instead out of disgust.

The fishing fleet unexpectedly managed to escape the harbour on the falling tide so Sennen crab and fish may be back on the menu again; which is a begger as I had to order the Newlyn lot his morning that seem to be half as feisty as ours.

For those interested enough there was a cracking good sunset just before another set of rain barged in. Our fingers and other appendages are crossed that the good souls of the Met Office have got it right for once about the coming weekend and that the weather will be kind for our last shot at fame and, particularly, fortune.

And lastly, three cheers to our venerable Head Launcher, who has eventually managed to grasp the fundamentals of the computer keyboard to establish contact with this page on the World Wide Web, (and thanks to MS Word for capitalising the last three words when, whenever we type them they are usually in lower case).

*August 27th – Friday* – And the sun it did pop its head out of the clouds and did a little sun dance. And the people all did jump and dance for joy and were joyous and later, merry. And the shopkeepers did throw a mighty whoop and they were joyous too and everything was happiness and light in The Cove.

Our international correspondent has been in touch but she isn't ever so joyous. It raineth in the big land across the water in big lumps of wetness so much so that their vegetables have grown to expanded proportions not seen since triffids wandered the Earth. A mighty watermelon of 44 pounds graced our reporter's allotment, which she transported home by raft.

Let's face it; everything's bigger in America.

Watermelon sandwiches, roast watermelon, stuffed watermel-on, watermelon on toast, watermelon flambé, water-flaming-mel-on surprise – what flavor, (they spell funny over there), pizza tonight, hun? Pepperoni. What? The dog ate the watermelon.

Closer to home, perhaps someone can enlighten me as to why we should have attracted the attention of the RAF Mountain Rescue service. By my estimation the nearest mountain must be 400 miles away by road. You would hope that the RAF's navigation isn't the issue. Perhaps they had to hand their sat nav back as part of the government cut backs.

Toyed briefly with the idea of going up the F&L tonight as they have a cracking good band on; oh, and a beer festival! Unfortunately we had two major deliveries today that need to be addressed and the bleddy hound needs her regulation run on the b-e-a-c-h (we can't say the word else she goes mad – we'll be absolutely beggered when she learns to spell).

Ooh I can feel the empathy from you all radiate through the broadband wires. Oh no, it's just the fan on my PC starting up.

So as the mountain rescue team of life abseils down the rock face of eternity and the rope of fate turns out to be thirty feet too short its time to say goodnight.

*August 28th – Saturday* – A bit of a Saturn V of a day, it went off like a rocket. (Yes, a very sad and contrived analogy. Boys and girls, Saturn V launched the Apollo series; c'mon you have the Internet, look it up.)

We were busy from the outset this morning and very nice it was too. Naturally it was on the cards that we hadn't ordered enough of everything. It wasn't this busy in the main part of the season, for heaven's sake.

We need Mrs Angry from Weybridge back again. Someone's parked a big van in the gap next to Salt House and it's blocking the public right of way, which is rather thoughtless. It confused the bleddy hound no end, not being able to dash through there on her evening stroll. The local constabulary has noted it and, no doubt, if it's not moved he'll have his bottom smacked.

Once again the day scudded by and we wondered where it went and what happened in it. I'm sure there were lots of exciting and interesting things happening all around us that you'd really love to hear about. Well if you find out what they were please tell us.

Ah, how it all goes whizzing by.

So it's off to the F&L for sure tonight to witness this festival of beers. I shall, of course, be the model of abstemiousness, at least once, probably to draw breath. Then wander back home the long way because the flaming path is blocked off.

Late breaking news: our local bobby, (off duty, no less), dashed to the rescue when a neighbouring house went up in flames, no, really. Dashed in with no thought of his own safety, doused the fire and saved the family guinea pig. Naturally I couldn't put a name to such a local hero. Just look for the man sans eyebrows.

Lastly, to shed any doubt that we live in God's own country, you should have walked home with me across the fields and down the lane with a three quarter, waning moon behind me and to see the retreating tide in such ethereal light. Just quite poetic, really.

Goodnight.

*August 29th – Sunday* – Early cloud shuffled off in a slow, ambling sort of way and left a nice big blue sky again. We did have a little nagging northerly draft but not enough to spoil the day.

Lifeboat Day seemed to attract a healthy crowd and the boat launched three times just for good measure. St Buryan Male Voice Choir adorned the evening service so that's all the local choirs come to Sennen in the last week. We must be in for a chance of Village of Culture this year, surely.

Our hero bobby donned his outer underpants again today. He was following a nice spanking new car whose driver became so overcome by seeing a bus on our roads he drove up the hedge and turned it over. We, who live here, of course, have become used to these rare visits.

And lastly, today was a bit of a turning point for us: it was our last day of eight o'clock closing this year. As well as heralding the end of another season this means a whole raft of changes in the household including being able to eat normal food again and at normal times.

With a little imagination and forethought you can dine from the shop over the period of two weeks without having the same meal twice. That's the aim anyway as most visitors will be here for a maximum of a fortnight.

We, on the other hand, are resident here for around six weeks with very little opportunity to gather supplies from elsewhere. (The first one of you to suggest employing the services of a certain home delivery service is going to get a clip 'round the ear 'ole.)

While our food is generally wholesome it can, over time, get a little tedious. It will make a great change being able to rustle up some more adventurous comestibles. Or, like as not, slip off to the F&L to be waited on hand and foot.

Bon appetite.

*August 30th – Monday* – The words are usually mutually exclusive in the same sentence so it gives me great pleasure to announce – Bank Holiday sunshine. Very fittingly it was a monster of a day.

The main competition today has been the Newlyn Fish Festival that, no doubt one day, we shall try and attend. I would think by then, if the doom mongers are right, it will just be the Newlyn Festival, the fish having long disappeared.

What we did have, though, was a coach load of pensioners wandering around The Cove. This was not just any bunch of senior citizens, oh no, someone had gathered together the most miserable, grumpy and surly bunch of old codgers imaginable and let them loose on an unsuspecting Cove. What a horror. If you were one of them and you're a happy soul I can only apologise. Please have a word with your chums. They're giving oldies a monstrous name.

I have to say I feel a bit like Frankenstein having created a monster because a new source has revealed themselves, (and played havoc with my grammar), to the hub of international news, here in Sennen Cove. It would appear there is a pre-existing link, of a horticultural nature, between MM and the *Cotswold Courier*.

I would have expected this humble page to expand organically over a period of time but I have to admit I didn't expect to have to open the gardening section quite so soon.

Nevertheless *Cotswold Courier*, your approach is most welcome and I shall look forward to hearing the finer points of turnip production on calcareous silty soil deep in the winter when I shall have begger all else to write about.

And why all the monsters and horrors today - Mary Wollstonecraft Godwin better known as Mary Shelley of The Modern Prometheus or Frankenstein novel. It was her birthday today in 1797. She lost three children before a lucky fourth, Percy, came along. Percy probably didn't feel that lucky and spent his life wishing he were born in Sennen Cove. Mary gave him a middle name after his birth place, Florence.

Though he did his best to avoid silly names in future life his, (adopted), daughter Bessie went and married Lieutenant-Colonel Leopold James Yorke Campbell Scarlett. They named their first boy Captain Mary Nancy-Boy Yoicks Shelley Scarlett, who later inspired a 1970's puppet show, just to annoy him.

Sorry, they didn't really, I made the last bit up.

*August 31st – Tuesday* – That little Easterly breeze seems to be a bit of a fixture this year. So while it looks rather pleasant, sunny and warm, if you're standing in the wrong spot it don't half rattle your knickers.

I've been keeping half an eye on the skies today towards Lands End Aerodrome. There was supposed to be a fly past over Sennen church today and I was rather hoping that LEA would wheel out their De Havilland Rapide. This is the plane that used to fly the Scillies run some years back. It would tickle Lillian no end.

Who's Lillian and Lillian who? I hear you ask all agog and on the edge of your seats with anticipation. Well it's all a bit odd really and even odder the salute should be organised here.

Lillian, Lillian Bland, that is, was the first woman to design, build and fly her own aircraft. She called it the Mayfly based on its expected ability to take to the air. She achieved this feat 100 years ago today, whilst in her early years, having been inspired by the likes of Bleriot. She pursued this interest until her father bought her a motor car believing it to be a safer mode of transport and a tad easier to park outside the shops.

However, she built and carried out her flying at Carnmoney in Ireland. Later she moved to Canada and, on the death of her husband, back to Kent.

Though certainly she had a full and interesting life in many fields there is no indication as to why she retired to Sennen, bankrolled by a habit of gambling on the Stock Exchange. Perhaps like many of us she came once and was hooked. She died here in 1971 aged 93 and is buried in the churchyard.

The Rapide never showed up.

And that's the end of today's history lesson. Tomorrow: Double mathematics.

# September

In the news: *Tony Blair, ex-Prime Minister, publishes his memoirs. Pope Benedict visits UK.*

*September 1st – Wednesday* – I'd thought about calling this August 32nd to try and eke out the summer season a little longer now the good weather's here. However the march of time is not something to be trifled with. So I'm afraid August has been consigned to the pages of the Archive.

141 cyclists left LE this morning on a Great British Cycle ride. How do I know there were 141? Well they all arrived yesterday in preparation and I painstakingly overtook every single one of them on my way back from Penzance.

I don't know if we're getting a little too sensitive or some customers are just getting a tad sillier. We shall enlighten you using two examples of silliness that, naturally, have been concocted for this illumination. Obviously no real person would be this silly.

First, a customer starts loading her shopping onto the counter as she collects items from around the shop. Despite a friendly suggestion that she might be better off using a shopping basket, she will refuse, preferring to clutter the counter. When the long suffering shopkeepers, in our made up example, can't see over the counter any longer they helpful move all the shopping to a basket, where it would have been better in the first place.

The customer, noticing that her shopping is no longer causing an obstruction, remedies the situation by picking up the basket and promptly placing it on the floor in front of the counter and wandering off leaving two other customers to trip over it.

Wouldn't happen in a million years, now would it?

What an imagination we do have, thinking up these crazy incidents. Here's another.

This gentleman comes in seeking medical advice, clearly unaware that this is neither a doctor's surgery nor a hospital. I shall spare you the detail because, frankly, it was distasteful, (er, I mean in this completely fictitious example), and I am keen to avoid distress among my readership. Now, I'm not a doctor, (although there was that doctors and nurses incident with Alice Mayband when I was six), but the product he is after is clearly, even for a layman, inappropriate.

So he spurns my advice, buys them anyway and complains that there should be some sort of drop in centre where these problems could be resolved. I, of course, suggest Cape Surgery.

He replies that he would have to wait two weeks for an appointment back home. At this point I consider pointing out that he isn't at home but conclude my breath would be wasted.

He continues that the problem has reoccurred over several months.

Well, yup, I guess if you continue to apply the wrong solutions and won't seek professional medical help then there's a fairly strong chance that the problem will persist.

All I can say is thank goodness these things don't happen for real. It would be enough to make a poor shopkeeper give up and go wurzel farming in Devon.

*September 2nd – Thursday* – Another sparkly day but getting a little hazy down this end. Any danger of getting overly warm knocked on the head by that, almost icy, easterly blowing through. You'd think we would be sheltered from it this side of the peninsular but it seems to channel down the valley, pick up speed and squirt down the road.

This week has been something of a bonus, or more appropriately a consolation. While there was a noticeable drop in visitors at the end of the Bank Holiday we have been quite buoyant all week. Long may it last.

Took the bleddy hound down to the b-e-a-c-h last night to mess around as the Missus was off getting her toes painted or some such. As soon as we got down there she found a comedy fish carcass. You know the sort, head and tail intact, joined by the skeleton. Knowing it would be confiscated she led me and a bunch of local children a merry chase up and down the beach for about half an hour. Laugh? I nearly strangled the little so and so when I caught her.

I wish I had the ability to draw cartoons to add to these pages, as that would have made a cracker.

So, any budding Giles, Cummings or Scarfe out there, The Sennen Cove Diary needs you to illuminate its gloomy pages.

*September 3rd – Friday –* I telephoned my publisher today and cancelled the publication of my memoirs.

I told him that a book containing a pack of lies, that stabbed my erstwhile friends in the back, was close to a work of sensationalist fiction and served only to further stuff my overflowing coffers had no place in the modern literary world. I can't see a book like that selling anyway.

So I'll concentrate on the Diary for now and see what fortune has in store for all of us.

I've said it before that some things over time change very little. For example, dictates from Europe being one of them. Today Brussels comes up with some spiffing idea and France and Germany generally implement them first, although very softly. After a lengthy argument and promises from politicians that they'll never happen over here we normally find them buried in the statute and irreversibly embedded in our culture quicker than you can cook a snail.

In 1582 most of Catholic Europe adopted the Gregorian calendar. We sturdy Brits robustly resisted this Euro-lunacy, thanks in no little part to good King Henry VIII, a principled Euro-sceptic, who kicked into touch the European Union President of the time, namely Pope Paul III, in terms of laying down the law in this sceptred isle.

By 1752 the Europhiles had inveigled themselves back into favour under George II. I mean, what do you expect, he was German for heaven's sake, and best pals with Pope Extraneous the 93rd, (look I'm on a roll here and don't want to dash off looking up who was Pope in 1752 – oh alright, it was Benedict XIV). So, guess what? September 3rd 1752, (a notable date too, when 187 years later we were minded to stand against European foes) became September 11th as we capitulated and adopted the Gregorian calendar.

The bottom line, dear readers, is that if it wasn't for all this Euro malarkey we'd still be sitting in August 21st, sun shining, kids off school and the Old Boathouse tills trilling to the sound of a thousand shillings dropping into the coffers.

But here we are instead; a day when Penlee launched and Sennen Cove Lifeboat was getting ready to launch for an aircraft. An aircraft, I tell you! The hapless aeroplane developed an engine fault returning from the Scillies but landed safely at LEA. Both boats were stood down.

And a day when the little boat got called out, several minutes later, to a venerated local fisherman and ex-Lifeboatman when his engine failed in a brisk sou' easterly in the bay. Such is this man's mettle that he ensured his box was full of 'ansum fish before he issued the call for assistance; he is the stuff of legend, no less.

*September 4th – Saturday* – We had a bit of the wet stuff come hurtling through early on this morning but the heavy stuff we were promised for the afternoon never materialised.

The first ever weather forecast appeared in The Times on this day in 1860. You'd think after 150 years they'd have got a little better at it. Still, the easterly has died off a bit and all in all quite a decent day.

A boat appeared in the distance across the bay today. Before we knew it she was in the harbour. Yes, it was TG, the fastest fisherman in the west.

There was no bow wave to be seen, as the bow wasn't in the water and neither was most of the keel, just a huge wake stretching out towards Aire Point. He has a sail wrapped up at the stern. This is not a sail for the wind to blow him along, oh no, this is only there as an emergency braking device. He spurns the use of a tractor to recover his boat preferring instead to aim the prow at his spot on the slip and let momentum carry him up. 'Course, at high water, that puts him on the doorstep of Myrtle Cottage.

Lifeboat exercise this morning: Saturday is usually a bad day for an exercise as many of the crew are busy. True to form there weren't many of us around shore side or boat side for that matter.

Our new slipway, wide enough to provide the walker with a sense of confidence, is dish shaped to guide the boat into the keelway on recovery. Pretty though it be, it acts as a magnet for weed. First job this morning, ahead of the launch was to clear a geet pile of the slimly stuff from the lower end of the long slip. We now understand why it is called a slip.

At this stage I presume there is no need to explain the order of events for this evening. Creature of habit? Moi?

*September 5th – Sunday* – When I retired last night I was comforted by the forecast's big sunny day ahead of me. At least that's what I thought those little yellow icons meant, running from dawn to dusk.

Oddly I woke to the pitter patter of raindrops against the window. What trickery is this, I thought, a major multi million pound, (our multi million pounds, incidentally), organisation couldn't possibly get a forecast so monumentally wrong, surely? Then I broke out of my half sleep state and remembered that it was the Met Office's forecast I had slept on last night.

It was a forgivable error; I mean they had, after all, attempted to forecast the weather a full twelve hours into the future.

We have always been aware that we have a cosmopolitan set of visitors in this part of the world. Yesterday we were visited by the Russians, or so I thought. They took ages and ages deciding on the gifts they wanted so they weren't Russian at all!

We had a Spanish party fishing in the bay today trying to cast a net. And, of course, the Frenchman who had his car clamped in the Beach car park. He had to pay £80 to let 'is car go. The Dutch were here in vast numbers to see our circuitous routes across the countryside. Yes, the Dutch like a road that will wind miles. Quite unbelievably we haven't seen any Italians this year. Perhaps it's because they stopped doing pizza down The Beach on a Sunday night. They ought to apply some pressure on the manageress down there because, as we know, you have to lean on to 'er for pizza.

I think I'll stop there before anyone gets hurt.

*September 6th – Monday –* A grim and grizzly start to the day; the rain came down until about lunchtime when we had a bit of blue sky and sunshine.

Took the opportunity to go into PZ to run a few errands. We had a fish order in with one of our suppliers in Newlyn so I told them I'd pick up the order on my way back. Having thought I saved a few ounces of carbon it wasn't very gratifying to meet his van later, coming back from Sennen.

Well, I could have stayed there for hours. There were a couple of chaps filleting various fish; it was nothing less than an art form. I tried, in my mind's eye, to slow down the process to try and understand where the cuts were and which way they were performed. A cross cut angled forward slightly, a slice along the belly about half an inch deep, a second almost to the spine and flipped out at the tail, then finally, knife flat along the spine and done. I almost bought a bag of random fish just to go home and try it myself.

It certainly makes you appreciate the importance of these trades' people in our lives. Where would we be without these fishmongers to fillet our fish, the butchers to slice our meat into presentable and manageable portions and the bakers to make our pasties, pies and bread?

But let us not forget the lynch pin is this underworld of public service, the humble shopkeepers who, uncomplainingly, make themselves available at all hours to purvey this smorgasbord of comestible delights. What a hardy and under-appreciated bunch they are. I would say something altogether proper and decent about these unsung heroes but I'm afraid modesty prevents me.

So as the fishmonger of eternity slices off a fillet of time, and the fishing inspector of fate tells him it will always be too short, it's time to head for the sandy sea beds of sleep.

*September 7th – Tuesday* – Sunny from the off this morning, despite yesterday's forecast of heavy showers all day long. An abundance of people buying things like beach mats and sun tents. Could be summer all over again if only for a day.

Decided to exploit our newfound freedom bestowed upon us by closing at 6pm; headed off into the big bad city, well PZ anyway. We're going to let some artisan of the gas cooker (they have draft gas in PZ, you know) rustle us up a culinary delight or, failing that, we'll just have a curry. Actually the intended curry house is one of the best in the area and does some interesting chef's specials amongst the normal masalas and biryanis.

To stop myself sounding too much like a travelogue, best I veer away and say a bit about this 'ere Devonwall constituency that's been proposed. It's part of the electoral reform to make all constituencies roughly the same size and this one will cross the border between Cornwall and Devon. Many hackles have risen over the proposal; even the Cornish Gorsedh has raised an ancient, worried eyebrow. By all accounts it's about as popular as a Katie Price single.

Talking of long legged birds, they have gone to some lengths to introduce cranes to the Somerset levels. They've had dogs dressed up as foxes and people have to wear gowns so they don't look like humans, in fact they look very much like Cornish Bards wandering around amongst the reed beds.

I feel there's much to learn here. I've been practising wearing shorts, loud shirts and socks tucked into my sandals so I don't frighten off the visitors. Can't say I've had much success though.

Missus reckons locking the door after they come in is a bit intimidating and I shouldn't smile as it scares small children.

*September 8th – Wednesday* – A nice looking day again and a lot of customers thought so too. Big tides all this week and a big sea at high water this morning that put off most of the fleet from going out.

But today is a particularly bad day for men that are roughly hewn from the bedrock of life. Men such as the hardy souls who enjoy their fishing while down here on holiday, of whom there has been a veritable army this week.

It is such a busy time for tackle that we had to call in our friendly tackle supplier for more tackle. Now that's a lot of tackle for one sentence, so you get the idea that we've sold a lot of tackle.

"Where do you go fishing?" They ask in manly, gruff tones. Well, we find the water is a good place to start, if we were to be facetious. Thankfully, though we are not, or not so often that you'd notice.

It is merely a fact, not a recommendation, that we tell them that many real men fish from the harbour wall. Real men ignore the big signs on the harbour wall saying don't go on the wall. Danger is a mere plaything to such swarthy types.

If you have an aversion to heights, like me, you avoid it like the plague anyway. If you have an aversion to getting pummelled by big waves and dumped into the harbour you don't go on there when there's a bit of ground sea running. We've seen chaps out there on the end with big waves crashing over the wall behind them, completely oblivious; real men, obviously, though a little dim. They will be out there in all weathers, strapped to the pinnacle by their belts, while the tempest crashes around them, casting into the boiling ferment.

"What tackle do you use?" You can feel the room resonate.

Good fortune has allowed for a friendly shopkeeper who is well versed in the kinds of tackle to use off the rocks and out on the breakwater. Fortunate too, that this shopkeeper stocks the kind of tackle that he recommends and at very reasonable prices, of course. Many of the spinners and lures are guaranteed killers, in the right, gritty, hands, naturally.

"What bait do you use?" Did the earth tremor at the sound of that voice? Mackerel, sand eel or rag worm all in nice tidy packs and at such a price I may as well be cutting my own throat.

"Live bait?" Nay sir, while you are a real man, our more sensitive customers are not keen to see worms co-habit with our Cornish mushrooms and potatoes and the sand eels tend to thrash about a bit next to the fizzy pop bottles. There is a plentiful supply, and free too, if sir wishes to purchase a spade and spend the evening on the beach.

All this testosterone, the rippling muscles, the deep and resonate tones are naught but useless frippery in the face of news as grim as that which broke today.

Cast yourselves down, ye men of greatness, and weep. Verily this weekend is the start of Strictly Come Dancing.

*September 9th – Thursday* – Another stonker of a day to behold.

Plenty of action in The Cove last night and today, unfortunately due to people hurting themselves.

Last night Rescue 193 was heard milling about but went quiet all of a sudden. Despite several enquiries it took until this morning to establish the facts. Our man in Vellandreath, who was on the spot for the incident, was a bit reticent in filing his report. Seems he was a little coy about getting his name in the paper and the subsequent awards for bravery and the obligatory OBE that would follow. I've promised to keep his name out of this report, haven't I Brian? Oops!

Anyway, it seems a chap had accidentally placed his foot down a rabbit hole and walked forward without taking it out first, in consequence breaking his ankle in a number of places. Our local hero, (the place is full of them), directed the Air Ambulance to attend. It was soon discovered that the Air Ambulance, being a small helicopter and the casualty being a portly gentleman were incompatible in a getting off the ground sort of way and the much bigger Rescue 193 was tasked.

Rescue 193 was with us again at lunchtime to attend a climber, possibly one of the Marines down here on exercise, who had decided to descend Pedn-men-du rather quicker than advisable.

A chance glance at the Parish Council report in the *Cornishman* has us a bit alarmed. It seems they will recommend having a 24 hour seasonal dog ban on the beaches next year. Currently dogs are allowed on the beach before 8.00am and after 7.00pm, a happy compromise.

During the summer months we are a bit limited on our options to exercise the bleddy hound. She has to be on her lead up the footpath due to the probability of adders lurking, so the beach after hours is the only option.

This bloodhound of a reporter, while having his beach access threatened, has bent the ear of his local Sennen Parish Councillor. It appears that Cornwall Council begged the question of SPC what sort of ban they would like to see. Rather than consulting, SPC unilaterally moved to suggest a 24 hour ban.

Unofficially, the blame has fallen to the minority of owners not cleaning up after their dogs, ruining it for the majority, a lack of dog wardens and the police with insufficient resources to monitor and prosecute.

Unfortunately the problem won't desist with the ban. Irresponsible owners will still let their dogs foul, just not on the beach.

Gird your loins, good Diary readers, it may soon be time to come to the aid of the party; stand up and be counted; all it takes is for good men to do nothing for evil to succeed and any other appropriate quotes and clichés you can think of.

*September 10th – Friday* – For a day penned in as grey and miserable it was actually quite warm, dry and happy despite being a tad grey. Big sea rolling most of the day especially coming up for high water.

Had a Lifeboat shout at around 2:40 pm with both boats launched in a bit of a hurry. *The Ripple*, a restored Cornish lugger was taking in water and had made it in as far as the Cowloes. All but the skipper were taken off, one with a minor injury from flying rigging, and a surplus Lifeboatman was sent for to assist on board. *The Ripple* made her own way back to Newlyn escorted by *City of London III* with a Lifeboat salvage pump keeping the water on the right side of the hull.

Recovery was something of a well crafted work of art by our coxswain as two hours before high water the tide was up to the rollers on the recovery slip with a big swell running. All done and dusted by 6.00pm.

It rather looks like full waterproof gear for a trip up to the F&L tonight, (yes, I know its Friday but there's a band on tonight too). Big rain expected overnight which looks like it might clear to give us a right good day tomorrow.

As it happened the promised rain fell elsewhere up country where it was probably deserved and I arrived home snug and dry, on the outside, at least.

*September 11th – Saturday* – It was the sort of day when nothing was going to happen.

The people sitting eating their breakfasts and lunches in the café next door sat there and did nothing. The surfers with their brightly coloured surf boards were on the beach and did nothing. The surfers with dark wetsuits with fancy names on them and surfboards with fancy names on them sat in the water and did nothing.

The girls from the village in their brightly coloured swim suits bought a pasty between them, then sat on the sandy beach and did nothing. The smart set, from up country, all took out their mobile phones and spoke about nothing.

The fishermen, with their small boat and long, long seine net stood on the beach and did nothing. The man with the big yellow kite swooping around and doing loop the loops stood there and did nothing.

The man in the shop watched the customers come in and do nothing. He watched the visitors from Essex come in and do nuffin' and the ones from Yorkshire do nowt.

The gaily decked horse and carriage came by and the cars backed up behind it did nothing. The wedding party in their pretty frocks and smart suits sat in the back and did nothing.

The gulls from The Cove sat out in the bay in a cluster doing nothing. The fish in their nets and the lobsters in their pots lay there and did nothing. The bright fishing boats laid up in the harbour did nothing, while the visitors took pictures and did nothing with them.

The sun sat up in the sky and did nothing, and the big low clouds that looked like they might have some rain in them, did nothing and went away.

And everyone seemed happy in their nothing sort of way and even if they weren't happy they did nothing about it.

And me, I'm looking at the list of things that I should have done by now and wondering what should be done.

Nothing probably.

*September 12th – Sunday* – I've been berated, or more of a ticking off really. I did know that it was DH Lawrence's birthday yesterday, no really I did. How could you forget Peter O'Toole and all that sand, or was that the other fellow? No, I'm joshing with you.

You have to remember that he lived not far from here and the wounds are still quite raw some 95 odd years later. You see he married a German and in 1915 that was a bit brave, or stupid, or both. And to flaunt a brash and forthright Teutonic woman in the Tinners Arms, (Zennor for the uninitiated), was just about enough for the locals, fed with tales of grimness from the front.

Not only was she German, she was a cousin to Manfred von Richthofen to boot, which allegedly he did on many occasions, DH that is, not the Baron. Anyway he was a tad strange and I desisted from mentioning the whole affair largely to protect the feelings of those well over 100 still living in Zennor that might remember it.

In one of those happy coincidences a chap today mentioned that he didn't know  DH had connections down here. Oh what joy, what self-satisfaction at being able to wax on all about it in a nonchalant, known it for years, sort of way. Oh, and by the way, did you know it was his birthday yesterday? I am sure it left the chap thinking that this neck of the woods must be full of intelligent, cultured and knowledgeable shop keepers. Oh, and did I mention – smug.

Putting aside these dark literary thoughts I must tell you what a cracking day it's been: sunshine and people in abundance.

Time now for a jolly good barbeque with our neighbours, I reckon.

*September 13th – Monday* – Well it all started a bit early this morning.

A drilling unit arrived first followed a little while later by something ominously called a welfare unit. Ah ha, we thought, this will be the start of the fish oil processing facility we've been hearing about.

Because of the increase in basking shark numbers for the past couple of years a few of our fishermen have been given licence to cull a percentage. These large fish will provide sufficient oil, along with other fish harvested from the area to resource the fish oil for a sustainable power programme.

The Harbour Commission applied for European funding for the project a couple of years ago and presumably this has now come to fruition. The plant will be on stilts in a corner of the Harbour Car Park to allow parking underneath. The first phase of the work is to drill a route for the pipe that will take the waste fish product out into the bay.

Talking of the bay, The Diary understands from a reliable source that Surfers Against Sewage want Sennen's Blue Flag status to be revoked. This is on the basis that our sewage system will discharge raw sewage into the sea on the occasion that we have, at the same time, a big tide, an unprecedented deluge of rain and a double pump failure; a situation about as likely as me catching a left breaking pipeline on a Saturday night. Well maybe a bit more likely than that.

While the SAS have done some excellent work in protecting and developing a £100m industry, some might say holding a noisy party in a quiet Cornish village and using environmentally un-friendly materials in your sports equipment might be a little hypocritical.

Expecting your sea water to be completely free of any risk of contamination might just be a little pernickety. After all the fish pooh in it.

*September 14th – Tuesday* – It bears some thought that the mere existence of this page relies on Mr George Anderson of Memphis, Tennessee.

In 1867 when Mr Chris Sholes and his mate Mr Sam Soule put their heads together and invented the first practical typewriter it amazed folk around the world; a machine that apparently had no purpose other than making a loud clacking sound.

It is a problem that I imagine besets many an inventor: that feeling that something's missing. Mr Bell with his first telephone; I mean who are you going to call when there's no telephone directory. William Webb Ellis; how was he to convert his first try before someone invented the first goal posts?

Things were looking pretty bleak for Sholes and Soule until nearly twenty years later, on this very day in 1886. Fed up with having a useless lump of iron in the corner of his room, whose sole advantage appeared to be letting him know that his secre-tary hadn't bunked off early, George Anderson invented the typewriter ribbon.

From there 'twas but a short leap to the first computer, printers and the World Wide Web and then this Diary. All of which are pretty much reliant on some poor sod tearing his hair out and wondering why it doesn't work properly.

As you might tell from the off-subject subject matter it was a quiet day in The Cove. Although we were promised rain in the afternoon, by the time we closed it hadn't arrived though the low cloud had. We all wait in breathless anticipation.

125

Still, I've promised myself an excursion tomorrow that's bound to be full of mystery and excitement. Bet you can't wait!

*September 15th – Wednesday* – Bit overcast first thing and no idea really what the weather had in store, so an ideal time to trip off to Hayle on a bit of business. Well I did promise you mystery and excitement. And what could be more exciting than crossing the West Penwith border and expanding one's horizons? That will have to remain a rhetorical question as I don't have time to write a list that long.

What better time, while I'm not there, to clear up the matter of the fish oil sustainable power plant that I said was being built in The Cove? After all there's been a group of environmentalists in the Harbour Car Park since yesterday, with placards and whatnot. I've had Surfers Against Fish Pooh on the telephone as well.

It was a joke, all right. What they're really doing is putting in a landing beacon on the end of the breakwater for the Scillies helicopter for when it moves to Lands End Aerodrome. It will also help when the new Eurofighter gets stationed there after the cut backs close all the other airfields in Cornwall.

And the mystery? What you think when you get to Hayle is, how do they make Philps pasties that good? And for heaven's sake keep that under your hat. Missus would go mad if she found out that I'd indulged in a Philps pasty without her.

And what you think while you're eating your Philps pasty, sitting in the van, looking at the East Quay is when on earth are they actually going to do something here? I remember visiting the proposals exhibition at least ten years ago. It looked amazing; such vision, such a vivid future. And that hole in the quay wall has got bigger since then.

And when you get back to The Cove with all its finishedness you think: Thank heavens for that!

*September 16th – Thursday* – The clouds parted in a bit of a Charlton Heston moment this morning and stayed that way. And lo did the sun break through and verily did it shine all day long. Still a bit of a nasty north westerly to worry your St Michaels, though. However I believe things will improve in all sorts of ways from henceforth: there's been a sign.

And talking of the sun there is an interesting picture of Godrevy Lighthouse in the *Cornishman* today. The photographer must have some lens on his camera as the title was Sennen Sunset. Beside it is a heading, Local & Trusted. If you say so luvver. Personally I think the *Cornishman* is a victim of its decision to outsource production to a firm in Shanghai.

And talking of slow boats to China, rumour has it the OS is rudderless again. Not that having a rudder seemed to make an awful lot of difference. Never before have we had a string of visitors through our door moaning about the place. It's of benefit to no one, not least the locals, that St Awful doesn't appear to be able to run a binge drinking session in its own brewery. The day its one size fits all approach works down here will be a very sad day for The Cove.

And talking of rudders, if it wasn't for one that worked, our International Correspondent would probably be sitting on an allotment in Solihull wondering why her watermelons are the size of garden peas. It was on this very day in 1620 that the Pilgrim Fathers, probably fearful of the latest round of spending cuts, took off for the Promised Land and found America instead.

And talking of pilgrimages there's a bloke with a funny hat doing a UK tour at the moment. I can't say I've got any of his albums but he seems to be making a bit of an impression some-where north of Launceston.

Now, I can't say too much about my source other than he taught me all I once knew and probably more, much to the chagrin of his Missus. This ancient, but reliable informant tells me that the God man is way on the side of the Cornish, revealed only to the knowing few by way of curious runes on the front of his transport. This oracle tells me that his registration plate, SCV 1, is Cornish.

Now tell me that isn't an omen.

I jest not, my source is seldom wrong and he has seen the light, well, the plate anyway. He almost came over all religious until a quick clout to the back of the head put him right.

Mark my words, good things is coming. If you're Cornish, obviously.

*September 17th – Friday* – Today was penned in as being the best of the week. So it was of no surprise that by mid morning we had a few squally showers come charging through The Cove.

Our crab fisherman has started to pull his pots in, so we have implemented our crab and lobster panic buying strategy. Looks like I'll be slaving over a hot stove this afternoon and the Missus will be picking well into the wee hours.

As it turned out our hearty fisherman dropped us round several feisty beasts, including a veritable monster of the deep. This fellow was, (note the use of the past tense), just short of a foot across and over three kilograms in weight.

I had not long committed the beast and three others to the icy depths of our upright freezer when I heard a clunk from the store room. I kid you not that one crab, presumably uneasy about being incarcerated with Mr Tyson of the crab world, had levered open the door and was making a bid for freedom.

You might imagine that such a display of heroics may sway a humble shopkeeper to stay his hand in despatching such a character. Wrong, he was the first in the pot. Got to set an example to the rest, you know.

Watching the news tonight it was apparent that our man, the Archbishop of Canterbury, known to frequent the environs of Treen, was getting all matey with his Catholic counterpart. It might take a little leap of faith, so to speak, but could we soon be seeing his Holiness dropping into The Logan Rock for a pasty and a couple of pints?

*September 18th – Saturday* – What an absolute rip snorter of a morning. We're going to have to have a till set up on the other side of the road and bask in this late summer sunshine.

Lovely day for a little Lifeboat launch and all the associated fun and frolic. A few kayaks out there in the bay and snorkelers doing their bit too and even a few basking shark sightings. Heck, if only we'd had weather like this during August we would have been laughing.

Word from our International Correspondent is that a new hurricane, Igor, is dragging its left foot and hump around the East Coast. No doubt we will have some echoes of this monster's side kick before long.

I've had some feedback from the Parish Council about the banning of dogs from the beach during the peak season next year. (For the unenlightened and those that just don't care see the entry for September 9th). It's gone to Cornwall Council now and will become edict unless a weight of opinion acts against it.

I was all for kicking off a petition etcetera, if it came to this. After a conversation tonight I'm inclined to suffer. The point being that if people, including and possibly, particularly, locals, can't be bothered to clean up after their dogs then collectively we deserve what we get. I might run a note up Terry's web pole and see what gets thrown at it.

And finally, up the F&L a new(ish) band; lone female singer and young boys on guitars. Sounds bad? Nah, she has a voice clear and crystal, them accomplished, pushy and together and they only play pubs during the summer as they're all at uni.

What's wrong I hear you cry: she couldn't smile. Man, you gotta smile.

*September 19th – Sunday* – Not quite as spiffing today but still calm and dry and plenty of good people about.

We do love this time of the year. It's difficult to nail it down completely but we think it has to do with how pleasant people are. In the peak of the summer people always seem in a rush, stressed and slightly annoyed all the time. Rolling towards autumn it's quieter and people seem in less of a hurry; the whole atmosphere is much more relaxed. Definitely a lazy summer Sunday afternoon. And, thankfully, that's the end of the gushy bit.

Having said all that we did have a succession of very oddly dressed chaps through the door. I can only assume there was a fancy dress party somewhere. First in was a man dressed as a construction worker; he was a very nice man with a big droopy moustache. A little while later a chap dressed as an American policeman, then a cowboy, an American naval officer, a motor biker and, weirdly, a North American Indian, (how pc am I?).

I should have asked them really but they must have been of the same political persuasion as they all bought the same newspaper. It was a shame as I was rather hoping there'd be one left as it had a jolly good disc in it by Kylie Minogue.

I have to thank G (who, incidentally, bought the last copy) for a timely bit of inspiration. Don't worry, we all like Kylie really.

*September 20th – Monday* – Phew, what a scorcher! As they say in certain red top daily newspapers. It's hardly cricket that we're getting this weather now instead of August, but then again neither is cricket by all accounts. I think I shall write to my MP. May as well give him something impossible to do and then I won't be disappointed when he hasn't done anything.

I think I've mentioned before how good our local doctor's surgery is. As soon as I turned fifty the arms of the welfare state wrapped themselves around me like a python on an Atkins diet. This time they've strapped me up in a device possibly last used during the Spanish Inquisition.

Apparently it measures my blood pressure and is an essential part of the programme designed to ensure my continued well-being. When it activates, not only does it encircle the wearer's arm with a vice-like grip, it also makes a sound reminiscent of a cow breaking wind, which in the privacy of your own home would be just about acceptable, especially as we have a dog. In the shop it can be rather embarrassing particularly as it does so every half hour.

The instructions are to remain still when the machine kicks off its little routine. All very well but when serving a customer this proves tricky. However should the wearer ignore the advice, the machine exacts its awful revenge by increasing its grip, fair near severing the limb to which it is attached.

I'm sure they have a better sense of humour in that surgery than I do. It wouldn't surprise me in the least if this machine did nothing at all but embarrass and debilitate the wearer and give the staff at Cape a bleddy good laugh.

It's going back tomorrow, probably floating across the bay.

And finally, apropos of nothing at all Coveish, there was a picture in one of the mainstream newspapers of a placard some wag had taken to one of the Pope concerts. Only relevant to those familiar with Monty Python's Life of Brian, (look it up if you will). It read 'He's not the Messiah, he's a really naughty boy'.

*September 21st – Tuesday* – There are some things that just shouldn't happen. Councils shouldn't lose money on pretty much safe bets and polar bears shouldn't turn up on the Cornish coast.

In fact, the second shouldn't, didn't, but that didn't stop ITV news reporting it. You might imagine a seasoned reporter for a top television news station might have thought twice about calling this one in. I mean you'd probably have a reasonable expectation that something which appeared on the ITV news was not only grounded in fact but also had been properly investigated.

In fact it probably went something like this:

Local: "You ITV noos?"

Seasoned reporter: "Yes. Right, where's this polar bear, then?"

Local: "Ees down there. That white thing bobbing around in the surf."

130

Reporter: "That's a polar bear?"

Local: "Yup. White, four legs. Sure as I'm standing 'ere."

Reporter: "Right. If we hurry we'll make the 7 o'clock bulletin."

Sometime after 7 o'clock and 1.5 million viewers later . . .

Local: "ITV noos man."

Reporter: "Now what?"

Local: "Might be a cow."

Reporter: "What?"

Local: "Yep, horns, udder. Definitely a cow."

Reporter: "Oh, bullocks."

I'll never believe another news report again. (Look up 'polar bear, Bude' on the internet if you think I'm joshing.)

Much as I couldn't quite believe that, Cornwall Council made a loss on issuing parking tickets. How on earth do you mess that up? There are private companies that make a living out of it. When you know the cost of service provision it's a short sum to work out how many tickets you need to bag. If you don't think you can get that many then you don't do it, do you?

Mind, if they sent a chap down to The Cove for a couple of days he could put his feet up for a fortnight and still turn a profit.

All this excitement and we had a double Lifeboat launch today. This was for visiting dignitaries who have signed up to the RNLI legacy programme who all enjoyed a little trip out. If you're thinking of signing up, don't worry; we did bring them all back again.

*September 22nd – Wednesday* – What a strange day. We were promised rain this afternoon but we had it this morning, just a small splash. The bigger lump blew up the Bristol Channel but it's dragging an even bigger brother behind it that looks like it will land this evening and tonight. What we did get was an oddly muggy, hazy day with a fair few people in it.

One of them asked why we didn't sell Cornish water instead of that 'French muck'. Although, as a fully paid up, card carrying chap, it pains me to say it, size does indeed matter, ahem, on this occasion. The larger bottles of the Cornish brew only come in two litres that don't fit in our chiller, not without upsetting the shelf heights, which would eventually mean losing an entire shelf.

I can see the point, although I'm not overly fond of bottled water. Down here I much prefer the draught, which, while being about as far from free as you can get, is still a sight cheaper than its contained counterpart and has some taste, the origin of which I dare not contemplate.

Which leads me onto poor old South West Water, which is in the news again. The water watchdog has told them to reduce the number of complaints they get. A highly commendable recommendation, I'm sure.

It's just when you're charging more than twice the rate for a comparable product in the next region up, you're bound to be in for a bit of a caning. They are doing their best to put things right, though. Reducing the bills? Nah, just spent £143m answering the letters quicker.

*September 23rd – Thursday* – Well here we are then. You, dear reader, were probably asleep when it happened, (with the possible exception of our international friends). I, of course, kept the vigil on your behalf, (at 03.09 UTC, did I, heck).

And there's an interesting concept, UTC that stands for Coordinated Universal Time, or rather doesn't. This is a time standard based on International Atomic Time or TAI. Oh, come on. If someone gives you a TLA, (three letter acronym), you normally have a bit of a chance of guessing the words but you're going to have real problems once they start going dyslexic on you.

After a little research I managed to discover the UTC 'acronym' is a result of a squabble between the English and the French, who wanted it to be TUC, (Temps Universel Coordonne). The UTC is a compromise between the two, suggested by some smart arbiter keen to avoid another 100 year war sparking off. Shame they didn't have a Cousin Jack on board; we would have ended up with DMA, 'Dreckly My Ansum'.

Oh and TAI? The French must have slipped that one in while the English were congratulating themselves on the previous compromise. It stands for Temps Atomique International.

Now, where was I before you rudely interrupted me? Ah yes while we dozed fitfully, we slipped into autumn.

Of, course, we're not allowed to call it the Autumn Equinox anymore lest it upset our southern hemisphere counterparts where, naturally, it's spring. It is henceforth our nights become longer as do their days, the leaves will go brown and fall from our trees, (if we had any down here) and theirs will blossom and grow. And I almost certainly will have to lose the shorts, which will be a relief to small children everywhere.

And down in The Cove visitors will become fewer and I will struggle to get my carcass out of bed in the morning. Time will become slower and I will have ample time to tell you, in graphic detail, about the mundane happenings you thrive upon – a, if there are any and b, if I can summon the strength.

*September 24th – Friday* – My bouffant hair, had I any, would have been fair tossed about this morning by a rather stiff northerly breeze. It had already tipped over our wheelie bin and later plucked one of our lightweight balls out of its stand and sent it sailing down the road.

Fortunately one of our more attentive and regular customers sailed after it, retrieving it with the grace of a gazelle. (I had to say that; she's a regular reader.)

The change wasn't bad for everyone, of course. Despite the beach being red-flagged, several hardy souls were out enjoying the new improved surf and a wind kiter fair rocketed across the bay.

Our ever-vigilant lifeguards sprang into action seeing a boarder struggling a bit in a light rip. The rescue involved driving the quad down to the surf line and blowing a whistle, "Hey, you're in a rip." "Yeah, thanks bud."

Had I fully appreciated the signs I should have been ready for this change of weather. However it wasn't until this morning that the Cover, the one who makes Methuselah look like a teenager, told me about the weather dog.

Yesterday afternoon we had a bit of a weather phenomenon. To the uninitiated this was a rather flat rainbow that hugged the cliff tops. Its base was broad; from where I was standing in the shop the red started the far side of Cot Valley and the violet ended at Nanjulian Cliff.

This is the weather dog: a harbinger of bad weather.

Mindful that a lump of weather is on the way, seasoned sailors would heave to and set heavier sails, fishermen would pull in their nets and smarter Covers wouldn't have put their balls out this morning.

Stop press: it took our International Correspondent to point out that last night, (Thursday), was this year's harvest moon. It was doubly special in that it was the first time since 1991 that it coincided exactly with the Autumn Equinox (and I can say autumn as this was not true in the southern hemisphere).

*September 25th – Saturday* – The wind dropped out today leaving us with lovely blue skies and, if you were sitting in the right place, a taste of summer. And some pretty impressive waves at 7.00am, but obviously hardened surfers don't do early mornings.

This, of course, is a simmering riposte to our International Correspondent who has been teasing me with tales of record temperatures and a sea that is near boiling point down there on the 32nd parallel. (I might have got that last bit slightly wrong; calculating the conversion from Fahrenheit to Centigrade was never a strong point).

At least if we take a dip in the water we have a fair chance of coming out with all of our toes.

On the basis that when a hurricane hits the US East Coast we get big surf two weeks later, if all goes according to plan we'll be basking in sub tropical conditions in a fortnight.

It will come as no surprise, to regular readers, that your Diarist spent his evening at the good old F&L. For tonight's entertainment the well-established Mississippi Burning's blues rock filled the air. They played, for a reason best known to themselves, a little bit of a Shadows number. A very underrated band that would, perhaps unkindly, have been better had they driven over a cliff.

I am sure I have mentioned this before, without even employing my CTL-F function to check, that a walk home, even under a waxing moon, is a wander to be cherished. When they mention, in songs, the silver moonlight, embrace it and be there.

*September 26th – Sunday* – Well I did open my big mouth and say 'a taste of summer'.

Let's get a few things straight.

"I don't mind", is not a helpful response to, "What class stamp do you want?" and parking in a place that has a big sign saying NO PARKING should not prompt the question, "Is my car all right parked there?"

In the height of summer these sort of things are expected, nay cherished, but in autumn? It quite disturbed my equilibrium I'll have you know.

As did finding a box of unsold pasties that had been there forgotten for a fortnight. Still, having brushed off the furry bits they came up quite presentable – I'm joking, I'm joking. Broke my heart consigning them to the bin, mind.

Today started gloomy just to show us what it could be like but the afternoon was lovely and bright though we did get several complaints of the cold. Looks like the week ahead will be something of a mixed bag according to the forecast but getting a tad warmer.

And we have October to look forward to and our last knockings in the shop.

*September 27th – Monday –* A blue sky morning that just got better and better.

Tripped over to St Just mid-morning and the place was alive with bustle. On the way back, the Scillies were clear and both Wolf and Longships lighthouses stood out in the crystal sea. What a corker.

By mid-afternoon it was a picture straight from high summer, (and I don't mean it was raining) except that there were few people around.

We had a bit of a coach party turn up; darned good job I've just ordered some more 15p postcards is all I can say.

Here's some happy news: Speedo, them of the figure-hugging briefs, have invented a waterproof mp3 player. Next will be a surfboard with those lighting-up panels on so you can put down some hip moves while hanging ten. Can't wait.

And lastly it was such a spiffing day it was good enough for a Lifeboat exercise. So we had one. While the boys had a jolly old time practising some search patterns, we, of the old guard, had time to shift a mountain of oar weed off the short slip. Pure heroics.

*September 28th – Tuesday –* Quite forgot to tell you that the lifeguard service ceased on Sunday. It was the absence of young fit types coming in for their croust and the lack of shrill whistles echoing across the bay that reminded me. So all you aquatic types: you're on your own.

I'm sure for many of you hardened surfers this will be akin to being let out to play without parental restraint. But a cautionary tale for all you fit running and sporty types out there: it's bad for you.

The Ancient Greeks had an inkling that things weren't quite right. It all started in 490BC with an Athenian goatherd by the name of Pheidippides. He found that all that running around after goats required something a bit more than the average sandal on his

135

feet. Being a bit of a smart lad he fashioned a light pair of sandals from goatskin that he found ideal for moving quickly over the rocky ground.

Things started to go a bit awry for him when he was conscripted into the army to see off the Persian invasion that had landed near Marathon. Standing in line while the top brass handed out battle orders one high-ranking officer noticed him.

"Nice shoes, son. Can you run?"

Being an honest lad he admitted that he could and was immediately handed the job of messenger. As a consequence he spent the entire Battle of Marathon running from the front to field HQ relaying commands and events.

At the end of the day the Athenians had more men standing up and the Persians went home. The elated field commander, sensing immediate promotion, thought it a pretty good idea to let his bosses back at Athens know how well he'd done.

Sitting knackered in the corner of the tent was good old Pheidippides.

"Nice shoes, son. Wager you're a bit swift in they things. Here, go tell the top knobs back in Athens, I won."

Knowing that you don't tell a Greek with a big sword to go hang himself, Pheidippides took off at top speed the 24 miles back to Athens.

Arriving at the door of No10, Athens Street, on his last legs by now, the top man waited patiently for Pheidippides to catch his breath. Glancing down he was amazed that the messenger's sandals still looked in good shape after such a run.

"Nice shoes, son."

Spurred on by the complement, Pheidippides managed to say with his last breath of life, "Niki", meaning victory in Greek, before expiring.

So inspired was the top man by this act of heroism that he decreed that henceforth a 24 mile race, to be called a Marathon, would be run on this day each year. He also decreed that the runners would wear special sandals named in honour of the runner.

And although the race has extended slightly and the name and shape of the sandals have been modernised, many runners, to this day, wear shoes called Nike.

So the lifeguards earn a, probably, long needed break after all their running around which might be poorly timed. I have been told that one of the Saturday mainstream papers named Sennen

Cove as top surfing beach in the UK. Expect a mob down here next week.

And we should remember that 32 years ago today The Covers put forward their own candidate for Pope after the untimely demise of Pope, John Paul I. Unfortunately he was not selected and it was back to obscurity for our man, George Ringo.

So at this point, while you digest these matters of huge import, I think it best I give you a rest until tomorrow.

*September 29th – Wednesday* – At last the press have cottoned onto something that we, in The Old Boathouse, have known for years: the big supermarkets are covertly ripping people off.

A major consumer group discovered that the supermarkets in question were selling "big value" packs that were more expensive than buying the same number of individual items and other, "honest mistakes". Also there was a customer who found a mouse in his Hovis from a supermarket online store.

Oddly the mice from my store seem to have disappeared – surely a coincidence.

But no such shenanigans from us, oh no! Our breaded mice are clearly priced and our two for one offer is a steal.

Now, I'm really, really sorry for this: our offers are clearly prefurable.

Such an awful joke deserves a really cracking day and, by golly, (can you say that?), we got one. Blue sky and sunshine, that's the way to do it.

Late morning we had a rather urgent Lifeboat shout. Big boat launched from inside the boathouse, that's the fast way, and the little boat on standby down on the beach; all that running around for what looked like a rather large inflatable pillow, mistaken for a capsized boat, but better that than the other way around.

Recovery was a little fragile, with a big swell on the long slip. Good job the firm supplies a good line in wellies.

*September 30th – Thursday* – As innocuous as this day appears we should not be fooled. Fair enough, we had some rain blow through in the morning and some more late in the afternoon, but the middle bit was pleasant enough.

We are hitting rock bottom on the visitor front, mind, save for a large group of German tourists that descended on us for half an hour. Their tour guide breezed into the shop and almost immediately out again.

"Nine sandwiches. Nine pasties.", he declared in a loud voice. I thought, I hope not, we don't have that many.

But, hold, things are not that jolly.

A new darkness is spreading over Cornwall from the east and we're not talking about the shorter daylight hours. No, this is an evil threatening the rights of passage of small boys everywhere and now, particularly in our neck of the woods.

They have given this satanic presence a name: It is Cameraria Ohridella, a name that will live in infamy for generations to come. Their common name, the leaf miner, gives only a small indication of this little caterpillar's devastating legacy. They favour the horse chestnut tree, you see, chomping away at the leaves causing them to go brown and drop off prematurely.

Small boys across the land will be looking down at their wizened, dangling spheres and ask, "Dad, why are my conkers so small?"

# October

In the news this month: *Poor showing at the Common-wealth Games in Delhi; the Government knocks child benefit on the head; thirtyodd Chilean miners are rescued from a collapsed mine and Cornishmen all protest at the prospect of a cross-border constituency.*

***October 1st – Friday*** – Another cracking good forecast from the Met Office who, at 6pm yesterday, had today pegged down as wall to wall sunshine while everyone else painted exactly the opposite picture. No prizes for guessing who was right.

I suppose it was a fitting day for the first day of October; a taste of what we can expect, perhaps.

I understand from our International Correspondent that the Met Office must have lent a chap or two to their US counterparts, the National Weather Service, as she's having similar problems.

And, with the weather, came the first of the post-season tumbleweed in The Cove. I always thought that The Specials had Coventry in mind when they wrote Ghost Town but clearly they were thinking of Sennen Cove on a wet day in October.

Apropos of nothing at all, it has been reported in the news that ADHD, Attention Deficit Hyperactivity Disorder, is caused by a physiological flaw rather than bad parenting or diet. (No doubt it will be revealed later that the research was sponsored by the Bad Parents on a Poor Diet Society.)

I shall bear this in mind the next time a little begger starts tearing apart the stock in the shop, and I shall sympathise profusely, shortly before it gets a well deserved clip 'round the ear 'ole.

And there was a little surprise sitting in my email inbox this afternoon. A lady from the BBC got my email address from the St Just Heritage website; though what it was doing there I have no idea, and sent me an invitation.

They are looking for gullible fools to go out and forage edible plants in the St Just area and later use them in a meal. The survivors will win a prize. This is for the *Countryfile* autumn special, (a BBC programme to remind people in towns that there's still green bits that Tesco hasn't built on yet), and they're looking for fifteen St Just residents. I did tell her in my reply that I was from Sennen Cove, but for the purposes of the programme I would be more than happy to drag my left foot about and carry a club. (Only joking, good people of St Just, honest.)

I'll let you know how I get on but I've ordered fifteen t-shirts with 'Sennen Cove Diary Rocks' on the front just in case.

*October 2nd – Saturday* – Not a bad start to the day although it did cloud over later in the afternoon, amazingly as predicted. There were a lot of happy surfers out there though, with some of the best waves for a long time.

Where would we be without Hans Lippershay is all I can say? The army of bird watchers we have down here each year would certainly be more challenged and astronomy would probably consist of looking at the moon a lot.

Hans, bless him, demonstrated the first telescope back in 1608 and we haven't looked back since, only forward and close up. I can, however imagine he faced a fair bit of leg pulling at the uncovering.

"'Ere Hans, did it escape your notice that we've all got two eyes?"
Still it didn't do Nelson any harm, though he did struggle a bit with the fundamentals. "Try it with your good eye, Nel."

Many thanks to R&C for pointing out that the Met Office have been busy, not predicting the weather accurately, but playing with their website. And very pretty it looks too, under the project name "Invent". How very apt, although you might have thought "Guess" to be more appropriate.

And yes, I did enjoy a perfectly reasonable night at the F&L in the company of Big Scott and the Blues Connection: they played some blues.

*October 3rd – Sunday* – A day far more pleasing to the eye than the last two; but boy did it rain last night; the run-off was still coming down the hill well into the afternoon. Our water feature in the shop returned too, giving a subtle hint that I need to get down and dirty again with the marigolds in the drain at the back. This time in the dry, of course.

We had a set of runners come through bit by bit today. They had completed three marathons in three days and were following the coast path out to Lands End, a privilege for which they paid good money. They all looked pretty chipper coming past the shop and were picking up a good speed. In amongst them, but not part of the group, was a bedraggled and knackered looking group from Sennen AFC. They had walked from St Ives, probably via The Tinners at Zennor.

Sennen AFC is currently third in the league. Looking at the motley crew that passed our door you have to wonder how.

So as the footballer of time, avoids the front page of eternity, until the call girl of fate calls to tell him he left his bike there, it's time to say goodnight.

*October 4th – Monday* – A spot on forecast for a change; beautiful day from the start although it did start to cloud over a bit in the late afternoon. It helps to liven the place up a little but at this time of the year we're still about as busy as a Delhi ticket office.

Completely forgot to excavate the drain today and with a bit of rain on the way there's an outside chance the rain will be inside tonight. Hopefully it won't be too heavy and we'll get away with it.

Perhaps with the demise of child benefit we shall have an increase in the number of small children available on the work market. Thus deprived parents could supplement their meagre incomes by sending their children out to work doing, say, drain clearing. What a delightfully progressive world we live in.

Also delighted is the bleddy hound as our part time neighbours are here this week. They are happy to take her down to the beach, which is now open all day to hounds, and on long walks hither and thither. Being a socially integrated dog she is unconcerned as to who takes her, as long as she is taken. So far our casual dog walkers have always brought her back again. I am ever the optimist though.

*October 5th – Tuesday* – A big swell starting building up towards high water today; a big boiling sea over the Cowloes and fairly huge waves running up to the beach with big combs of spray tearing off the top. Down on the surf line the water was churning up to at least head height. I dare say we'll have a sight less sand down there tomorrow morning.

The spectacle drew in a fair crowd from all over and boosted our camera sales. By high tide geet lumps of water were coming over Pedn-men-du and about half way up Nanjulian cliffs. Not a surfer in sight; don't you just hate these fair weather sports people.

141

We were treated this morning with a new, bright red, shiny dump bin. What joy I thought. The clever bit about this one is, it has a locking lid. This will not only ensure only our rubbish will get into it, but will also frustrate me no end as I arrive at it with bags in hand and no key. It will also upset the poor dispossessed soul who is used to helping himself to unsaleable foodstuffs from it.

I almost forgot: the ongoing saga with my 'lecky company losing my bank details has finally come to an end and no, my mortgage hasn't been paid off. (See July 19th and July 30th if you really can't remember – am I wasting my time here I wonder?)

The first letter, if you can call it that, was largely unintelligible. Incomplete sentences, bad spelling, where, where were should be, etc. Do they not teach written English in schools any more?

Escalation ensued and they kept upping the compo hoping I'd go away, (and I would, if they'd paid me enough, shallow? Me?), when all I really wanted was some straight answers.

It arrived today. Chapter and verse on how they took details, processed them and eventually messed up. No life changing sums, however. Can't say I didn't try.

We're getting the gas in next week.

*October 6th – Wednesday* – A star is born.

I told you on Friday that I had been asked to go and forage edible flora for the BBC and to be filmed doing it. Well, it all came to fruition today and along with around a dozen other people, none of whom were from St Just, we stomped around Perranuthnoe in search of things green.

In fact I felt a little fish out of waterish as all the people that turned up were, more of less, professional foragers. I also got the impression I was in deep veggie territory and seriously lacking a kaftan.

The maid that led us runs a business doing much the same. She also prepares meals from the collected greenery. This added a little edge to the proceedings in that if we got it wrong our stomachs would punish us.

James Wong, he of *Grow Your Own Drugs* fame, (no, I hadn't heard of it either), fronted the programme. Let's face it, if it had been Alan Titchmarsh the Missus would have trodden my nose in the dirt as she rushed out of the door.

We spent about five hours collecting and being filmed walking, then doing it again and again for successive 'takes'. I asked James how long the slot was for *Countryfile* and he told me seven minutes. No wonder our TV licence is so expensive.

Being the only non-professional, (and clearly carrying the mark of international film stardom), they wanted a few minutes with just me and James on camera. I had considered throwing a hissy fit, in the manner of all such stars, but I didn't have a dressing room to lock myself in and standing in a bramble patch was severely limiting.

After collecting our green bits we retired to a farmhouse in St Buryan where we crammed into the kitchen to prepare the meal. A show of hands was required for numbers willing to have the mackerel, showcasing the apple mint, sea beet and tri-cornered garlic salsa verde. My worst fears were confirmed when I realised I was in the minority; my fellow foragers looked down on me with scorn. They all favoured the falafels that only required the murder of a few innocent plants.

The main course of mixed green salad, (not a lettuce leaf in sight), was served up with a risotto flavoured with stinging nettles. Perhaps I was trying my luck suggesting it might have been improved with some foraged steak.

To be entirely fair, (and honest), the salsa verde was first class and the green salad was an explosion of different and palatable flavours. The demonstration made its point that a whole meal could be made from these ingredients, though I seriously doubt you'd ever want to try it at home.

In reality many of these free foodstuffs could quite easily be used to supplement a normal meal to good effect.

Perhaps it would be cruel to say it had the whiff of elitism about it. How many working Mums or Dads would be able to nip out for a couple of hours to forage and then spend as many, if not more, in preparation to put some free food on the plate? No, I suspect, for all its history, this is the plaything of well off idealists, (with the emphasis on idle), or the brainchild of people that will make serious money out of it.

Despite my misgivings, all in all an interesting and fulfilling day spent in the clear sunshine and a stiff breeze. And let's not forget fame and fortune are but a short step away, (if the previous paragraph hasn't seriously stuffed my career, Tom Cruise style, before it's started). I will, of course, have my agent send you all a signed photograph and a complimentary copy of this month's fanzine.

143

*October 7th – Thursday* – Another stunning start to the day, though a little breezy, and did, as forecast, cloud over a bit in the afternoon.

Had to trip into town again today for a spot of shopping. I know it was a foolish risk but I wore my dark glasses just in case I was recognised. On the way out of the car park I did my first good turn of the day, (other than opening the shop, of course).

A lady was struggling with a couple of boxes and I asked her if she needed some help. It was clear, from a brief look at the contents that she was on her way to one of the charity shops. In fact she was going to two and asked if I could take the box she'd given me to the closer one.

Quite unsuspecting I gave the box to the rather proper looking lady looking after the busy shop. I was turning to leave as she nosed into the contents while thanking me for my donation. I was half way to the door when she added the word, "Chippendale".

Now, it has to be said that my first reaction was that some priceless piece of woodwork was in the box and that somehow I'd missed it and my potential fortune. It wasn't until I turned around to look that I saw that she was clutching to her bosom a dusty videotape. She was referring, to my horror, to the group of strapping young men who take off their clothes to music and, at whom, women of a certain age toss their underwear.

You just instinctively know that there is no amount of vociferous protest that will convince the assembled company that the tape is not yours. Thank heavens I was wearing my dark glasses.

*October 8th – Friday* – Bit of a grey day today but not as bad as forecast earlier in the week. In fact in the afternoon it brightened up tremendously. Even that nagging east wind was relatively warm. Nothing quite like a warm nagging on a Friday afternoon, I've found.

I was left in no doubt that it was indeed windy as every customer that came in told me that it was. I am grateful to the one person who told me it was much worse up top. It at least gave me something to reply with for the rest of the day.

The warm winds of change also appear to be blowing through the OS with the new managers on board. It is early days, but the change in atmosphere was almost palpable - in that there was some.

There seems to be some professionalism at work here, but I'm sure St Awful will address this failing as soon as they find out. The restaurant appears to be going back to being a restaurant, the managers were there in person and the staff was doing something completely foreign to them- working. We shall watch with renewed hope.

Exercising the bleddy hound seems to have taken on a life of its own. Three times she was taken out yesterday for fairly extensive walks/runs. Just hope she doesn't start thinking this is normal or we're going to be run ragged during the closed season.

*October 9th – Saturday* – Purple haze!

Hendrix must have had this morning's sunrise in mind when he penned that. Black as pitch when I got up this morning, the sun slowly edged up through a mix of high cloud, low cloud and mist turning the whole sky a weird mix of colours.

And if we thought it windy yesterday it was just a practice session for today. JC's website had it recorded as 23 mph but I suspect his station must be a little sheltered from the east. Even the incoming waves this morning had a tough job making headway. Later on he recorded 51 mph which was more like it with averages in Gale Force 7 gusting to 9.

Consequently it was a blustery day of no consequence. So inconsequential was it I may have been tempted to join the Devonwall protests up in Morwenstow, just for something to do had they been held in Sennen. I wouldn't have travelled any further for it.

I think Che Guevara would have approved too, although he might have gone for something slightly more flamboyant than waving a few flags and messing around in the Tamar on small boats. At least he might have approved if he hadn't been captured and shot 43 years ago today.

With the man himself in the picture, Cameron might have reconsidered his, 'not exactly the Amazon', comment although it wasn't until after he got popped off did his status become iconic, Che that is, not Cameron. Not bad for a lad from Tooting, I say.

And last, a small addendum. A Lifeboat shout at around 11:30pm in response to flares spotted somewhere off St Just. A French vessel in the area helped co-ordinate the search along with the Lands End coastguard team. The Lifeboat investigated several radar contacts until it was recognised that the flares 'lit up the cliffs'. With a bit of Holmesian logic it was reckoned that, taking into account the wind, the flares were launched from land.

The Coastguard team found a parachute and some very likely lads. The search was called off and the Lifeboat recovered at around 2.00am.

Che might have had a thing or two to say about that too.

*October 10th – Sunday* – 10-10-10. A coincidentally arranged set of numbers, aesthetically pleasing perhaps but otherwise not terribly special. Something similar will happen next year. Odd then that the radio stations and certain newspapers make such a big song, (in one case literally), and dance about it. I was going to say, have they nothing better to write about, but since I'm writing about it I perhaps I shouldn't be too harsh.

Come first light, at ten past seven, I came down our twelve steps, naturally missing the first and the last to get the shop ready for opening. Amazingly I had ten Sunday Telegraph newspapers to pack and toyed with the idea of disposing of two Observers just to make that amazing too. At the end of the day I sent back ten Sunday Times.

When I checked the lottery numbers I missed out because I didn't have a number ten in my line, or for that matter five other matching numbers.

It all looked at bit misty and overcast this morning. Then, blow me, at ten past ten it started to brighten up a little. With mist all around us a little patch of blue opened over Sennen and stayed for the rest of the day, probably for ten hours had we had sunlight that long.

Head Launcher and I settled, alongside the eight other diners, in the Breakers Café for breakfast that was a bit of a treat. The ten items on our plates took ten minutes to arrive and it took us ten minutes each to clean our plates. And very nice it was too.

The afternoon got very busy indeed, tens of people at a time flowing through the shop. We can only hope we get similar weather for the half term.

It was very quiet later and I considered shutting the shop ten minutes early, but then a chap came in and browsed for ten minutes before buying ten cigarettes. He paid with a ten pound note.

So as you can see, apart from the weather, a completely unremarkable day after all that fuss about the date.

Nearly ten o'clock and it must be my bed time.

*October 11th – Monday* – An absolutely cracking day for a long walk.

One of the favourites around here is to catch a bus to St Just and walk back along the coast path. It is probably a little more than five miles if you account for the bits of high rocky headland and the deep Cot and Nanjulian Valleys. Along the way are ancient monuments and old mine workings to wonder at. It also gets a bit hairy in places if, like me, you're not blessed with a head for heights.

The riskiest part of the whole journey, however, is nothing to do with terrain, wild animals or the elements. No, if the bus isn't running you're knackered, as discovered by a bunch of intrepid explorers this morning.

They were even willing to take a taxi. Unfortunately, if you're a good way downstream of the bus breakdown point, there are plenty of other people en route to get to the taxi first.

Note the use of the term, 'the taxi'. Yup, there's only one in this neck of the woods, probably due to the fact that it's becoming exceedingly difficult to cut a living off a business based on using lots of diesel. Mr P only keeps going because he's probably sponsored by Mr Depp and the Archbishop of Canterbury: difficult to stop on a mix of star power and divine intervention, I imagine.

A glimmer of hope announced in the paper for us poor country folk caught with high fuel prices, long distances to drive and poor public transport, (all together now, ahhh!). Danny Alexander, Chief Secretary to the Treasury, is to implement a pilot scheme of lower fuel duty on the Isles of Scilly. Don't hold your breath, though. The trial needs the backing of the EU and is on their to do list somewhere after standardising European time for high water and maximum depth of bath water directive.

The moral of this story is if you want to walk back from St Just, ask someone to drive you there who's quite happy to come back and wait in the pub until you return. My rates are fair, given the prices of diesel and beer at the OS and I'm available from November 8th.

*October 12th – Tuesday* – We get some pretty odd questions asked of us from time to time. None for a long time have stretched us to answer it like this one.

The lady caller wanted to come on holiday when there is a spring tide and low water during the main part of the day.

From November onwards the new tide time book is out and answering this question would be a synch. Before then it is almost impossible to gain access to the tide data for next year, for free anyway. Although nailing down the spring tides was relatively easy, full and new moon dates being readily available, I can assure you, (though someone will doubtless prove me wrong), that the high and low tide times for next year do not exist in tabular form on the Internet; at least not outside those locked and chargeable portals.

I was close to giving up when I found it, an application available to download, for free. It was in the deepest darkest corner of the web, a recess so remote that it had a layer of electronic dust two inches deep on it.

It was a program so old that it was first written for use on a slate board with a piece of chalk. Initially converted for use on a steam computer it required a bit of tweaking before I managed to crank it into action. Even then it required the patience of a saint, together with judicious use of a big stick, to extract the required information.

I had fully expected to have to apply some adjustment to the output to calculate Sennen Cove time, hopefully from a nearby port. There is a preferences option that allows the user to choose the target location and another to select the period of time for which the tides times are required.

Having managed to find England I then looked for Falmouth, Newquay, Penzance. Not there. The closest was St Mary's in Scilly, which was manageable, but I felt keen to search some more. Quite unbelievably, there in a sub list, was Sennen Cove. I can only guess that Michael H, who penned it, has some connection here as it is not the most obvious location. He might even be a reader.

As I was saying it is a very well written program, has a clear interface and feels so modern and user friendly. Thank you, Michael.

The upshot, of course, is that I was able to furnish our lady enquirer with the pertinent details for her holiday. All in a day's work ma'am.

I shall now get on with the simpler tasks of the day like ending poverty, (particularly my own), creating a vaccine for the common cold and implementing world peace.

*October 13th – Wednesday* – A morning as joyous as a Chilean miner. Clear skies, crisp and fresh.

Had a letter this morning, (for you technophiles out there, that's a piece of paper with writing, or in this case a picture, on it folded inside another piece of folded paper with a destination written on the front that used to be a form of communication between two remote individuals), from our International Correspondent who has given up with the vagaries of trying to send a photograph of sufficient quality across the Internet wires.

Her point, other than that technology can be challenging at times, is that if we think we have it tough with a proposed dog ban on the beach next year, think again.

The picture is of a sign erected at the entrance to a beach, a stone's throw from her mansion in South Carolina. You will get some inkling as to the message that the sign conveys when I describe that the full expanse of the upper left quarter of the sign carries the word NO in bold red print.

Allow me to appraise you of some of the activities and contraband, the undertaking or possession of which will earn you prosecution and a fine up to $500 per offence – sorry, offense.

Picnic on the beach with a small glass of wine, perhaps? Not a chance. No alcoholic liquor, beer, wine and certainly not in a glass container.

An ice cream from the local kiosk? No unauthorized commercial activity, I'm afraid and don't for heaven's sake think of slipping out of your trousers, er, pants, as indecent exposure of the nudity kind is completely out of order.

Stunt kiting and sand-sailing are limited to mornings and evenings only between April and September and if you have an ordinary kite don't let go of it. Kites not under manual control will land you in the clink.

Animals may, or may not, be allowed on the beach and sometimes on a leash dependent on the time of year. You will, though, require a keen understanding of the dates of some key American holidays including something called Memorial Day, originally remembering only Union casualties of the Civil War, and Labor Day.

Having scared the living bejaysus out of you in so many ways the sign then urges you to have a safe and enjoyable day at the beach.

Ok, perhaps a dog ban isn't so bad after all.

Gosh, you're being treated today, (or tortured, depending on your point of view), there's at least another five paragraphs to go.

A bit of musical Lifeboats today:

Our boat is being whisked away for a bit of mechanical maintenance that could not be carried out in the station. In order for this to happen and maintain continuity of service, another Tamar class boat needs to be here before ours goes away. So for a short period we will have two boats on station.

The process, in case you're interested, involves launching our boat, then recovering the relief boat. The relief Tamar is then dropped down onto the short slip and secured. Our boat is then recovered and secured on the long slip. After that the relief boat can be winched up onto the cradle and swung around behind our boat. Simple when you have the odd three hours to spare.

Then, just in case you haven't had enough playing with Lifeboats, you can get up at 5:00am the following morning to send our boat on its merry way to maintenance land.

I clearly haven't had enough and will be there tomorrow morning, hankie in hand, to send the boys off on their way. This being the case, this is the very last paragraph for today. I imagine you're delighted.

*October 14th – Thursday* – Oh yawn. Yes, that 5:00am start really set me up for the day.

I expect I should tell you that we're into squid and oyster season. Not, to my knowledge, that there's any oysters here abouts and even if there were it's very unlikely we could get at them, at least not using the usual dredging method, akin to running a plough along the sea bed.

You see, very recently a sea conservation area, (Marine Conservation Zone), has been set up, (possibly still proposed), roughly from Runnel Stone to Cape Cornwall. Quite what this means in reality I really have no idea. I understand that fishing is still allowed, although I think they might have something to say if you tried to run a beam trawler through there.

However, do not be disheartened. We have some of the country's best squid hunters in these parts. The squid hunters are highly recognisable; the Black and White Minstrel Show comes to mind. In fact I am in possession of the fruit of their labours as I pen this very page. It will, very shortly, be treated to a couple of minutes in a pan of melted butter with garlic and rapidly consumed with some freshly baked bread, (please, do stop dribbling on the keyboard).

The method for catching these cephalopods is underhand; something of a nasty business really. Jigs are used that resemble a female squid. Clever fishermen paint long eye lashes, ruby lips, long blonde hair and large tentacles to their jigs for good measure.

By the time our frisky male realises he's been had, he'll have been whisked away from the fun life he had with all his mates. Not that different from the human world, then.

Oysters, I know, are not everyone's cup of tea. I have tried them on a number of occasions and never better than with a very good friend of mine. He and I, dressed in our finery, a gentleman's measure of g&t in hand and we ate them with condiments of Tabasco and Worcestershire Sauce and perhaps a little pepper. A very special moment – we almost held hands. Had we one free we might well have done. Still brings a little dampness to the eye when I think of it.

I have tried to convince the management of the F&L, without success, to echo the Falmouth Oyster Festival with a few of the bivalve molluscs. I shall never get to the real thing as the shop is always open when it's on. I'd ask at the OS but they'd probably come in a packet.

PS. I've been asked to make an apology for the cheap, unnecessary, pathetic and sexist attempt at humour in the squid catching paragraph. There was some reference about my tentacles and a sharp pair of scissors if I didn't.

*October 15th – Friday* – Grey these last couple of days and getting noticeably colder too. Not too sure how much longer the shorts and flip-flops will last.

So quiet and unassuming was the day I could hear the breeze rattling between my ear 'oles. In reality, all today happened to be was a filler 'cos in the evening The Blues Busters were playing – in Camborne.

Yes, assuming safety in numbers, eight of us happy Senneners procured, at reasonable expense, the excellent taxi services of Mr P and headed off up country. We dropped short of the border and, cunningly disguised, made our way under the wire.

What a rip roaring, top hole, evening we enjoyed. Big Scott on vocals and the singeing notes from the guitar of Mr Stingray. We could almost have been in the smoky haze of a Chicago blues bar.

All too soon it was over. Our disguises wearing thin, the locals looking restless for blood, we cut our losses and called in Mr P and his medevac solution. What a jolly bunch of chums we were, threading our way home.

And just to think if it hadn't been for The Blue Busters we would have had a three line Diary entry. Heaven help us all come November.

*October 16th – Saturday* – Sun came up into a few dark clouds lighting up in a very colourful display. The clouds, moving our way, dumped a fair bit of rain on St Just, as they do, and gave us a little sprinkle as they passed out to the west. We were left with clear blue skies for the main part of the day and a keen easterly.

A fair few people around today; probably the advance party for the half term next week.

The fishing fleet were out in force this morning. Even the youngster RS, who hasn't been out much this year, took to the waves for a bit and was rewarded by hooking up a cod.

I've been reading in the news that it would be even more amazing if he hadn't caught one, perhaps. According to the Norwegians there are more cod than at any time since the last war and they fear overcrowding, that may lead to food shortages resulting in the older cod eating the little ones.

Now, I know that they were talking specifically about the Barents Sea but I can't see the Norwegians being slack in the fishing department, at least no less than us, even if their national dish is farikal, (lamb in cabbage). So if the Barents Sea is full of fish why shouldn't our bit of water be, unless cod have suddenly decided North Norway is the fishy equivalent of Notting Hill, don't you know, darling.

Anyway RS was happy enough with his catch and didn't seem too keen on sharing any about. I'm still partial to a bit of pollock, but you try and get some battered at any of the chippies around here. It's all cod, so can't be too much of a problem with the supply chain.

Someone, somewhere is telling tall stories about the state of fish stocks. The fishing industry, the conservationists and EU all have vested interests which means it's hard to get an objective truth.

Meat curry tonight chaps.

*October 17th – Sunday* – Another rip corker of a day and still as the grave; cold in the shade but blistering sitting out on the sunshine Whatever next in mid-October.

You're probably wondering why there was no report from the F&L last night. Did the sky fall in? Was I ill? – About the only two things that would prevent me from attending the usual Saturday night shindig. I can assure you all is perfectly well in The Cove and I'm as hale and hearty as medical science allows.

No, the thing that interrupted the usual flow of events was one of our randomly spaced 'Curry and Cards Nights'. Mainly held during the off season, as all of us tend to be busy during the summer, we will descend on the home of one of the attendees for a home spun curry and then proceed to play poker for the evening. There may, or may not, be the consumption of some alcohol during the event, I forget.

It is a loose arrangement and relies on the host having been able to negotiate with his spouse, often a costly affair, the use of a cooker and a dimly lit, and preferably, sound proof room. Last night it was my turn to cook and provide the venue.

Fortunately the shop has the use of a large industrial sized waste bin in which to dispose of the detritus and by this afternoon, with the deployment of copious quantities of 'Au de Pong-all-the-Same' air freshener, the room was mainly habitable again. I'm sure that by the end of the week the Missus will have resumed civil communications unless, of course, she discovers the red wine stain on her best rug; it was a stroke of luck that the bleddy hound moved when she did.

At last knockings we had a bit of a Reginald Perrin moment. Our neighbour, walking her hounds, discovered a neatly folded pile of clothes, shoes 'an all, stacked in a corner of the Harbour Beach, under the slipway. A detailed scan of the bay revealed no obvious owners.

Having acquired a second opinion from the Lifeboat coxswain, the alarm was raised and an army of Her Majesty's finest Coast-guards arrived. Naturally as soon as they had, the Regina Perrin, as it turned out, emerged running, Baywatch style, waist high through the surf.

A brief, explanatory note among the clothes would have been useful. However we can appreciate that such precautions are not always obvious to the uninitiated.

*October 18th – Monday* – Oh dear! A lot of dark clouds around today and the boys on the radio telling us that some rain is on the way 'mainly in the Isles of Scilly and West Cornwall'. Thanks for that.

It was noticeably chillier today and set to get colder. I'm afraid the shorts and flip-flops have a very short life now.

I did have to slip on some over-trousers for the Lifeboat exercise; that would have been a hairy leg too far. We were a bit short handed with our Head Launcher in dry dock for a spot of maintenance but managed with a bit of running around.

The launch was to assist the National Coastwatch Institute (NCI) in their training. They are a bunch of volunteers that run the watch stations around the coast after HM Coastguard bailed out a few years ago. They do an excellent job in monitoring ship movements and have been instrumental in more than a few inshore rescues. We are flanked by one at Cape Cornwall and another at Gwennap Head. They are well worth a visit as the chaps are often on their own and are happy for the company.

The Lifeboat drops a target and steams off for a while. The NCI then track the target and guide the Lifeboat back in via Falmouth Coastguard.

A couple of hours later the Lifeboat was back home and tucked into the station.

I note, from the newspaper, that Iran is planning on chopping off the hand of a shoplifter. I feel this may be a tad extreme although, I imagine, quiet effective. Naturally I couldn't advocate such barbaric punishment over here, at least not for a first offence. Perhaps we could start with a finger then maybe work up to a thumb if the light-fingered begger, (perhaps a poor choice of description) got caught again.

Got to dash now; a bit of sea bass for tea and just remembered my filleting knife could do with a sharpen.

*October 19th – Tuesday* – These cold, dark mornings are certainly not conducive to getting out of bed early. For the last few months I have made sure things are on the move in the shop then have got the bleddy hound and taken her around. Usually all I have had to do is call softly from the door and she'll come, not exactly bounding, to get her collar on.

This morning I called, then called louder and eventually went to the bedroom to get her. She did raise her head momentarily before giving me what I can only describe as a doggie "V" sign then plonked her head back down. She eventually got up with the Missus well after the shop was open. Looks like I'm the only stupid one in our household.

Wind up today and the sea in an awful state. Kept the fishing fleet in for the day but we have higher hopes for tomorrow as we have some fish orders in.

154

All that wind kept most people away today although we did have some milling about, wondering what to do with themselves. You'll be pleased to note, and no doubt fair awe inspired, that the shorts and flip-flops have endured for yet another day. I felt positively under-dressed compared to some of the customers. I just hope we don't get the weather they're expecting.

Missus and family have gone out deep to the big city lights. No doubt the van will be creaking on its springs on the way back filled with goodies I didn't know we needed.

I'm beginning to wonder about this 'partnership' deal.

*October 20th – Wednesday* – Dragged myself out of my pit again, to a sparkling new day. That breeze has kept up a little longer than expected and the temperature has definitely dropped a degree or two. And yes, in case you were wondering, I'm still wearing them.

Someone took the trouble to walk all the way from the other end of The Cove to tell us that there was a dead seal on the beach. I did check but I'm ok for slippers and there probably wouldn't be enough for a coat. So I telephoned the Council but the person I spoke to said he was the last one there and was only employed to turn off the lights on his way out.

Our friendly little thrush is back. At least I think it's a thrush as it does look like the picture on the Internet although we're not exactly in a wooded area, which is apparently where they're found. Ok, I'm not a bird expert! This could be a greater spotted song twerp for all I know. Does it matter? This one is quite happy to hop into the shop and have a little nose around when there's nobody about. Unlike the dumb sparrows, (which I can identify), it also appears unfazed by the enclosed surroundings and will find its own way out without having to fly up and down the shop crashing into things.

The way things are going we shall be grateful for the company after the half term week. Yes, we're only a couple of weeks off closing now after which your Diarist will be regaling you on yet another interesting walk down the beach and how many cobwebs there are on the living room ceiling.

Buckle down, it's going to be a rough ride.

*October 21st – Thursday* – Well the sun came out into a big blue sky. The temperature lifted a degree or two and the wind abated. Guess what? Today I got into my grown up trousers and a pair of warm shoes.

The seal on the beach turned into a Harbour Porpoise overnight with some expert picking over the bones this morning. I wish I'd known as I suffered some sort of Chinese in a box affair this evening for tea, dolphin steak would have gone down a treat.

Fickle lot these fishermen we have down here. All I wanted was a couple of brace of mackerel but not a chance. They're all chasing the squid at this time of year and the fish have a stay of execution. Unfortunately I ordered one squid too many for another customer. Oh dear, I'll just have to eat it myself.

Did we know that Dylan Thomas frequented this neck of the woods during the mid 30s? Not until we picked up the latest edition of the local magazine, we didn't. Seems he spent some time in Mousehole and Lamorna and is very likely to have trekked a bit further too.

He married Caitlin down here in the same registry office that the Missus and I got hitched in and, no doubt, drank in the same watering holes. Given he was a bit of a dysfunctional alcoholic I'm sure he was not out of place, probably why I feel so comfortable here.

I'd treat you to a few Thomas lines but some of you might have sharp implements within reach. After the second stanza you might be tempted to use them. Not that I'm suggesting any of you are suicidal; it's my own safety I'm thinking of – some of you live quite close.

Had to trip up to our mouse store today. We felt it was appropriate to make the effort to try and stock the shop, looking like we expect it to be busy next week. Have you seen the forecast?

At this time of year we also have the legal opportunity of disposing of anything that might be combustible. In the field at the back of the F&L is a giant pyre ready for firework night. My remaining lumps of cardboard, old shop fittings and displays all went to a good cause. The bonfire ends up an enormous stack and the night is a big one in Sennen.

More of that come the time. So that's at least one diary entry taken care of. Bet you can't wait.

*October 22nd – Friday* – Started off a bit cloudy today but soon brightened up and we ended up with another cracker. Set to get gloomier tonight with a big lump of rain waiting in the wings.

Lots of pottering souls around today; wandering aimlessly into the shop and just as aimlessly wandering out, mainly without buying anything. It was rather reminiscent of a George A Romero film set but more Afternoon of the Slightly Mystified rather than Dawn of the Dead, where the characters were a sight more animated than our lot.

There I was, minding my own business, leaning against my door frame, as you do, when all of a sudden: B-BOOM. And, no, Basil Brush hadn't made a surprise resurrection with David Nixon's hand up his rear end. This was a sonic boom of a jet breaking the sound barrier, I'd stake my trousers on it, unless the gulls have learnt a trick or two recently. It fair rattled the whole building.

I had already seen a vapour trail up to the north, at least 30,000 feet, of an aeroplane that had performed a very tight turn and was heading back east. This is highly unusual as I'm pretty certain that aircraft of any sort are not permitted to break the sound barrier anywhere near land.

An investigation is obviously required, but where to start. I'll pop an email to Radio Pasty if I don't hear anything on the news tomorrow. Stay tuned for breaking news, and I'll try not to break it too fast.

*October 23rd – Saturday* – Do you remember those pictures years ago, from children's books, where the wind was depicted as a cloud with a face with 'o' shaped mouth blowing. Well that's exactly what happened this morning except this time the chap had a mouth full of water too.

We were lucky, again, that the shop remained dry because I only remember to clear out the drain at the back after the rain starts. It does look like we'll have rather a lot this week. I suspect this is largely because the schools are out and it would be terrible to spoil this year's record of having rain through every  school holiday so far.

It's also spoilt the chance of having one last fling with the fish sales. The only viable day looks like Monday. I've started a marketing drive to try and squeeze as much out of the one day as possible. Marketing as in, 'look you're going to have some fish whether you want it or not and it's going to be on Monday. Alright!'

And having thrust squid down everyone's throat, what's our favourite fisherman doing Monday? Fishing for bleddy mackerel.

Not to be fooled by the Met Office's promise of a sunny afternoon we battened down the hatches while more showers piled through in the afternoon. Nice to see the MO continues to uphold its fine reputation. To be fair(ish) the big lumps of cloud didn't deliver much rain in the afternoon – they were moving too fast.

In the face of all this adversity I'm firmly of the opinion that I should conform to the authorities' view that alcoholism is rampant in Cornwall with over 23 per cent in the at risk category. I'm off up the F&L to drown my sorrows and once they're drowned I'll wring 'em out and drown the beggers again.

*October 24th – Sunday* – Here we go again. The good old MO had us down as having lots of lovely sunshine today so the water running down the back of my neck is merely an illusion. And those big black clouds up there, a figment of my active imagination, no doubt!

Here's a salient tale if you find yourself in trouble down here. In all cases we will do our level best to find you a solution, bend over backwards we will, or at the very least point you in the right direction. However sometimes we are completely stumped. That means there is absolutely nothing we can do, really, honest, no kidding.

Getting sharp, snappy or grumpy isn't going to help any and will make me wonder why we bothered trying in the first place. And if you're going to get into that sort of state because your car doesn't work it may well pay to spend a few bob on a roadside assistance plan.

But enough of this ranting. I'd quite forgotten how good it was to see the wealth of happy faces. Some new, some old and being introduced to the twin girls who looked so awe inspired, as if the mysteries of the Universe were being unveiled before their eyes, as they got their very first bucket and spade. Or the little old lady content to push her wheel chair around in front of her, very slowly, including down the middle of the road. As she put it, "I'm not in a hurry any more".

And I don't think I will be by the end of this week. We have a house full of women for the duration so please excuse the shaky handwriting as I fear the start of slow descent into deafness and lunacy.

*October 25th – Monday* – Bit on the chilly side this morning but a clear sky and a pretty little sunrise thing going on. High cloud moving in this afternoon, then that very welcome high pressure system moving out the way.

The squid marketing plan worked; we're still cleaning up the ink. Mackerel and megrim too all played their part in the biggest fish day this year and more orders coming in. In fact we cleaned out two Cove boats to fill our squid order and they were so fresh they were still kicking in the bags when we sold them.

The child labour put in a late appearance this morning. Child may not be entirely accurate any longer as age has started to take its toll, which is a shame as they're slightly less malleable. Labour, as you can imagine, might be a bit of a stretch as well although they did a pretty palatable impression of a butternut squash soup that was very welcome. Of course, I told them it was awful – you don't want to encourage self-satisfaction at that age, do you?

With a little pointing in the right direction we'll be having three course, cordon bleu cuisine by the end of the week. If things go awry it will be one course of penicillin.

Rounding off the day with a Lifeboat exercise launch that will at least get me out of harms way for a while, particularly if they've caught a sneaky read of this entry.

*October 26th – Tuesday* – Backlash day today in a number of ways.

First the weather has closed in on us: overcast and rainy this morning, clearing up but still cloudy in the afternoon. While yesterday was slow to start, today never really got going. That's the payback for two rather buoyant days of business.

We didn't feel it much in The Cove but I imagine the wind was fair ripping across the moor at the top. It certainly didn't blow anyone down here though.

Given the inclemency of the weather the Missus took our young guests off to our award winning farmers' market and thence onto St Ives which will no doubt be packed; everyone goes to St Ives when it's raining. And with even less doubt, our sturdy van will come back laden to the roof with more things I didn't know we needed. It is therefore easy to understand my aversion to rainy days.

In the number two spot of backlashes, was a news item. This morning the Isles of Scilly Steamship Company have decided not to back the chopper move to Land's End aerodrome. They have, probably wisely, decided to keep a few shillings back to replace the *Gry Maritha* and *Scillonian III* or, if the Link Project fails to attract the appropriate government funding, to maintain the two existing ships for a further period.

This will delight the anti bodies and the 'nimbys', fearful of noise and pollution up at LE. It would be nice to think it would also scupper the sale of the existing Penzance Heliport to yet another supermarket. However, the likely result will be for the area to lose the link altogether, along with the jobs and the visitor potential that goes with it. Of course, IOSSC may now go ahead with their plan B with the helo gone. They have an agreement with Ryan Air to fly 100 seater jets out of Lands End to take up the slack.

We've been promoted to the front line in the fight against international terrorism that blights society at this time of the year. Devon and Cornwall Police have presumably spent a small fortune in producing the tools and training we retailers need to combat this onslaught.

We at The Old Boathouse have, naturally, stepped up to the mark and are doing our bit. To demonstrate our commitment we have placed our credentials in pride of place on our notice wall – a poster kindly provided by the police. It leaves would be perpetrators of heinous acts in no doubt that we mean business. We shall be scrutinising our customers thoroughly, and like the poster says, our stocks of WMDs, (namely flour and eggs), will be sold at our discretion this Halloween.

*October 27th – Wednesday* – I feel there is some affinity between The Cove and our International Correspondent's small corner of the USA, Hilton Head. It is as genteel and law abiding as our own little neck of the woods, so I'm led to understand. The areas are similar in every respect, with the exception of the weather, temperature, longitude, animal life, language, (to a degree), flora and size.

While across the Atlantic they're after some rain we were very pleased that the weather sorted itself out again for today and with it came an influx of visitors; fair-weather friends, I ask you.

A busy day down here out of season does cause its own problems, though nothing on the scale reported in the *Island Packet*, our adopted community's local newspaper.

For example, to save a couple of bob, many of our visitors feel it appropriate to park on the double yellow lines. While, after

September 30th, this is perfectly legal it does require a modicum of responsibility and common sense on the part of the parker. I fear these commodities may be in short supply as today cars are parked from the OS to the bus turning point without a break.

A driver, therefore, needs to ensure the whole stretch of 150 yards or so is free to traverse before embarking on the attempt. Not an easy task when you cannot see round the corner at the OS end. Of course if you own a Land Rover it is clearly appropriate to complete the whole route on the pavement, irrespective of it being used by pedestrians.

I seem to be on the receiving end of a bit of a Chinese whisper from a reliable, though mischievous, source in this country; our International Correspondent is in a bit of a spin. "Bust yields seven kilos . . ." reported in the Island Packet seems to suggest that Hilton Head is a hot-bed of vice where illegal drugs are transported and concealed about a certain part of a ladies anatomy. The news, I contend, has clearly been misrepresented and I feel duty bound to correct it.

Quite obviously the report relates to a head and shoulders sculpture cunningly contrived to allow the storage of perfectly legal medicines and pills, a drugs bust, albeit a large one, and clearly nothing to do with illegal substances. I have one myself: a colourful Rastafarian smoking a strange looking cigarette upon which I hang my hat. It has a funny little three cornered leaf on the front by way of decoration.

These newspaper reports can quite easily be misconstrued and lead to an unnecessary slur on the otherwise unblemished character of a community. It could so easily have been Sennen Cove.

And for those of you, dear readers, who haven't got a clue what I've been going on about for the last three paragraphs you are in good company. I think your Diarist has, at last, reached that place between genius and insanity without having been troubled by passing through the genius stage. I am, after all, sharing quarters with five women. I'm sure you understand.

And having completed about the twentieth draft of today's page, wiped the sweat from my brow and let the smoke clear from the overworked keyboard, I shall never again attempt anything so daft as to tie a completely unrelated report in the *Island Packet*, South Carolina, to The Cove Diary.

Although by the middle of a dead December I reserve the right to revise that last statement.

*October 28th – Thursday* – The return of some more good weather after a shaky start was welcome, as was the return of some of my equilibrium after apparently slipping off the rails yesterday.

I think I may have found the answer after a little light reading today. I was browsing the snappily titled, "Consequences of Feminisation in Breeding Groups of Wild Fish". I can heartily recommend it. It is well written and has some surprising twists in the plot but it leaves a bit of an open end. I suspect the author is working on a sequel.

Its main thrust is the feminisation of fish, particularly river fish, from swimming around in waters laced with EDCs. Oh, do I have to explain everything? Endocrine Disrupting Chemicals from sources as diverse as the contraceptive pill and washing up liquid, like Fairy, perhaps. Apparently the male fish studied have turned a bit girly and are up to 76% less likely to breed.

The report postulates that there may be knock on effects further up the food chain, namely us, and could lead to erratic or unexpected behaviour. Since I've consumed rather more fish recently than is probably good for me I can only assume yesterday's Diary page is a direct result.

It was suggested that I wean myself off The Cove a bit. Since the shop will be shut in little over a week, and I may have to take journeys beyond the top of Cove Hill, I braved the journey to Newlyn to pick up a particularly small order of fish. I also wanted to make sure they were real blokey sorts of fish and we didn't get passed off with the girly ones.

Nasty little accident on the way back, just by Crows-An-Wra, though fortunately it didn't look like anyone was hurt. Half a dozen cars had stopped and a very organised bunch of chaps were directing traffic. Well done! Could have been there all morning else.

R and O, two of our staying visitors, have asked me to mention just how much of a pleasure it has been for me to have them here. There, I mentioned it and I better mention P as well, else she'll be upset. I just hope they don't forget to go home tomorrow.

I have to sign off now as my girdle's killing me and my stockings are falling down.

Steak tonight, I think.

*October 29th – Friday* – Ooh what a grey day with a little rain first thing but brighter later. Big sea running too, though that didn't stop a pod of dolphins from coming in for a play around in the surf.

The fish factory ship, *Athena*, is still giving fire fighters some trouble. She's being held by the tug *Anglican Princess* just outside Falmouth harbour limits. Due to the big seas and high winds she's turned into the wind and from what I hear that means smoke and fumes run the whole length of the ship so the firemen have nowhere to go for a breather.

There are some upsides, though, succinctly coined by our Lifeboat Cox, there'll be no shortage of smoked fish on the market when they eventually bring her in.

If that wasn't enough a training ship with 36 children on board was dismasted in heavy seas 100 miles off Scilly and in a spot of bother. She also couldn't start her engines for fear the tangled rigging would foul the propeller. With two tugs caught up with the *Athena*, a fishing boat, *Nova Spiro*, out of Newlyn has gone to her aid and will tow her in. A tug from Alderney has also been despatched and the St Mary's Lifeboat is going to assist.

It would be interesting to see what would have happened in this situation next year after the Emergency Towing Vessel (ETV) service is scrapped with the Government cuts.

Lightening the mood slightly it's off to the F&L this evening for a long awaited auction. In the chair is the very excellent Mr Hocking, a professional agricultural auctioneer. Last time we saw him I had an itchy nose and came away with three pigs and a combined harvester.

*October 30th – Saturday* – Halloween must be approaching fast. We had two small child incidents today, on which we will not dwell, but did put us in mind of a little devilishness.

The rain held off until late afternoon, which was nice of it, and there was a good manageable swell for the surfers. The dolphins put in another couple of appearances as well until they chased the Lifeboat out of the bay.

The Lifeboat was on her way to relieve the St Mary's and escort the *Fryderyk Chopin*, the no longer tall ship, along to a hand off with Falmouth Lifeboat. They launched at 3:00pm today and will be out all night. Recovery expected around 10:00am tomorrow with a very tired crew, no doubt.

And I shall leave you with this, before I dash off to the F&L, yet again, (before you mention it), that a bumper of good liquor will end a contest quicker than justice, judge or vicar.

It was only right that I finish this, fearfully short, entry with a quote from Richard Brinsley Sheridan who was born on this very day in 1751. And as a little link to our revered county, in 1804 he was appointed Receiver-General of the Duchy, whatever one of those is.

*October 31st – Sunday* – Bit of a quiet start today and a drop in the swell that let our fishing fleet get out for a while. Didn't find out what they caught but I imagine squid featured quite prominently.

The Lifeboat arrived earlier than expected after a little confusion with the clock thing. We still had a little time, though, to watch the dolphins put on a rather impressive display quite close in.

I'm beginning to hear some encouraging noises concerning matters at the OS. Service is on the up it seems, though that wouldn't be hard; it couldn't have got any worse. My informant, who is best known for complaining vociferously about most things, tells me that not only did the OS have some Sunday roasts after 12:30pm but that it was actually quite palatable as well. The tattler also noted that it was very quiet. Well one swallow and all that.

It has also been pointed out to me by a reliable source that the OS does not do what I, rather unkindly, referred to as 'boil in the bag' food and never has. My mistake and I offer heartfelt apologies. It is clearly testament to the professionalism and superior talents of the then kitchen staff that they managed to turn out perfectly fresh meals that appeared and tasted like they were boil in the bag, then.

Nice to see our efforts at controlling our vast array of WMDs paid off. We had a succession of young, blood dripping creatures come to the door this evening and not an egg or flour bomb in sight. One of them even took the bleddy hound around with her.

Talking of talent, ahem, there was a chap with burgeoning stardom and dashing good looks due to be on telly tonight. I had taken the precaution of hiring two burley minders to stave off any over enthusiastic teenage fans that try and storm the shop in the morning, (or afternoon being teenagers). In case you try and call tomorrow I'm afraid the telephone has been switched through to a call centre in Delhi.

But disaster! My acting prowess and fame guarding tactics have come to nought. I've been dropped in favour of some Essex lad hacking away at a bunch of pumpkins and a herd of rutting deer that will probably be looking out of some rich bloke's wall by now.

What a senseless waste of raw talent. Me, that is, not the deer.

# November

*November 1st – Monday* – I've been thinking about painting the shop ceiling. I feel inspired. Naturally we can only do this when the shop is shut but I'm not sure I'll have enough time.

Mind you I could have started this week. We noticed on Sunday that business had taken a bit of a dive. Today was even worse despite the weather being quite clement and mild. Bit of rain headed in by late afternoon, though, and that really put the mockers on it.

Both the Ice Cream Parlour and Breakers have shut now, leaving us to fight off the hoards all by ourselves. That is if the hoards can get here through the preponderance of tumbleweed heading down Cove Road. Still, the main reason for staying open the extra week is to get things cleared up.

I know for a fact had we shut on Sunday we would have risen late, then spent the rest of the day, and probably the week, cooped upstairs doing not a lot. There would have been promises of doing this and that but always later, or more often tomorrow. And we all know where tomorrow comes in the pecking order.

Which is why, if I'm going to do this ceiling, I'd best get on with it. I was thinking we'd not just go with plain white this time but have something a little more interesting, maybe a picture or two in the form of a fresco. While not easy to do, it would certainly pull in the crowds some. Of course we'd do it properly, using the buno fresco method, where the paint is applied while the plaster is still wet. This would give a longer lasting job than, say, fresco secco or finto fresco but clearly is a lot more difficult to do.

It may be that we have to get a chap in to do it and I've looked at the Internet to see if I can find anyone. There were a few painters and decorators but I could find only one with the right set of skills.

His website says he's done the sort of work we're after and been established for quite a while. I'm a little worried because the last job listed took him four years to finish and it was a while ago now. In fact the firm was having a bit of a celebration because it was finished today in 1512. It's been retouched a bit since but, fair play, it's still there.

I was keen to use a Cornish company but this Italian sounding chap, Michael Angelo, will have to do.

*November 2nd – Tuesday* – It is a wild and stormy day in the making. Just right for a Lifeboat launch it was felt. This was for the BBC *One Show* programme who are making a bit of an article of the rescue in 1907 from the liner *Suevic* of 456 souls by Lifeboats from Lizard, Coverack, Cadgwith and Porthleven. I presume they would have filmed from Lizard if the new station had been built yet.

It was a bit touch and go whether the boat would launch, which it did at 10:30am The recovery was a little dicey with a fifteen to twenty feet rise and fall on the short slip. I don't think there's any danger of your Diarist being featured, but you may hear the sound of loud raspberries being blown in protest at their dropping me from *Countryfile*.

This is the time of year, with only a few days left of opening, we start to consolidate our freezers so that they can be shut down and cleaned. It's quite amazing the build up of ice that accumulates, especially in the public ones. It is also amazing just how much water is contained in those inches of ice.

For those interested, over the next few days we will be running demonstrations of just what will happen when the polar ice caps melt; though I suspect that we will need something a bit more effective than a mop and bucket to clear up that mess.

Naturally the designers of the freezers place the drain at the bottom of the unit. Well you wouldn't put it anywhere else given the laws of gravity and water finding its own level. What you might have done, is provide some sort of tube to enable the water to be directed to a bucket. As it is, the hapless defroster, must either find a container sufficient for at least a gallon of water that is only one inch deep, the height of the drain hole above the floor, or resign himself to mop up said gallon off the floor the following morning.

In between penning the last paragraph and this I have fashioned a cunning water extraction system. If it works I shall patent it. If it doesn't I shall be on hands and knees tomorrow and we shall say no more about it.

And last in this cornucopia of disconnected tit bits, George Bernard Shaw who died sixty years ago today once said that if you laid all the economists end to end they'd never reach a conclusion.

This struck me as an odd thing to say for a man who co-founded the London School of Economics. Given he hated school, perhaps he was suggesting an institution that kept them all in one place.

*November 3rd – Wednesday* – It's taken me a while to get started on the Diary today. It's quite time consuming mopping up a continuing drip of water as the ice in the freezer slowly melts. And don't even think of asking about my water extraction system, okay!

Still, it's better than trying to mop up the water in the bay today; a large swell still going on from last night and crashing over the breakwater even at mid tide. We even have a little wet stuff falling from the sky.

The whole day was grey with sporadic visitations from passers by. It has made me wonder why we did open this week although we have got rid of the ball and windbreak stands and emptied one freezer – in three days.

Our over-enthusiastic running down of stock has forced us to re-order various things. It is interesting, in retrospect, to think that opening the shop without certain items is unthinkable. Bread and milk would almost certainly fall into that category along with perhaps butter and eggs. It is, though, a damning indictment on our marketing led consumerism that one of those essential items that we ordered for today was Coca Cola.

As if to rub salt, (of which we have plenty), into the wounds of our shameful capitulation and a fact that would have John Montague spinning in his grave, we care, not a jot, that we have run out of sandwiches. John, whose birthday it was today in 1718 was the 4th Earl of Sandwich without whom we wouldn't have any to run out of.

*November 4th – Thursday* – A rather curious day for weather, with big blue sky and high cloud in equal measure and warm with it. It was certainly very bright first thing with only a cloud of gloom over St Just way.

While the sea was very big it didn't stop three windsurfers taking to the waves. I suspect that they were professionals as they went out a fair way and were dancing on top of the Cowloes for a time there.

They also appeared to have a photographer in tow. He was obviously brighter than the surfers as he preferred to stay on dry land and use a camera with a particularly large lens. I have to say I haven't seen one that size outside of sporting events on the telly. It amused me to note that it was camouflaged, as if you could hide something that size.

The Missus obviously feels that our impending incarceration and excommunication from the public view will lead to a rapid increase in body weight. It's probably not far from the truth as we munch our way through the winter darkness. She feels the ultimate answer to us not becoming another unfortunate Health Department statistic on obesity is the procurement of technology, namely a Wii Fit.

In my view the only pounds this toy will shed are those paid for it.

In setting up the device I had to endure its initial assessment, which meant jumping on board and being measured. It told me I was overweight. True, but it also pointed out that my ideal weight was eleven stones. Now the last time I was eleven stones I was about twelve years old.

While in the latter part of the intervening years I have been of, ahem, comfortable weight, the earlier ones I was slim as a board. I still have the limbs of a gazelle, albeit an old one, its just the middle bit is a little rounded. Dropping to eleven stones now would make me look like a ball cock with two arms.

I doubt that I need worry too much though. I imagine, ere the batteries expire, it will be enjoying the company of the step machine, the bullworker and the running shoes.

We had a sales lady dare enter the shop today. She was proffering the wares of a certain TV chef who, apparently, in his spare time, makes pots, pans, crockery and cutlery. What a busy lad.

There were several can't-do-without items highlighted by my guest including a cooking pot with a cone lid. This marvellous invention, used by the Etmegramma tribe of North Africa, will 'cook vegetables from raw in just a few hours'.

"Similar to a saucepan, perhaps?" I enquired.

"Ah, but this one has a cone shaped lid where the steam collects, cools and runs back into the vegetables."

"Ah, similar to a saucepan with a lid on," I suggested.

"He does saucepans too." She offered.

"I already have one of those." I replied.

I suspect our TV chef won't be inviting me to any filming in the near future.

*November 5th – Friday* – A grey and mizzly day cheered by the welcome return of the boys who built the slip and did the work on the Lifeboat station.

It's nearly a year since the work was completed and they've come back to make sure there are no outstanding issues before the work is finally signed off. Most of the same crew are out at Chapel Cove working on the rebuild of Lizard Lifeboat Station that will look like a mini version of Padstow. If you're interested they have about a million photos of the work on their private website, as opposed to the RNLI official one.

Guy Fawkes Night: Odd to think we were once compelled to celebrate on this day by law. No one needs to compel me to venture up to the F&L for a hog roast, free firework display and all round jollity tonight. It is a well-practised and organised event and raises money for local charities. It would be a crime to miss it.

I can confirm that there were more oohs and aaahs than you could shake a sparkler at, or in this ultra safe modern world, a light sabre or spinning LED device, that some enterprising soul had the foresight to purvey.

You should have seen the looks on the faces of the small children as they commemorated an event whose perpetrator the authorities planned to hang, eviscerate while still conscious and pluck, before his living eyes, his still beating heart, bless them. Guy, not too keen to provide such entertainment, took a dive off the scaffold before they could get a rope around his neck.

Fortunately the rain held off until the very moment the fireworks started to fly, soaking all and sundry. The bonfire, being of gargantuan proportions, survived the storm and burnt well into the night.

*November 6th – Saturday* – Cleared up nicely today with some wintry sunshine. The weatherman wasn't kidding about the drop in temperature with a bit of an icy blast coming in from the North West.

A fair few people around today as well. Our meagre supply of pasties for our penultimate day opening was nearly wiped out. The shelves are looking so empty now and drawing comment from customers. Sorry chaps.

I meant to tell you yesterday that a man from the Ministry telephoned. I had responded to the email the MOD had sent me telling me I was silly thinking that we'd heard a sonic boom the

169

other week. Despite my insistence that a 999 call had been made and HM Coastguard had been involved, he was equally insistent that I was the only person to contact him, which meant that I must have been hearing things.

I'm sure I said before that my name is probably on some list of radical dissidents, buried away somewhere in the vaults of the secret police. I think I've just earned myself another black mark against my entry.

I shall, of course, be attending at the F&L tonight where a rather good band will be knocking out a few banging tunes, (hip language or what – how cool am I?). Unless the other dozens of people there start up online diaries tomorrow to corroborate my report, you must conclude that it is a figment of my over active imagination.

I expect that there will be men in white coats arriving shortly to take my delusional soul to a place of quiet repose. I think I should quite like that.

*November 7th – Sunday* – Well, that's it. Last open day until Christmas time and possibly the first mention of the 'C' word but probably not the last.

The weather certainly gave us a mixed send off. First thing was foul with high winds blowing the rain straight in to the front of the shop. It got so bad at one point we had to close the door, as the rain was hosing so far into the shop our newspapers were getting wet.

The main part of the day brightened considerably and attracted a few ambling visitors before a big blanket of cloud came in mid afternoon and put paid to that.

But the real game for today is counting up all the food items that will go out of date before we open again. It is always challenging getting the ordering just right so we run out on the last day.

Some things, butter and bacon for example, can be frozen and picked at during our closed season. Others like milk, while it can be frozen, is inconvenient in such a state, mainly because the tea's already poured when you find out your last bottle's empty.

Actually it is far worse finding out the milk has turned to sludge. I tend to push the boundaries on the use-by date for our own milk, (not the milk in the shop I hasten to add – honest, guv). It is at the point when you shake the bottle and nothing happens that you remember yesterday's tea tasting a bit tangy and that you made a mental note to get a fresh one and then promptly forgot. And now you are holding a slightly aromatic bottle of cheese wearing just your bed socks, (sorry for that mental image, ladies, please do try hard not to swoon), and you realise that the nearest milk is a) downstairs in the shop and b) rock hard.

Much of the wastage gets bagged up and handed out to regular customers, whether they needed it or not, rather that than see it dropped into our bin. By and large, though, there wasn't a huge amount with a couple of notable exceptions, yep, you guessed it, bleddy milk was one of them.

*November 8th – Monday* – Sea building for a big finale at high water this evening it seems. Fair bit of sunshine and some showers mixed in. When it came to it, the sea made a lot of noise but didn't see much as darkness fell.

Now here's something I didn't anticipate - with the shop shut we are no longer tied to being here, and it is from this very seat of power that the Sennen Cove Diary is cunningly contrived each day from Cornish artifice and essence of small wicked children. I'm sure you can see where this is going.

It is with great regret I must inform you that your trusty Diarist is having to go out deep for a few days, ergo no Diary entries. I will, of course, endeavour to make up ground on my return with tales of derring-do in the far reaches of the cosmos, or North Devon as they call it there.

Thought I'd get a bit of practice in and trekked off to PZ. I managed to get back before the withdrawal symptoms kicked in and the rain started. I think I managed to get everything, you know, Kendal Mint Cake, thick woolly socks, malaria tablets and oxygen. It will be all right, I'm sure, as long as I don't stare at the upside down cream teas and the funny looking meat pies that they have the temerity to call pasties.

Well dear readers, that's about it. I'm going outside now. I may be gone for some time.

*November 9th – Tuesday* – Left The Cove this morning with the sea crashing over the harbour wall and the wind howling in my left ear.

The dogs were baying all night long in the wind and the roar of the sea. It took a while this morning to calm them down and fit them into the harnesses for the long first leg. *Wolf* and *Cottontail*, (had to let the Missus name one of them), the lead dogs, took off at a tremendous pace with the point, swing and wheel dogs all falling into step behind; hopefully a good sign for the tough journey ahead.

Disaster. Reached the end of The Cove and found the dogs couldn't pull the sledge up Cove Hill; went back for the van. They struggled with that too so had to use the motor in the end.

Better progress this time, but noisy with a dozen bleddy hounds in the back.

Reached our first supply camp with time in hand. We're heartened that Mrs Philps had seen fit to provide an abundance of her finest pasties.

Onwards from Heyl camp the route became ever more difficult and the weather closed in around us. Though frostbite was some time off, Titus caught a nasty cold and had to go home to his Mum.

The remaining party pressed on. There were times all you could see was the flailing of ice picks. Scant use in the pouring rain, I felt.

Food running short. Had to ration remaining supplies and improvise where we could. It was a desperate business.

At last base camp is in view just beyond the last housing estate. Last few drops of fuel and no food left; we were all in joyous mood.

We are lifted by our warm welcome. We are given blankets and cot for the night. Not least comforting is a tot of Her Majesty's Navy's best which brings a warm glow to the cockles that haven't yet dropped off in the cold.

Lastly we are asked how the dogs were. Harrington started coughing badly and Caruthers pretended he didn't hear, leaving it to me to say, after relieving myself of a little trapped wind, that they were very nice, thank you.

Dreadful business these expeditions, you know.

*November 10th – Wednesday* – Last night I dreamt I went to Sennen again. It seemed to be I stood by an iron gate leading to The Cove, and for a while I could not enter for the way was barred to me.

Waking in a strange place, far enough from the sea as not to hear it, discomforts the soul. And that it be someone else's house is a queer feeling indeed.

This is the abode of the parents-in-law.

Worthy of a visit? Of course, they are. After nigh on fifteen years it's a wonder that I'm still welcome at all. Time, I imagine, tempers the spirit but I fancy that I'm tolerated on the basis that I bring their little girl back to visit.

The bleddy hound, at least, has a small garden to run around in, although she's not keen to use it for her ablutions. This, then, still requires donning a harness, (for her, not me, as she can easily slip the lead if so she chooses), and dragging her around the estate. There are busy roads to be wary of and there are no places to hand for her to run around untethered. There is a small park but even there, bleddy hounds must be 'kept on a lead at all times'. This is not a dog friendly place.

Father-in-law is not as steady on his pins, as once he was, and has acquired a small, battery powered, scooter. It is decided it should be employed this morning on a run down to the town. It fits easily in the back of the van, though fairly weighty, and with a trusty 'blue badge' we are able to park in a privileged spot.

I'm looking forward to some sport here. These scooters are near silent and are known to drive fear into the heart of casual shoppers. You can see them diving for cover as these vehicles approach; worse still the yelps and the look of loathing as one is caught from behind. It's a bit like a Sam Peckinpah, (Quentin Tarantino if you're under thirty), version of ten-pin bowling.

It is therefore a grievous disappointment when the old boy mounts up, turns the key in the ignition, sets the controls for maximum disruption, presses the go button and nothing happens. A blue warning light hints at a terminal problem.

The instruction book is consulted on returning home. The book has clearly been translated from the Mongolian, by a dyslexic Norwegian with a strong Breton accent. We conclude, independently, that since the machine hasn't been used for a month it probably needs recharging.

I decide to accompany the all female party to the out of town shopping centre. My plan, doomed from the outset, is to avert the over use of precious funds. Instead my purpose is confounded by the application of bribery, by way of chocolate, for which I am a sucker, so to speak.

There is something to be said for living forty miles from shopping civilisation.

*November 11th – Thursday* – Day two in the Big Family house and all the hoose mates are asleep.

Well not quite. Words cannot adequately describe trying to sleep in a bed, smaller than the one you're used to, with a bleddy hound who thinks that there should be no difference, regardless that the space she normally occupies contains your head.

It's blowing a hooley out there but this should not prevent the Missus from sallying forth, with her mother, on another shopping trip. It is understandable that when you're used to shopping in PZ, the bigger towns up country are akin to London, Paris and New York rolled into one. Standing in her way, on such an occasion, would merely leave an impression of me, cartoon-like, on the carpet.

I resolve to take the bleddy hound down to the beach at Instow Sands. There is a strip of sand of varying widths, depending on the state of the tide, alongside the broad mouth of the River Torridge. Today the receding water is whipped to a boiling cauldron by the stiff westerly breeze and the loose sand is blasting cross the beach.

We are not alone, despite the wind and occasional horizontal shower. The bleddy hound is, at first, keen to enjoy the first belt over open ground in a couple of days. The added encouragement of a thrown ball has her chasing around like a whippet. It is not long, however, before the constant sandblasting against her flattened fur evaporates her enthusiasm like spit on a blacksmith's forge. If she could have raised two claws in my general direction I believe she would have done and, thus disgusted, headed back in the general direction of the van.

The cruel curtailment of our expedition led us, prematurely, back to the family home where a far greater torture awaited us.

It is widely known that there is a gulf, nay a chasm of biblical proportions, that lies between the televisual tastes of ordinary people and those whose great age affords them the irrefutable advantage of choosing which channel to watch. Not only that, but to have that luxury without paying a penny for a licence.

In our case, that is the bleddy hound and I, found ourselves at the butt end of the Father-in-Law's recorded collection of *Last of the Summer Wine*. First aired when Edward the Confessor sat on the throne, this British comedy classic must have more episodes than a horse has hairs. So long has it run that some of the characters have been replaced by their real life offspring. It is now repeated three times a day on satellite television. The F-in-L has them all captured.

The sound of the Missus's credit card being swiped, in the back of my consciousness, was almost drowned out by the sound on the television, set at a volume that, as any full blooded 'bloke' knows, should only be reserved for war films and computer games.

You will know the depth of my despair when I report that it was of great relief when the Missus returned with her mother, the former burdened down with expensive frippery that I will, one day, understand and appreciate the necessity of.

Perhaps, on this day, we should temper these frivolous thoughts with just a moment's worth of pathos.

*Do not despair*
*For Johnny head-in-air;*
*He sleeps as sound*
*As Johnny underground.*

*Fetch out no shroud ~*
*For Johnny in the cloud;*
*And keep your tears*
*For him in after years.*

*Better by far*
*For Johnny the bright star,*
*To keep your head,*
*And see his children fed.*

John Pudney

*November 12th – Friday* – Home is where the heart is.

I always regarded that phrase, not only an overly romantic notion, but somewhat devalued by over-use. I can assure you that, with only a few days away from Sennen, it is most apt.

Our journey home was as beset with foul weather as the journey out, but was pleasantly free from too many other travellers. The sense of relief in the van as we dropped down over the hill towards home was almost palpable.

The Atlantic Highway is the most grand sounding road but in reality fails, for most of the journey, to live up to its name. It does however pass through or by some interesting sounding places. We would have stopped at Box's Shop had there been one and possibly strolled slowly around Chapel Amble had it been the Sabbath and we very clearly would have been home sooner had we started at Advent.

We stopped at a lay-by with three huge transporters parked up. They were loaded with parts of the column and the blades of one of the new 400 feet wind turbines, bound for Delabole, I think. Being so close you can understand why they generate more controversy than electricity.

175

We were home sufficiently early to let the bleddy hound loose on the beach for an hour. Despite the wind chucking in the last of its fury, the harbour is sheltered so she was quite happy.

The Cove is almost deadly quiet, the nearest big shops are sufficiently distant to be of little threat and traffic is no more than an irritating notion.

'Tis rather nice to be home.

*November 13th – Saturday* – A corking day to start and well into the afternoon.

So much so it was well worth taking the bleddy hound out along the big beach for a darned good run. Now, be prepared, you're very likely to get a lot of this in the Diary this winter much like you had a lot of fish during the summer. Tune in, turn on, drop out.

The new fitness model of the Missus came too, but parted company when I decided to drop into the OS to see the lay of the land. Quite a good job I did, as I came away with some information from the horse's mouth - one of the chefs. I can confirm, as this particular chef is to be trusted and believed, that all the OS meals are now home cooked. Whoopee!

It is still expensive in there so I didn't stop for food and only had the one pint, honest. Home to do some home cooking of my own if we can scrape together some food from our dwindling supplies.

Then naturally it's up to the F&L where a new band is strutting its stuff. A group of players more technically perfect you wouldn't find, heck, they spent half an hour doing a sound test. Good though they were they didn't quite capture the mood.

Good then that the rain clouds had disappeared and I had a starry walk home. I might have said this before, (has he ever), but you need to be there, you really do.

*November 14th – Sunday* – Started off a bit showery, nothing too awful but noticeably colder.

The sea was a bit choppy but clearly excellent weather for doing a bit of a survey. A small survey craft spent the entire day out there steaming up and down. I guess doing this sort of thing on a Sunday avoids all the working day traffic and, very possibly, pays double time at the tax payer's expense.

Blue sky in the afternoon and pleasant if you wrapped up a bit.

So pleasant in fact that our neighbour suggested a walk, another for us, down the big beach. This soon turned into four dogs and several other friends and family, not ours, family, that is, not friends. As so often happens on a Sunday afternoon with a bunch of affable sorts we repaired to the pub for what has been termed, for generations, the Sunday Afternoon Session.

What a splendid time was had by all. More acquaintances came and went, plenty of chit chat and a few beers. What more could a couple of off duty shopkeepers want from their spare time?

In the cold light of day I also recall offering, (note, bleddy offering, volunteering as opposed to being cajoled, tricked, black-mailed, beaten with a stick), into looking after the neighbour's hound while the girls go off on holiday.

Ah, the demon drink! I'm off down the Methodist hall to sign on and I'll shun John Barleycorn for good – erm, from tomorrow.

*November 15th – Monday* – A right cracking good day and no mistake with lots of blue bits and reasonably warm too. Even the fishing fleet was out and about for the first time in a while.

Also out in the bay the small survey boat's mother ship has come on scene. Still out there well into the evening, lit up like a Christmas tree – oops, there you go, mentioned the C word again.

Now I have some time on my hands I thought it worthwhile doing some research on solar panels. When you start getting four figure 'lecky bills for a quarter it's time to start thinking about alternatives. In fact it may be too late as I understand the Government has withdrawn its Low Carbon Building Programme grant due to the cut backs.

Nevertheless I found a local supplier with good credentials. I took a little look at their application form online and, heavens, the amount of information they want is legion. I need to collect the measurements such as pitch angle of the roof, quote from local scaffolder, shading in 10ths, space between batons in the loft and the estimated length of cable from roof to fuse box,( assuming I know where it starts from, of course), my inside leg measurement and a signed picture of Elvis.

Once they have all that they send around a few panels and a page of instructions. Given that the roof is west facing and is buried at the bottom of a north facing cliff all I really want is someone to tell me how feasible all this is. Of course I could go back to that lay-by, (see November 12th), and see if the boys will divert that 400 feet windmill. Sure that would go down a storm.

To soften the blow we could put fairy lights on it for the coming season and run tours up it during the summer. Gosh, I'm almost sold already.

**November 16th – Tuesday** – Bit of a greyer start this morning but with a calm sea the fishing fleet are out again. Bits of blue later in the day before a big daddy of a weather front came through in the evening and overnight.

Our neighbour has been out sanding down his tables with clouds of sawdust flying everywhere in the breeze; clearly an advertisement to come hither to some people. It must have been sore tempting to respond with a less than convivial remark when he was asked if the café was open.

I bravely took a trip into PZ in the afternoon and not just the outskirts either. Right into the centre, this was, (I can tell you're impressed), and up Market Jew Street. All right, it was midweek, lateish in the afternoon and the weather was on the turn but 'twas a scene of utter desolation. A handful of shoppers milled about but many of the 'extras' on the scene were Humphry Davy school children lazily making their way home.

Oddly, the wharf car park was about a third full, at least on the north side. So I have to ask, where was everyone? I suspect a black hole in the Oxfam shop or perhaps we have a demon hairdresser, after all there is a preponderance of pasty shops in town.

"I'm sure Tarquin will be able to help you madam, that's him sharpening his hairdryer. He's a whiz with a pair of curling tongs and his permanent wave will be the last one you'll ever need."

I have to say it was a bit spooky down on the wharf with the wind picking up and rattling the rigging on the masts of the yachts parked up there. It could quite easily have been the set of the latest zombie thriller. I'm sure the undead would be right at home in PZ on a day like today – well most days, possibly.

I scurried off sharpish in the direction of the harbour and across the Ross Bridge. Hadn't really noticed before but they've done a good job on the Abbey Slip, sensitively converted into apartments. When you think of the ramshackle building it was before you wonder why the cultural protection mob made such a fuss. Okay it doesn't take homeless people off the street but neither did it when it was a rotting shell and I know which view I'd prefer to look at.

I'd still be cautious about living down the promenade though. High water was some way off and the waves were already starting to come over the wall. This was not going to be the evening for visiting the Queens Hotel, for sure.

Tied up the evening by attending a poker night at, you're going to be shocked, the jolly OS. Yes, I voluntarily spent an evening there. The new couple are moving the place ever forward and, bit by bit, a little atmosphere is creeping back into the place. They laid on a bit of grub for the card players, chicken curry, and I must report it was a proper job. Beer is still prohibitively expensive but at least you're being fleeced in what's fast becoming a proper pub again.

Crikey, and I thought I wouldn't have anything to write about when the shop shut. Best I shut up now or all you'll get tomorrow is a weather report and a walk down the beach.

*November 17th – Wednesday* – The bit I dislike most after the shop shuts, is the level of isolation to which we subject ourselves. While the shop is open there is always someone to have a meaningless conversation with; it is sociable and keeps us connected to reality, albeit by a gossamer thread.

Therefore it was with some bemusement, that I treated the first telephone call of the day. It was from a friend asking if we had escaped the flood. Given that I was looking out of our window on blue sky and a drying street, I felt confident that our concerned friend had given leave of her senses, or had immersed herself too deeply in the Book of Genesis, chapters six to nine, (it's the bit about Noah, for all you Godless readers out there – ok, I had to look it up too).

I turned to our trusty steam radio and immediately tuned into the Home Service. It seemed that our little bit of rain had ganged up, rather, on the unfortunate chaps in South East and North parts of the county. Had it only teamed down on a certain brewery in that neck of the woods, I would have felt quite smug that the big pub lover in the sky had visited his wrath upon them for ruining the OS. It seemed a little unfair to smite the poor beggers living in the general vicinity.

The telephone rang a further six or seven times, which was gratifying to note that so many friends and family have our well being at heart. With more rain on the way I'm minded to take a trip down the wood yard but finding a chippy able to build a boat to take, 'two of every sort . . . male and female . . . everything on the dry land in whose nostrils was the breath of life', in just seven days might be a bit of a challenge.

One thing continues to bother me in all this blotting out of people, animals, creeping things and birds of the heavens and saving the privileged few; how come the fish get away so light?

*November 18th – Thursday* – I woke up to the shop alarm going off this morning. As it happened it wasn't ours but a car alarm somewhere behind us. Disconcertingly it went off at the same time I keyed in the reset code into our alarm, which had me worried that it may have been our alarm with a fault. All these pressures I have to bear, it's a wonder I sleep at night.

A tidy old sea running today and threats of rain that never came our way. I didn't poke my head out much today, save to take the bleddy hound out to service her needs.

When eventually I did venture forth the tide was fully in so I took her up the back of Shannon's and down by the lifeguard hut to the beach that way. The sun was all for setting over the cliff just east of Pedn-men-du and made a real feast of it; geet shards of sunlight cutting into the sky behind dark clouds rimmed in gold and reflecting fully on an angry sea.

I'd forgotten to take a ball but she was quite happy chasing balls of foam thrown around by the wind. It was hard going as we had to trek through the soft sand. Felt like we had walked miles more than we actually had.

Bleddy tough life, this.

Lifeboat practice tonight and we'd decided to take the winch engine to pieces to pass the time. Having just removed the starter motor the pagers went off for a shout: a fishing boat off Runnel Stone taking in water. Seasoned professionals that we are, we managed to get everything in order without missing a beat.

Both Sennen and Penlee attended for what could have been a potential sinking. Penlee carried out the tow with Sennen in escort. With the swell somewhat ten feet off Seven Stones it was felt best to leave our boat in Newlyn for the night and recover tomorrow morning.

With nothing further to do, our stalwart Shore Crew retired to the OS for the first quiz night in a long while. What a splendid night it was too, despite our trusty crew losing by a fraction. It will be a different story next week when our intellect and cunning, that have sometime been unkindly referred to as cheating, will come to fruition.

Now, you will be well versed in this Diarist's observation of natural phenomenon. So here's another, spied on the way home. Caused by stratospheric hexagonal ice crystals that refract the light, it manifests itself as a ring of light around the moon. It is often a harbinger of poor weather.

Now here's the technical bit: scientists call this a Ring Around the Moon or a Moon Ring. It must have taken them hours to come up with that.

*November 19th – Friday* – Nothing like an early morning Lifeboat recovery to get the old life force juices flowing: a textbook performance even though we do say so ourselves.

The boys on the boat said there was a big lump of pitch black cloud out to the south. This never amounted to much and even the big "rain event", warned of by a very nervous Met Office, didn't materialise for us down this end. I think they were more concerned with South East Cornwall again and we shall have to wait until tomorrow to see if that came to anything.

Largely another day of watching the Missus get ready for her big holiday adventure. It is leg tanning today, which, I believe, offers some level of protection against the sun. She does like to have her feet rubbed while watching TV, (I know, a little too much information, but relevant, I'm afraid), and, noticing my concern, assured me that it would not come off – the tan, that is, not the foot.

Later in the evening she was upset that the tan had not taken effect. I can vouchsafe, as I finish off this entry on Saturday morning that it works very effectively: the palm of my left hand is orange.

I tripped out to St Just to visit our favourite butcher in the afternoon. I think I may have mentioned before that when we place our orders by telephone, he always manages to tempt me into buying something I hadn't intended to have. When I visit the shop it's even worse. I'm already like a small child in a sweet shop as everything looks so attractive. I'm sure he knows this and does take advantage so.

It doesn't take much encouragement. The skirting looked so good I'd already felt the onset of a pasty making session. Naturally you'll need some lard to go with that etcetera, and so it goes on.

It doesn't go all his own way, I did manage to duck a rather nice looking Beef Wellington.

There were a few ladies in the shop. I did not know them but it was a convivial atmosphere with a bit of friendly banter. One of these strangers called me by name, which was most disconcerting to say the least: a hitherto unnoticed stalker, perhaps, and I haven't even been on telly yet.

Needless to say, I was in there a while. I now needed to go back to the green grocer for turnip and 'taters but I'd spent so long at the butcher it was closed.

I now have to settle for making the pasties tomorrow. I hope my orange hand doesn't rub off on the pastry.

*November 20th – Saturday* – Altogether a pleasant enough day but a bit of a biting east wind first thing which is when the bleddy hound got me out of bed.

A visitor arrived overnight into the bay. She's a biggy too, weighing in at 7,700 tons; looks like she's here for a spot of maintenance on the transatlantic cable that runs into Gwenver, as by evening she had crept in almost to the beach. Come night fall she was lit up like a Mississippi showboat, bet you thought I was going to say Christmas tree – oh, darn, mentioned that word again.

All in all I had the most incredibly lazy day; hardly had to stick my head out of the door once except for the usual walkies. The neighbour even saved me the trouble of taking the dog out for a longer blast, which was just as well since I was in the middle of making my pasties for this evening.

Trouble with lazy days is they give you hardly anything to write home about so that's where I'll leave this one for today.

Of course, next week, with the Missus away, there'll be plenty to write about: wild parties, dancing girls and the like. I shall be relying on your discretion not to let the cat out of the bag when she comes back or I shall never talk to you again – mainly because I shall be unable to from hospital.

Naturally, being Saturday, it's off to the F&L for the best band they have up there - Devils Creek. If you get the chance they're well worth a look, or listen rather, at their Face Space on the Internet. If you like a bit of blues-rock, then you can be incredibly jealous that I heard them live.

*November 21st – Sunday* – Well I think I'm still due 14 minutes and 55 seconds of fame after last night's televisual performance.

Despite the very warm comments, thank you, the only offers I had in my email this morning were to improve my performance in bed, to increase my length and a very nice letter from a gentleman in Nigeria offering me an awful lot of money. I have written back on numerous occasions to the two former telling them that I already sleep very well and I am quite tall enough. I suggested to the Nigerian ex-Foreign Minister that perhaps Brian Cowen, the Irish Taoiseach, might be in greater need of his Naira.

All in all I don't think I'll be giving up the shop for a teaching job at RADA just yet.

Besides the pen is mightier than the sword, if you want to interpret M. Francoise-Marie Arouet in a modern day context. He was born today in 1694 and with a name like that, no wonder he wrote under the pseudonym Voltaire. It took him three days to complete Candide, one of his greatest works, which is some feat since I started this Diary in March and still haven't finished it.

I see we're in for some colder weather, which is nice, while the Missus is sunning herself on some hot and sunny shore. It was cold enough down on the beach this afternoon. I suggested to her that I might have to find something to keep me warm in bed while she was away. Nice of her, therefore, to make sure the electric blanket was turned out before she went.

So as the Viagra salesman of eternity stiffens his resolve before the portals of time, and the Lorena Bobbitt of fate sharpens her knife, it's time to say goodnight.

*November 22nd – Monday* – Bit blue and showery and starting to feel that cold bite.

I am minded to post an explanation after last night's *Countryfile*, to allay readers' fears that we are destitute and wholly reliant upon comestibles foraged for free from our hedgerows. While the offer of food parcels and largess are profoundly appreciated they are, as yet, unnecessary although the artisan offerings from TC's bakery sound very attractive.

Thanks too to MM. I would have thought that being across the water and unable to watch *Countryfile* would have been an enviable position. However, her suggestion that, with the use of a dull blade, Mrs Bobbitt's action would have been more effective, I can only see as a veiled threat. She has requested that, somehow, I make the piece available to her. I shall have to see what technology can provide.

Time seems to have disappeared rather quickly today. The Missus needs a last trip into town for some necessities for her impending voyage and we have had to co-ordinate this with a visit to the vet, for the bleddy hound. The attendance is for a routine, though unspeakable procedure, lest you were concerned, and needed to be fitted into a tight schedule.

The aforementioned rush was to permit us and the neighbours to go to the F&L for a pre-departure meal.

They have some very nice nettles, Alexander, Pennywort, Plantain and tri-cornered garlic roots in a field behind the pub that should go down very nicely with the Sea Beet and Laver we collected earlier.

There is a nice seat in the garden that affords a view through the kitchen window where we can watch meals being prepared that we can only aspire to enjoy as we tuck into our free fare.

*November 23rd – Tuesday* – We were woken during the night by the needs of a small, sick dog. This was not a good sign for the Missus is departing today. It is not a good sign for the dog and it is especially not a good sign for me, as I have not been blessed with the patience for patients.

The sickness proceeded to escalate throughout the day, the details of which I shall spare you. Suffice it to say it ended with another trip to the vets. Her previous trip being so recent, the bleddy hound was a tad reluctant to return and, had she not been tethered to me by way of a lead, would have been half way home before I got to the door.

Had I been called to the veterinary vocation, it is clear now that I wouldn't be standing in these rags and living off foraged food from our hedgerows. They should have a sign above the counter, "Open your wallet and say after me, Help Yourself". An ounce of lead would have been cheaper and more effective.

So my cunningly intricate plans for long walks, broken by wholesome lunches in rustic hostelries have been struck a fell blow. The bleddy, sick hound is on a diet of medication, chicken and rice and I shall be eating something unidentifiable from our freezer with *Jeremy Kyle* and reruns of *Last of The Summer Wine* to pass the time.

I shall, of course, not be at all jealous of the Missus sunning herself on some sub-tropical beach, drinking fruit cocktails and gorging on fresh seafood. I doubt, very much, the thought will even enter my head.

*November 24th – Wednesday* – A bit less panic today with the bleddy hound getting back on form, you may be pleased to hear.

It's turned very wintry down in The Cove. Very grey out there and some nasty little showers coming through every now and again, mainly when you're trying to exercise the dog, or dogs as it was today, as we had a visitor from next door. The sea has begun to stir up a little and I suspect this will be the last day for a while that the fishing fleet will be out.

It is also very cold and if this keeps up I may be tempted to turn what little heating we have on.

We are blessed with those overnight storage radiators, well two anyway. They are extremely useful if you want to be tepid between midnight and ten in the morning and are absolutely purposeless at any other time. They are not even good to look at.

This is not good if you are under house arrest due to your bleddy hound's condition. Makes me wish I kept up my collection of goldfish scales. At least I could have had some fun putting them in different orders or polishing them or something.

With snow on the way for the weekend I might have to venture forth tomorrow for some survival rations, unless the anticipated excitement of it all consumes me before then.

*November 25th – Thursday* – The last of the tallow candles ran out last night so I've had to fall back on the electric light. I've also capitulated to the cold and turned on the electric fire – one bar, mind you.

A very weird wind this morning. Sounded very much like the roof was coming off at one point but the anemometer on the Lifeboat Station roof was hardly moving and the direction, all over the northern quarter. Unfortunately JC's weather station at the top of the hill is down for maintenance so I have no idea of the actual wind speed. The shipping forecast is giving variable five to seven but it sounds much stronger than that, but the variable bit I can believe.

Had the neighbour's dog again today so there was nothing for it but a darned good run down the big beach. Did I wrap up warm?

I'd say: a vest, two fleeces, overalls, thick socks, gloves, over trousers, waterproof jacket and a cuddly toy. I could hardly move. To say we were lucky is an understatement because as soon as we'd left the flat, the sun came out. We managed the run to end and back with only a smattering of light hail but that North wind was vicious.

Oh my, has it come to this? This page used to be such a hot bed of intellectual profundity with undertones of political satire, (all right it wasn't but it scans well). I felt like Jean-Paul Sartre, Melvyn Bragg, *Spitting Image* and the bird from *Countdown* all rolled into one and now I'm reduced to telling you about a walk on the beach with a couple of dogs; more Janet and John meets My Little Pony. I can't even get my days of the week right, (yesterday was definitely Wednesday, I realise now). Oh woe, oh woe is me!

*November 26th – Friday* – Another grey, grim and stormy day with regular lashings of hail charging in from the north. Our butcher said that it was snowing heavily in the village first thing but, to my knowledge, we saw none in The Cove.

The bleddy hound is nearly fully recharged now. Adjudged it safe to voyage to St Just today, with dog in tow, (not literally, honest). I have some idea for Saturday, or possibly Sunday dinner banging around my head that I just have to experiment with. I know that shopping in St Just ticks all the self-congratulatory boxes but, by and large, I know I can get what I want there at an honest price, and the goods haven't been half way around the country first.

Bought a *Cornishman* newspaper as Sennen Cove is on the front page, unfortunately not for a good reason. A bit of a major upset seems to be on our doorstep with the Sennen Surf Club being given notice, by the Parish Council, to quit the old Men's Institute building that they have spent some time reinvigorating. The *Cornishman* has given little detail, although more can be determined locally and there are clearly divided views. We hope the issues can be resolved swiftly to the satisfaction of all parties as it is good to see this community resource being actively used.

As you may well guess another sojourn along the big beach was in order again this afternoon. The weather wasn't half so pleasant, (pleasant!), as yesterday and the wind seemed to get stronger towards the north end as you would expect, nearer the source.

The bleddy hound clearly took pity on me, sensing another dumbed-down Diary entry, so she proposed we discuss Nietsche's concept of the Superman in the context of socio-religious culture of his time, in between chasing a ball.

I said I rather thought he was just using his position to pose an anti-Lutherian stance and the subsequent intellectual debate was misguided. She disagreed and said that his work on Superman shouldn't be taken on such a literal footing. She reckoned it was a reaction to the overbearance of religious dominance of the time and that the people needed a far greater power to aspire to and postulated the 'will to power'.

I told her that anyone who could come out with the quote 'a pair of powerful spectacles has sometimes sufficed to cure a person in love' and wear a moustache the size of a floor brush shouldn't be seen in such a complex light.

We agreed to continue the discussion over a pint at the OS but unfortunately she fell asleep on the bar floor.

The loneliness of the long distance beach dog walker; I can promise you it hasn't affected me one little bit.

*November 27th – Saturday* – What a difference this morning, well looking at it, at least. Bright blue skies, sunshine, the wind had moved around to the east and it was bitterly cold.

I went up the top for provisions early on and heard reports of snow in PZ. Later I was told that Heamoor roundabout was near enough closed with thick snow, (that's thick for these parts, maybe three inches, but that it petered out by Drift and nothing much else further west on the mainland. Almost unheard of, Scillies had a blizzard.

By late evening ice was forming in The Cove, which is unusual. I'm grateful I have no plans for driving up the hill in the morning.

But no amount of weather is going to stop the main event of the day. A clay pigeon shoot is held twice a year up behind the F&L, one on Boxing Day and the other at Feast, and this weekend is St Sennen Feast weekend.

Once Feast days were raucous events, where the pubs would stay open all day as a special concession. Of course, the all day pub is no longer something special and the celebration of the Feast is very much an understated affair.

However the shoot is a happy and sociable occasion attended by the real men of the Parish, oh, and me as well. While I don't have a big weapon like the real men, if I'm lucky someone will let me use theirs. For the last few shoots I've made myself a bit useful by doing some of the administration, like taking the money and recording the names on the shooting order.

The event commences with 'the sweeps', a set of five guns shooting from five positions in turn. The winner of each sweep gets his entry money for that sweep back. Then there is the Parish Cup, open to only those living in the Parish and the 'Open', available to all, as you would imagine.

Naturally we all repair to the F&L afterwards for some warming stew or other and a libation or two to celebrate the winners and commiserate with the losers.

Fortunately the neighbour had the dog for the duration, as the field used for the shoot is her rabbit field. Had I taken her there she may well have taken off after the little furry creatures and possibly been mistaken for one herself. Not an ideal circumstance in a field shared with five guns, although it would save a fortune in future veterinary bills.

Being shackled to a bleddy hound that is none too keen on her own company, I was rather hampered for a return to the F&L for the usual Saturday night shenanigans. As she doesn't share my taste in music, taking her with me was out of the question.

We settled for watching a movie on the television with a shared tub of popcorn. Front row seats, of course.

*November 28th – Sunday* – Up with the lark, if we had any around these parts, as I am looking after the neighbour's hound from early doors.

There's ice on the ground here this morning, which means it's twice as bad up the top. Beautiful blue skies in the east but out to the north west geet gatherings of cloud and a nasty black line on the horizon that looks like's it dumping serious amounts of snow or hail. Looking at the forecast it seems they may well stay there. Fingers crossed for that then.

Prepped up the nosh for this evening's tea while the two hounds looked on licking their lips; I hope it turns out like they seem to expect it to.

I left it late for, what is fast becoming, a Groundhog Day run down to the beach. The two hounds have distinctly different behaviours when they're out. Ours has a ball fixation and will, given the chance, chase the ball and bring it back until Doomsday, given the opportunity. The other, a shaggy Tibetan terrier, wants to run around chasing and being chased by other dogs. This is mainly because the Tibetan, *Dolly*, can't see the thrown ball through her fur unless you throw it in front of her nose and not very far.

The two characteristics are not necessarily complementary. Therefore Dolly goes off at any chance to find other less tunnel-visioned hounds to play with, not all of which welcome the prospect of a gangly bundle of fur leaping all over them.

Having irritated every other dog walker on the beach I decide to see if we can annoy a few more in the OS which is fast becoming a pleasant, if expensive, hostelry to frequent again.

Even on short leads, with the bleddy hounds pulling in opposite directions, supping a quiet pint becomes something of a trial. When you add the landlord's two dogs into the mix it's time to throw in the towel and return home.

With this Diary fast becoming a dog's 'what I did on my holidays' page I'm tempted to let the bleddy hound do tomorrow's page.

*November 29th – Monday* – It's a jolly good wheeze to wake the old man with a tongue in the ear 'ole. You have to be quick though, because he usually throws a swipe in your general direction when you do.

As you probably worked out this is the 'bleddy hound' penning today's page.

When Christopher Sholes invented the qwerty keyboard he didn't have p[wes poqws – blast it – paws in mind, so this ain't as easy as it looks.

Let's start by exploding a few myths that  might have misled you. First this is *my* house. The woman that usually lives here reckons that they are Mummy and Daddy, and treat me like a human child, which is pathetic - hello, I have four legs and a tail. I'm a dog, (and not a bleddy hound, either).

Most times I get my own way. The woman is a bit of a harder case to crack but the old man is a push over. For example - tongue in the ear, it's time to wake up and take me for a walk. I shall act like I'm just about to wet myself until you get me out the door, whereupon I shall wander around, sniff every blade of grass, and generally procrastinate. When I sense the old man's tether is near the end, then and only then shall I have a pee.

189

There was snow on the hills and ice on the ground when we first got out, but it was starting to rain. I share the old man's frustration as the rain was not forecast. Not having waterproofs I get wet when it rains which doubles my frustration.

The old man wanted to go into town. I was given the choice of staying by myself, which I detest, or going in the van, which I loathe. I went in the van, which I loathe less than the detestation of staying on my own.

Of course it couldn't be a simple trip into town, oh no! We had to take the winding road out to St Buryan first, then into PZ that way. He left me in the van while he went off shopping, but fortunately wasn't long. Then going back it seems it was imperative to go via St Just.

By this time it started snowing pretty heavily. There was snow all over the moors up by Leswidden, that apparently looked quite pretty. It's hard to see that well when you have your head between your legs trying to stop being sick.

We stopped at my favourite shop, the butchers, and he came back to the van with steak, yes, it definitely had the whiff of steak about it, then he got us a pasty to share.

Back home I gave him some peace while he ate my pasty. I always give them some peace when they're eating, as there's pretty much an odds on chance that I'll end up with some. I find sitting with a paw on his foot and my head between his legs generally lets him know I'm there.

Having taken the miserly portion that he saved me, it was time to exact my revenge. This involves waiting for him to get settled and comfy. Then I get my chicken and bring it to him. It's a toy chicken I like to play tug with and chase – ok it's pretty simplistic, but it means he has to move and give me some attention. Here's the ritual: I drop the chicken at his feet, he ignores me, I paw his leg and look doe eyed, he tells me to wait, I bump his leg with my nose several times, he gives in and comes to play.

Aw, I'm so cute; he's so dumb.

By mid afternoon even I could see that the tide was on the way out. I wonder what will happen next? What a surprise; a run down on the big beach. Now, don't get me wrong, I love a nice long run down on the big beach, chasing a ball, digging in the sand, chasing the ball some more, but the old man has absolutely no imagination. Oh, and we stop at the OS on the way back. Another big surprise.

Just to add insult to injury, there I was pretending to be fast asleep on the sofa next to him, when, up, off we go again into the cold and up to the F&L for a quiz night. I really wasn't expecting that.

I spend the entire evening trying not to get trodden on and looking doe eyed at the landlady who often gives me titbits. She was obviously on an off day - no titbits. They apparently call sitting around in groups, answering dumb questions, fun. By the last round I was bored witless and made my feelings known until I got taken home.

We walked home. For heaven's sake, it was cold, dark and icy and we slid all over the place coming down the hill. It was horrible.

One thing's for sure: he'll be wanting a lay in come morning. Hah! No chance. My tongue's poised for another ear licking, bud!

*November 30th – Tuesday* – Can't understand why there's sand all over the keyboard this morning and there's muddy paw marks on my seat.

A beautifully bright day in the offing, miles of blue skies and sunlight dancing on the hills; gulls are balanced delicately on the wind and a glittering, crystal sea lies spread out on a pushing tide. Amazing how deceptive looks can be, isn't it? It's freezing out there.

Didn't want the bleddy hound to feel I have no imagination so took her for a walk over Mayon Cliff late this morning. Run offs from the springs up the hill have frozen in their path making the going a little treacherous and there was me thinking running water didn't freeze that easily.

It's well worth a little trip up there on days like these. You can see all the way down to Wolf Rock Lighthouse and as you walk back towards Maria's Lane you can look out to Chapel Carn Brea and Boscawen beyond. They all seemed rather frosty, but the snow has largely gone.

While being poetically transported, the bleddy hound has found some fox or badger pooh that she likes to spread behind her ears. Fortunately, it too is frozen and the aromatic disaster is averted. I should have realised that this was only a portent of worse to come.

We fell in with some other dog walkers, visitors who knew me and the dog but, as is even more frequent recently, I didn't know them; the price one has to pay for global fame, I suppose. I shall have to start carrying a pen for when the autograph hunters arrive and, of course, I am ever mindful of the risk of stalkers. Even Jeremy Clarkson paid some homage in the *Sunday Times* this week, though he didn't mention me by name, but when he wrote, "a bunch of bulldogs chewing on wasps" I knew. I am, almost as I write, contemplating an advanced driving course for when the call comes for a *Top Gear* appearance.

Naturally I couldn't resist a run down the big beach, especially as I was encumbered with two hounds again. This is where I realised that even international fame can't save you from the vagaries of a curved ball from fate's humourist. I shall spare you the finer detail but suffice it to say that the pair of bleddy hounds found a way of covering themselves in some unspeakable mire almost as soon as they hit the sand.

It wasn't until we got home, that the pungent aroma became obvious and left me no choice, but the fearful act of having to shower the pair. This requires: a dedication to the care of dumb animals, the patience of a saint, the arms of an octopus and oilskins, the antithesis of all of which I have in abundance.

Having divested myself of my winter layers; cleared the bathroom of all breakable objects; acquired a bundle of towels and adjusted the shower head for maximum effect, all while holding two dogs that knew exactly what was to befall them and were keen to escape the action in as many different directions as they could conceive; I managed to get them into the bathroom and lock the door. There then followed a period of carnage similar, I imagine, to a re-enactment of the Battle of Agincourt in a swimming pool staged by a bunch of small children that had been on a diet of blue Smarties and fizzy pop for a week.

All in all pretty much a quiet day really. Next week – how to redecorate your bathroom in five easy steps.

# December

In the news: *Vince Cable, the Business Secretary is castigated for making unguarded comments to a couple of undercover reporters from* The Telegraph.

***December 1st – Wednesday*** – Bitter cold from first thing with clouds rolling away to the west, leaving a bright and clear day again.

Think I best spend the day clearing up the evidence of a wild and debauched week. On reflection, since I didn't have a wild and debauched week I think it more beneficial to leave or create, more like, some evidence. I wouldn't want the Missus thinking I've been all saintly while she's been away, that would never do.

As it happened I had more than enough to do with two demanding hounds. There was the walk up Mayon Cliff again, although the bleddy hound had been up there yesterday to see all the glories of The Cove from above, the visitor hadn't. Then there was the obligatory run down the big beach.

The tide was only just retiring today as we took our constitutional. With the sun in its last gasp above Mayon Cliff, the sand was golden and pure looking and our shadows stretched long before us. Unfortunately the sand was also soft and deep on the ridge where we were and I reached North Rocks sweating and gasping. My quads will be like tug boats by tomorrow morning.

The OS was a waste of time, only because our visiting hound has not been adequately trained in the required behaviour of being tethered to a bar stool. I used to enjoy those winter, late afternoon visits, brief though they usually were. It was quiet but there was always someone to have a light conversation with.

For the previous year or so it was like visiting a pox clinic, (I can only imagine, honest), for all the welcome you got. Now, though, a little warmth has settled back into the place.

Bleddy hound and I took our last walk late evening; more bitterly cold than the morning and a clear, starry sky. Not much evidence of a flurry or two as the forecast has it.

Stop Press: I couldn't wait to tell you. As I put the finishing touches to today's entry, (Thursday morning), I'm looking out on three to four inches of snow in The Cove.

193

*December 2nd – Thursday –* I know, I spoiled the surprise yesterday but by now someone will have told you we're knee deep in the white stuff, well all depending where your knees are, of course.

There was very little evidence of vehicles moving about. Even in a 4x4 you probably would have been chancing your luck going up Cove Hill. TG was last seen heading in that direction but he borrowed the Harbour tractor and apparently he struggled.

This rather put paid to going to pick up the Missus from Newquay in anything like a timely manner. Fortunately someone else was passing from up country in this direction and was diverted to save the day. By the time he got here Cove Hill had been cleared.

No sign of our Postie today either. He has been taking liberties all week by strutting about in a pair of shorts. I shall look out for him tomorrow and ask, very dryly, why a bit of snow prevented a big strapping lad like him from carrying out Her Majesty's delivery. He'll probably give me some excuse that his speedos were in the wash and he needed a new pair of flip flops or some such.

The snow has, at last, given me the opportunity to exact my revenge on the bleddy hound. I took her up to Mayon Cliff again this morning and it was on a whim that, having gazed up the snowy path to Lands End, I decided to walk in that direction. We were not the first to travel that path, for sure, and judging from the sets of errant footsteps not everyone knew the track that well.

By the time we reached the complex the dog's little legs were hanging with snow balls. If you have seen pictures of bearded polar explorers with geet lumps of ice hanging from their whiskers, you'll get the idea. Much to my shagrin she didn't seem to mind one bit.

We came back via the cycle path to Maria's Lane. I'd quite forgotten the Missus didn't have a key and my unscheduled detour was beginning to close in on her arrival time. I had also neglected to consider how we would get back down into The Cove. Having battled through a few further snow falls I decided to forgo the pleasures of sliding, base first, down Stonechair Lane and elected to go down the less precipitous way we came up, via Mayon Cliff. It was a smart move, as even that was getting slippery and, as I learnt later, some small children had turned Stonechair into the Cresta Run.

We arrived back home just as a heavy sleet storm moved in. Having dried off the bleddy hound she has, thus far, failed to move from a curled up ball on the sofa. Maybe I'll see if I can get her off down the beach for a run in a minute. I'm guessing by the end of the day it will be a long time before she ever asks me for 'walkies' again.

Now, it should never be said that our Lifeboat coxswain hasn't got a sense of humour. Half way back from Lands End my pager went off. In the height of a blizzard I concluded that exposure was taking its toll, until I met up with the First Mechanic on the way back into The Cove – Lifeboat exercise at 17:30, if you please. I'll have to check if the bleddy hound has been at the telephone to arrange this. It would be just like her to have the last laugh.

If it wasn't her, the last episode of the day certainly had her mark on it. I took her for the final constitutional of the day by which time the road was nothing more than a skating rink. At the bottom of the Lifeboat car park I suddenly found myself gazing up at the stars from a recumbent posture, still clinging on to a lead connected to the most unconcerned dog in the world.

Either someone close by was watching a re-run of the cartoon series, *The Wacky Races*, or the bleddy hound was doing a passable impression of *Mutley's* sniggering laugh.

*December 3rd – Friday* – Signs of a little warming up today; I use the term 'warming up' somewhat loosely; it's still darned cold. After last night's little mishap I was a tad ginger about where I stood and was quite keen to let the bleddy hound off the lead before she pulled me over.

The pair of us, that is the Missus and me, gathered both our own and the neighbour's dogs and set off on a route designed to minimise the risk of further injury to my rather aching frame. It was a good call as there was still plenty of snow up through Vellandreath and the slopes beyond and also on the beach above high water mark. The dogs had a whale of a time.

We came back through the Beach car park as the tide had cut off the main slipway. The whole area still sported a rather thick covering of snow, ideal for sledging. This had attracted the small children of The Cove and the small twenty something child, oft seen behind the bar of the F&L.

I also understand that a certain member of the Beach Politburo had also attempted a bit of sledging in his smart BMW 4x4 earlier,

195

which had ended with it buried in the wall at the bottom of the slope. Whoops!

Late rain made light work of clearing up the remaining snow, leaving just a few patches of ice to snare the unwary. By late evening it was positively balmy by comparison to our previous days. If this carries on we might even lose our heads completely and venture out of The Cove tomorrow.

At the very least we need to go to the Post Office. Some foolhardy soul has noticed that we actually sell things on our website and has placed an order. Will wonders never cease?

*December 4th – Saturday* – Overcast and showery all day but much warmer than of late; an out and out lazy day and, but for the dog, I should have stayed in bed.

We couldn't even muster the enthusiasm to go forth and explore the brave new snowless world; although I did run up to the Post Office, it was hardly the stuff of adventure.

I can tell you, though, that our fishing fleet, or at least the hardy ones, have been doing some sterling work over the last few days. I understand that the Frenchman has reinstated himself as the Squid Hunter, a name conferred on him by a national newspaper some years ago.

Although I would be pegged out on the beach if I told you the exact weight of his catch, I can say that it was a harbour record. He was lucky to bring his boat in on top of the water the haul was so prodigious.

Naturally, now that the Missus is back and my dog sitting duties are reduced, I shall be visiting the F&L again. I shall, no doubt, be ragged for my lack of attendance last week but I shall take it on the chin.

Only another three bands till Christmas!

*December 5th – Sunday* – Looking like rather a pleasant day out there. As the meteorologists would say, about four eighths of cloud-cover, and if they can mess up their fractions like that you can only wonder at the rest of their calculations.

By afternoon it was getting noticeably chilly and by evening we were getting a frost, which again is unusual in The Cove.

A little less lazy today; we went with the neighbour and the hounds up the hill and started out on the top path across the fields before descending to the beach via Vellandreath. I say a little less lazy as we did get a ride to the top of the hill, tusk, tusk!

The route passes a wartime pillbox down below Carn Keys, that's the little, black wooden chalet almost on the beach. Would you believe there is a website that lists them all, their situation and condition? Pillboxesuk if you're interested. The pillbox is still open, while most have been sealed up, and demonstrates how short our troops must have been at the time. Not the most perilous situation, however, I still wouldn't have liked to be stationed in it on a cold winter night, waiting for who knows what to happen.

In the end I understand the closest action seen here was a sea mine drifting into the bay. The local commander refused to take action and the mine exploded close to shore. You will need to buy a copy of the Book of Sennen to read that full story; I don't care if it is nearly Christmas there's no freebies here, luvvers. Or, if you dare, you could always ask FT who will give you a colourful, if possibly over embellished, account if he hasn't chased you off with his stick first.

The Missus has gone down with some bug, which will teach her to go off to foreign parts. Not wanting the heating on when the temperature drops by half a degree is a sure sign of her definitely being unwell. Either that or it's a ruse so that I have to take the bleddy hound out in the icy air.

I have some errands to run tomorrow and some shop-type administration to perform before that. It's amazing how quickly you can get into the old dreckly frame of mind after we close. The paperwork's been piling up for weeks so I'd best knuckle down – tomorrow, obviously!

*December 6th – Monday* – Boy, was it cold this morning. It was that kind of dry cold, which I can't help feeling is crisp and clean. Not a cloud in sight and we certainly have had some full on starry nights to gaze up at. Of course, with very little light pollution even the smallest stars are visible. I can't say I know many of the constellations, but I do know they're very distracting and you end up walking into more earth-bound objects, if you're not careful.

As I alluded to yesterday, a trip into the big city, well PZ anyway, was on the cards this morning. Even at midday, when I eventually completed my administrative duties, the van was frosted up. I don't ever recall having to clear the windscreen of ice down here before. Having frozen my hands offchipping away, I

197

resorted to a bottle of warm water, which is where I should have started.

After executing my duties to the Revenue men and bought myself some much needed waterproofing for my old walking boots, I stopped by the Police Station. I hasten to add that the latter visit was purely voluntary and involved enquiries concerning a shotgun licence.

Having been involved with the Feast and Boxing Day shoot it was suggested to me, by one of their number, that I invest in a gun. This makes it a little more convenient, rather than having to borrow one. Additionally, by exploiting some contacts in the farming community, I may also supplement my meagre diet of foraged greenery with hunted pigeon, rabbit or, due to a lack of accuracy, possibly some lamb.

I had this in mind to tell the officer, by way of explanation, but only got as far as telling her I ran a shop when she stopped me. She said she fully understood that interfacing with the general public could, at times, be testing but the use of a gun to defer complaints or, possibly, to boost sales may not be seen by everyone as reasonable.

I have to say that I hadn't considered this perspective, but now I come to think of it . . .

*December 7th – Tuesday* – Cold again last night but it doesn't seem quite so cold first thing this morning. Maybe that's because the sun is out in a clear blue sky, sea is calm with a few of the fishing fleet out and everything is in its rightful place.

The beach looked so inviting at low water with its big open space and sun drenched, golden sand, it was irresistible. Are you jealous yet? It was so irresistible I didn't resist and took the bleddy hound down for an extended run, right along the water line; it was positively balmy at the far end. Shame, then, that we had to make our way back with the obligatory stop at the OS.

The Missus is obviously on the mend; food shopping in town today.

Now I don't want to start a battle of the sexes here, but I think, ladies, if you search your heart of hearts you will hear a ring of truth in this. By and large, (as I would hate, for the sake of my health, to generalise,) if a chap goes food shopping he gets what's on the list; if a chapess goes food shopping there is rather more in the cart than is on the list. I have to ask, God bless me, "Do you have a second list that we mere males are not privy to?"

Heaven knows I'm grateful if you do, with my shopkeeper hat on, but my enthusiasm dampens slightly while on the buying end.

If there isn't a Diary entry tomorrow it will be because the Missus read today's or my computer has sunk under the weight of irate emails from offended lady readers.

Ah, the thrill of living dangerously.

*December 8th – Wednesday* – I had contemplated just writing the words, "See December 7th" for today's entry, but then again the Missus didn't go shopping today, the weather was a tad different and I didn't want to upset lady readers all over again.

The sea was whipped up into a bit of a frenzy this morning, although that didn't stop a couple of fearless fishermen hauling in a few catches. It also didn't stop the divers here to maintain the channel markers, but I reckon they were wishing they got here a day earlier.

And I was wishing I didn't have to take the dog out. The forecast said that it would be warmer today but with a strengthening northerly wind it would feel cold. Oh boy, did they get that right. It was flaming freezing and that wind cut straight through you.

As if it wasn't cold enough in The Cove, I decided to take the bleddy hound up Mayon Cliff to get the full force of it. There's no good having an ice cold wind if you're not going to take proper advantage of it.

I like to introduce a bit of variety in the route and decided to go beyond Stonechair and take the path down beside Cove Hill. Well, you'd think I was asking the dog to walk into the fires of hell. She was utterly determined to head down Stonechair, and home by the shortest path. Fortunately I'm bigger than her but it still took an encouraging boot up her rear end to get her to traverse the last bit of Maria's Lane. I can't imagine where she gets her stubborn streak from.

You can always tell when there's a lone talker in the OS; someone whose conversation is a bit one-sided and the subject matter is a little, how can I say this politely, esoteric, maybe? I should have noticed straight away, but he'd gone out for a smoke when I arrived, and the barman was just poking his head around the corner from where he was hiding.

It wasn't until after I'd ordered a drink that the smoker came back into the bar. It was only when the barman suddenly evaporated, that I realised I was alone in lone talker territory, save for my (full) pint and a dog.

It is maybe, at this juncture, I should explain that I was there for what, in these parts, is known as the Samurai Steve incident. Samurai Steve was a lone talker whose residence was some distance beyond the edge of reason. On this occasion he was clearly deciding to decamp to a place that you can't see from the edge, even with a good pair of binoculars.

When the police eventually arrived it appeared that their operational plan was to wait for the offender to pass from natural causes, although they said later they were awaiting the arrival of a firearms unit.

It is, therefore, with no apology, I put in practice the family motto of cowardice being the better part of valour and legged it. I finished my pint first, of course. I'm not completely without ethics.

*December 9th – Thursday* – Phew, what a scorcher; positively Caribbean. Thank heavens it was overcast today, else we would all have been roasted alive. According to the weatherman we are the warmest part of the country today and tomorrow as well, apparently.

It was, of course, an excellent day to go and have one's eyes tested. It has, after all, been two years since the last time, or so my optician tells me. She has all sorts of clever bits of equipment to measure the performance and health of my little peepers. However the main thrust seems to be the age-old use of a card with letters of various sizes upon it at the end of the room, though nowadays it is projected onto the wall by electronic wizardry.

I did my best to read the entire card, the last line of which that I could read, seemed different from the rest: J Smith & Son Printed in Birmingham, copyright 2009. Very odd.

The upshot of all this testing was that my eyes had changed very little in the preceding couple of years. Though I'm sure the lady is a first class optician, she is a poor salesperson and we agreed that I'd stick with my current reading glasses.

Having checked the health of my eyes by various methods she then offered an optional extra – a picture of my retinas. Again she wasn't ever so good at selling me the benefits but, I confess, I was intrigued and coughed up the extra shekels. It was like looking at a picture of the planet Mars. Fortunately there was no sign of any meteor craters though there was a red spot, which, I am told, was the optical nerve.

I am sure you will all be very interested to learn that everything is in perfect working order including a first class macula and a fovea that a fifteen year old would be proud of.

I still needed a telescope, mounted inside the Lifeboat Station, however, to see what the fire engine that arrived at the top of the hill was up to.

Late in the afternoon there was a hang glider soaring in the thermals over Carn Olva. When it disappeared I thought nothing much of it but when I returned from the Post Office there was a couple of worried looking chaps in jump suits milling about at the top of the hill.

On closer inspection, through the telescope, it was plain that one chap had decided to practice a bit of early Santa antics and had landed on the roof of one of the houses up Cove Hill. The Fire Brigade, brave lads, arrived in timely fashion to assist the hapless, and fortunately unhurt, venturer from his lofty crag and to release his kite from the chimney.

Operation clean up at Lifeboat training tonight in preparation for a big inspection tomorrow. The exercise must have kick started the synapses as our motley collection of hangers-on won the quiz at the OS. I don't think we cheated either, well not a lot, honest.

*December 10th – Friday* – The application for my shotgun licence came through today, and a memorable date it was for it to arrive. I had expected some keen questions such as, why would I wish to possess such a deadly weapon, and to which purpose I would put it? As it happened I'm rather glad they didn't press too hard, as today it would have been a tad embarrassing to put to paper that, apart from some rather vicious clay pigeons, I might add to the notches on the stock with some real pigeons or the occasional rabbit.

Now I know that this kind of activity is not to everyone's taste but, from a personal point of view, I've never seen the harm of it but there again I've never been a rabbit. I can assure any sensitive reader that I will, naturally, be consuming whatever I despatch and those occasions will probably be few and far between. My aim is such that I am much more likely to be putting holes in thin air.

No, my embarrassment stems, as any keen conservationist and protector of defenceless animals among you would know, from the fact that today, in 1903, saw the formation of the Society for the Preservation of Wild Fauna of the Empire. They were the first

201

society for the preservation of wildlife in Britain and would, no doubt, have furrowed their brows at my planned activities.

I made some amends for my dark thoughts by suffering a two dog sort of day. Our neighbours had set off early for a day of consumerism in the big city up the line and left their hound with us. The Missus, being still being plagued by the plague, meant the bleddy hound and friend were attached to me alone for a drag down the beach.

Had I my wits about me I could have taken a rubber pigeon with me instead of a ball and had them practice some retrieval. Judging from the state of the ball at the end of our jaunt I can only conclude that any felled game would be consumed long before it reached my table.

I have erstwhile, spurned attendance at either the F&L or OS on a Friday night for some while, to the benefit of my pocket and my sanity. However these long winter nights and the day long presence of two lunatic dogs swayed my judgement and I elected to walk up to the F&L.

As it happened the neighbours made a timely return and I was taken up the F&L by a rather nice young lady in a fast car tonight. PR remarked that he'd much rather be taken somewhere by a young lady in a slow car, and I could see his point. Nevertheless, it was a very pleasant evening spent in the most convivial of company, to the extent it might persuade a chap to do it all again the following week.

*December 11th – Saturday* – Overcast again today but still mild and the sea still good enough to keep the fishing fleet happy. In fact the mackerel are back in numbers, a gem that someone let slip round Newlyn; we've had foreign boats out there for a few days sharing in the rich pickings.

Also the smaller survey vessel is back again and this time was hard in at the west end of Tribbens, disturbing the morning peace with the chug of its engines. I've still found it impossible to discover the status of their work and whether the MCZ is active or not.

TG wasn't at Lifeboat practice this morning so I couldn't ask him; he was out sharing in the mackerel boom. Young DS was at the helm today and with the good doctor in attendance they were out for a good two hours. Our Head Launcher is in dry dock again with a self-inflicted  injury but still managed to put in a late appearance. I know how he feels. Whatever your circumstances it's hard to stay away from a launch, it just seems wrong somehow.

The Missus managed to drag herself off her deathbed for a shopping trip up St Agnes with the neighbour. Yup, you guessed it, another two dog day to endure and another run down the beach. I left it a little late and it was getting gloomy when we eventually hauled ourselves up the slipway. Avoided the OS this time as dog two seemed a little under the weather.

So just another ordinary day in the seat of loveliness that is Sennen Cove; and just another trip up the F&L for the band and rough chap-type banter and an ale or three. Also heard from a man that knows, that our roof bound hang glider from a couple of days ago, (now, is one who hang glides a hang gliderer?) was a sprightly 85 year old. At his age you'd think he'd know better.

I think if I'm still writing this and running dogs down the beach at 85 I'll be centrespread in *The Lancet*.

*December 12th – Sunday* – Gosh, I'm quite worn out. I don't think my behind has left the sofa for more than twenty minutes today, which is a tad disgraceful, but hang it anyway. It was the sort of day to do nothing in particular and maybe tune in the wireless to something pleasant, just because, thanks to Guglielmo, we can.

It looked a bit grey out there anyway, although the sea's been calm for most of the week. I understand that the cold weather is heading back again towards the end of the week with easterly winds expected from tomorrow. I might just venture out tomorrow; I'm fed up with being warm.

In the van you don't hesitate to turn on the radio and think nothing of it. The last person you would probably think of is Guglielmo who, on this day in 1901, fired off his first radio transmission across the Atlantic from not a stone's throw, all right, a fairly hefty stone's throw away from where I'm sitting. Actually, Mr Marconi, as you probably know him better, was in St John's in Newfoundland where he was extremely fortunate to find that someone had invented the radio receiver, else you would probably have never heard of him at all.

And because I did absolutely nothing at all today there is very little else to tell you. I shall leave you, therefore, with the line, 'Rats!', which you will, of course, immediately recognise as the work of Mr Robert Browning, who died today in 1889 just as the Venetian council approved his housing application. And you think the waiting list for council housing is bad today.

Oh, go on then. I'll give you a little more since you asked so nicely.

> *They fought the dogs and killed the cats,*
> *And bit the babies in the cradles,*
> *And ate the cheeses out of the vats,*
> *And licked the soup from the cooks' own ladles,*
> *Split open the kegs of salted sprats,*
> *Made nests inside men's Sunday hats,*
> *And even spoiled the women's chats*
> *By drowning their speaking*
> *With shrieking and squeaking*
> *In fifty different sharps and flats.*

**December 13th – Monday** – Still a bit grey this morning, but the easterly wind that has indeed developed is thankfully light and the chill, not as severe as first forecast.

Grey though it may have been, The Cove had a bright star on the wharf this morning being filmed for a documentary. Quite right and deserved too for this was Poland's latest hero and respected Newlyn skipper, Shaun Edwards. Shaun is skipper of tuna boat *Nova Spiro* that went to the aid of the tall ship *Fryderyck Chopin*. They towed it for in excess of 72 hours, through heavy seas, from the other side of Scilly to Falmouth. For a cracking and unsensationalised report on the incident have a look at Newlyn's fishing website, blog.through-the-gaps.co.uk, for Friday 5th November.

Given that yesterday was my laziest day on record I decided to make amends today. I girded my loins, or would have done if I knew what that meant, and sallied forth, heading east beyond PZ to, what turned out to be, a sunny Helston.

The in-laws arrive tomorrow and before any in-law visit, the Missus has a blue fit of house cleaning. It is a far, far better thing I do now than I have ever done, that is being as far away and for as long as possible when this event takes place.

I gauged that, if I arrived back late afternoon, the dust may well have settled. Although my plans would not take me that long, the fates were kind to me, and I was caught in some traffic mayhem around Helston that extended my journey beyond my wildest hopes. As luck would have it, the traffic reports on the chaos arrived over the airwaves only after I was well and truly stuck.

Some ill placed temporary lights on a three way junction, that had clearly not taken into account the permanent lights preceding them, had some unlucky travellers trapped for more than an hour.

Having extricated myself, I spent a while touring the busy high street in search of the post office. I congratulated myself on finding the longest queue with the most awkward of customers in front of me. I detained myself even longer in searching for, and finding, a device that would stop our tumble-dryer shaking itself forward off its perch, as it had inexplicable decided to do after a year of static, shuffle free, operation.

Such was my earnestness in vacating the scene of the pre in-law deep clean I had completely omitted to feed myself breakfast. This I remedied at dinner time in the car park of some superstore on the edge of Culdrose. While I feasted I was treated to a display by a couple of BAE Hawks, dog fighting at low altitude over the airfield. No doubt this sight will become a thing of the past when the defence cuts start to bite. Pilots will have to content themselves by running around the NAAFI with paper planes held aloft making whooshing noises.

Though still before three in the afternoon, the sky had become dark as night, but as I travelled back west the clouds broke up and the sun squirted straight into my eyes. I endured this all the way back to PZ for another time-waster, before detouring via our butcher in St Just on the way back home.

We are to have a faux Christmas dinner with the in-laws before they depart home. The beef, or perhaps fatted calf, such was its bulk, and the turkey crown, clearly riven from a fowl the size of an ostrich, are for this purpose. I have no doubt that we shall still be consuming the left-overs on the real Christmas day a week later.

Looking at the forecast for the weekend there is some risk that the in-laws may be snow bound here. Despite there being no shortage of provisions for them, I am sure they would be devastated should they have to extend their visit.

Such is my commitment to their well-being, I shall scour the planet for an available snow plough and snow chains for their car, in the certainty they would feel more comfortable in their own homes, two hundred miles away.

*December 14th – Tuesday* – The wind was a bit sharper this morning and thus a little colder. Still dire warnings for the end of the week, but the picture on the television forecast showed a little bit of green down our neck of the woods, while everywhere else was white; we live in hope.

There was a little more blue-fitting as the last of the cleaning and polishing was carried out and I again bailed out, sharpish, in the direction of St Just, this time for last minute provisions. The light bulbs were still being polished when the party arrived.

It was like a grand safari of another era. All that was missing was a line of little natives in loin cloths with boxes on their heads; I half expected David Livingstone to come charging up the steps. They sure they're only staying for a week?

Took the bleddy hound out of the way later, down the big beach, of course. The sun was on the way down behind Mayon Cliff, breaking through some big dark clouds from time to time. From the far end of the beach it was a magnificent sight. The sun shining through the clouds like a big search light beam, variously lighting up features across the bay: first the Cape shining gold at the end of a line of black cliffs, now Brisons, then North Rocks.

Out on Longships the whole reef was shrouded in a pink-red mist. The crashing sea, on the horizon from where I was sitting, sending up plumes of spray, was caught in the vivid beams of sunlight. For all the world it looked like the sea around the rocks was on fire, flames licking around the lighthouse. It only lasted a moment, as good things often do, but I did feel rather privileged to see it.

Lost my shirt at the cards night down the OS, as usual and took the bleddy hound out for her last run when I returned. Coming back off the harbour we were greeted by the hound from the chip shop. Never will you have met such an errant beast, stubborn as a mule, big as a bus and coming on like an elephant in full charge. The two hounds, ours and theirs, are great pals and were off back down the beach in an instant; intervention, at this moment, is pointless.

I looked around for someone carrying a ship's hawser, about the only lead worth using on this animal, but no one appeared. Thinking it best to bring the dogs to our flat and call the owners from there was, it turned out, an over optimistic objective. Chip shop dog had no intention of moving in that direction and no amount of pulling or encouraging boot in the rear would convince him otherwise.

Eventually, with the strategic use of our hound as lure, I got the big beast to the foot of our steps, three feet at a time. Once there, in true comic form, chip shop dog suddenly went from being rooted to the spot to shooting up to the door. I, of course, went, just as suddenly, from pulling to being pulled, sending me flying up behind it.

I was very grateful when we tracked down the owner. One bleddy hound is more than enough, thank you.

*December 15th – Wednesday* – A bright start that continued through the day with a few big white clouds drifting about. With the sleeping arrangements in a full house as they are, the Missus even took the dog out first thing.

It has been decided that this household's Christmas will come a week early this year, as the in-laws will depart on Sunday, weather permitting. This, apparently, meant a trip to one of the big supermarkets to do what everyone else will be doing next week. I told them I couldn't go as I needed to shampoo the goldfish and was happy to wave them off. Thankfully they didn't notice that we don't have a goldfish.

Mother-in-law is partial to a bit of fish and, as it happens, we had some left over in the freezer from our bumper fish year. Lemon sole and a megrim are now nicely prepared for an oven baking for me and her, while the others enjoy some battered fish and chips from a decent chippy in town.

With the proper fish prepared, and the women folk out deep, I took the bleddy hound out again for a trip over the hill, down Maria's and down to the big beach.

I meant to report this last time but other matters overtook me, but the path down Cove Hill is tortuous. Erosion has had its way with this path for too long and the steps, in the first part of the descent, are precipitous. Had I packed my ropes, belay devices and carabiners it would have been a synch, but on foot and with crumbling knees, such as mine, careful avoidance of the full height of the steps is essential. How families with prams and beach equipment are supposed to traverse this path, the main one from the upper car park to the beach, is a wonder. Not surprising that most risk life and limb and go down the road.

Having made all that fuss I was met, on my descent, by a frail old lady coming up. To say that she was bounding might slightly overstate the case as it took her about five minutes to mount one of the steps. Nevertheless she was a game old bird and must do this route regularly as I have seen her on the beach before today. In another couple of winters I'd say she'll be carrying a ladder.

The wind dropped out and I was melting when we got to the beach. By the time we reached the slipway there was a terrible thirst upon me. My thoughts strayed to the hound that had run most of the journey. Unusually I succumbed to my empathy for her and let her detour to the OS for a drink. It would have been unsociable to let her sup alone.

By evening the wind had got up again; a storm is on the way. Batten down the hatches, I reckon.

*December 16th – Thursday* – A right big blustery start to the day, continuing from overnight, with force seven winds heading into us from the north west. Not ever so cold during the day and a bit of wetness joining us later in the afternoon. Later in the evening the temperature took a nose dive.

Had to trip into PZ as it was my turn to do a bit of shopping and to visit the bank; I've just noticed a few old twenty pound notes peeking out from the lining of the mattress that need to be changed. As it turned out it was just as well I had them.

For the first time in years I remembered that some people send Christmas cards in the post, and I thought I'd give it a go. Seems you have to buy them first, where previously I've always thought the Missus had an inexhaustible supply she simply pushed under my nose, with threats of punishment if they were not completed.

I ventured into a shop that was purveying several thousand of them. Slowly the reasons for ceasing to buy Christmas cards returned to me - they are, in the main complete rubbish, with sentiments inside that you wouldn't convey in the secrecy of a confessional, for fear of embarrassment, let alone to someone you actually liked – not without the aid of a nearby bucket, anyway. Others were simply crass, immature, pathetic, insincere or a combination of any of the above.

I selected four that displayed the least concentration of any detractions and pottered in the general direction of the counter. Now, what I did not appreciate is that none of these cards display a price. I am led to believe that they have a code instead, printed on the reverse in the smallest font imaginable. If you have been lucky enough to be blessed with magnifying eyesight, and were able to determine the code, you then have to find the price list secreted in the least obvious location in the store.

Naturally I was unable to complete any of the above tasks. I was therefore at the mercy of a tinsel decked shop assistant, who was able to deliver a surprise coup de grace, by telling me, in delighted tones, that I owed her a tenner for the four printed pieces of thick paper I held in my hand.

I enquired of this purveyor of seasonal joy, whether the price included entering my personal message inside each card in hand crafted, illuminated writing, a maid's silky tongue proffered to dampen the gum on the envelope and personal delivery to its destination by winged servants of Mercury himself.

Apparently not, although I could have a carrier bag for a further five pence that would go towards relief of distressed reindeer. I considered that, for a tenner, I could probably buy a distressed reindeer and a second hand sleigh and deliver my Christmas greetings personally.

If you are a lucky recipient of one of these four cards this year, treasure it. It will be the last.

As if to placate my sense of utter disgust, a little pleasure was dropped into my lap this evening. As ardent followers of my weekly routine will know, tonight was a quiz night at the OS. Attendant were only the mighty Head Launcher and myself, under dogs to a man if ever you saw us. Nevertheless, bolstered by a friendly soul half way through, we surfaced as victors for a second week running beating five other teams to the prize.

Such was my elation I even forgot I have to fork out another £1.64 on stamps. I'll have to see what's left in the mattress.

*December 17th – Friday* – Well, we escaped the big deluge of white stuff, at least for now. We did have a few sleet showers come through from time to time, and the wind did gust now and again. Still cold.

The Missus mobilised her voluminous handbag of disparate skills and completed the Christmas window display down in the shop. It is a wonder to behold and means that you happy customers, may have to squeeze yourselves around the shop when we open next Wednesday. Believe me it's worth every press and squirm and if you're unable to attend, shame on you. I shall do my best to put a little moving picture show on the website.

Despite the whipping wind and scarring hail showers, I took bleddy hound and her mate down along the beach again. This served two purposes, one of which was to exercise the dogs; the other was to avoid the gruesome and tortuous process that is preparing Christmas dinner. You will, of course, remember that today is faux Christmas Day at The Old Boathouse, for the benefit of our in-law guests.

We had Jamie sprouts, Nigella roast potatoes, Heston turkey, (cooked with an oxy-acetylene torch), and Delia beef followed, undoubtedly, by Andrew's salts. I am fortunate that we shall not have to repeat this grizzly performance next week. One Christmas dinner a year is surely sufficient for anyone, whosoever it was.

And talking of salts, Cornwall's favourite chemist started today in 1778 in PZ. No, not the one synonymous with footwear but the one who discovered potassium and calcium, by means of electrolysis, and invented a lamp that enabled the user to see the end of a mine, instead of the end of his days. This, of course, was Humphry Davy, possibly the only man in history to be awarded a medal by a dictator of a country with which we were at war at the time.

And any proper Christmas would be incomplete without a trip up the good old F&L. The staff, having enjoyed their own Christmas party, were in such high spirits they found it requisite to contract in a customer to run the bar for them. What an all round, jolly Christmas it was. I can only imagine next week will be an utter disappointment by comparison.

*December – 18th Saturday* – What a bright and shiny new day we have, despite being bitterly cold. But there's one thing in our favour – not a flake of the white stuff to be seen anywhere. Unlike many of you we can get in our cars, even the two wheel drive ones, and go hither and thither on a whim.

Well that's what I thought, but our range appears to be somewhat limited. I caught up with SN, who found a road mounted ice rink on her way to Helston this morning and did a bit of skating. Unfortunately she was in her van at the time, which is now a different shape from the one in the brochure.

As the tides are all wrong for a stank down the beach today it was off to LE with the bleddy hound. You can almost guarantee that on that particular jaunt she will seek out some badger or fox doings, (sorry if you're eating your sandwiches while reading this), to dab delicately behind her ears. Do not try this at home; the stuff has a distinctly different odour from Chanel No 5 and is not half as alluring, unless you're another dog.

This, of course, leads to a washing, a description of which you can enlighten yourself with by reading November 30th's entry. It seems churlish after she went to so much trouble to adorn herself but we clearly do not share the same values in aromatic delights.

I shall spare you the boring detail of the regular Saturday night entertainment. Needless to say a desperate, music filled night was enjoyed by all.

And I almost tripped up with the birth of another chap by the name of Wesley, today in 1707. Wrong Wesley, however, this was Charles who had very little to do with Cornwall, but wrote a lot of hymns. Over six thousand in fact. It was an easy mistake to make, he was one of fifteen little Wesleys, (yes, fifteen). I'd wager in the end, dear old Susanna would lock herself in the bathroom when Sam came home from the pub on a Saturday night.

Anyway, while some spotty kids are outside your door, tunelessly belting out, *'Hark! the Herald Angels Sing'* for a few of your hard earned shillings, it's Charles you can blame.

*December 19th – Sunday* – A rather delayed entry today and nothing to do with a sleety rain, freezing cold morning or the rather brighter freezing cold afternoon; no, this was all to do with a Cornish christening.

Now, a Cornish christening is something of a special event that involves around thirty minutes in the church followed by eight hours in the pub. As I rather hazily recall, the small child that is subject of the christening doesn't seem to feature very much, apart from a minor part at the outset of proceedings.

We repaired to the OS, that I am sure you will remember me saying is much improved lately, thanks, in no small part, to C&J at the helm. On this occasion we all had a chance to sample a selection of their fare, laid out for the celebrations. It is only fair to report, having previously used this page to denigrate their offerings, that it was all rather lovely. For those actually having to pay for the privilege, it is fairly priced too, unlike the beer, which, unfortunately, is the only downer on an otherwise wholesome experience.

On the basis that I believe I left the contents of my head at the home of the proud parents, that is about all you're going to get out of me today. You must hope, as indeed do I, that normal service will be resumed tomorrow.

*December 20th – Monday* – Quite a few big fluffy clouds around today but some nice blue bits too. It hasn't let up being cold though.

I hardly know whether to be proud of this achievement or outraged that I should be cut off so early in my literary career. You see I have been censored, blocked, curtailed, unmanned, (possibly), consigned to the bonfire of lost words.

I cannot be specific as to which establishment has seen fit to snip my little ribbon of bits and bytes off in its prime, for fear of a backlash. I can tell you it is an educational institution and, since it is probably fed its Internet capability from a single source, I am also likely to be barred from all such schools in the Local Education Authority area. Worse, if this bastion of early teachings is part of a Grid for Learning, I could even be excluded from an entire region.

You will understand that I cannot name the whistleblower lest she be castigated, or worse, in this obviously backward corner of our otherwise enlightened land. Needless to say, if you are able to read this page from some underground Internet café that has not yet been uncovered by the jack boot agents of your local authority, we are behind you all the way.

We had considered dropping printed versions of the Diary over your area but have been unable to find an airport open in the snow. Do not despair, however, rise up and resist the oppressors at every opportunity.

In the face of such suppression I must console myself with the fact that I am in good company: Voltaire, George Orwell, D H Lawrence, Salman Rushdie, Enid Blyton and Richard Neville have all been in my position at some point.

I have to go now, there is someone at the door. It will be my team of personal detectives I expect, provided at the taxpayers expense, and, in my view – possibly solely in my view - I'm worth every penny. If everything goes according to plan, as with all banned things, I shall be more popular than ever: number one by Christmas I reckon.

Oh and Richard Neville, (thought I might have you there), – *Oz Magazine*. And that two word phrase has probably got me blocked from the rest of the Government's Internet streams too.

*December 21st – Tuesday* – Happy Winter Solstice, one and all and a bit of a special this morning – a total eclipse of the moon, if you could see it, and the first time it has coincided with the Winter Solstice in over 500 years. I'm sure some sage or soothsayer would translate this as a sign that the end of the world is nigh. They aren't far wrong as, let's face it, Christmas feels pretty much like it most years.

But let's not jump the gun. There's plenty happening before then, the shop is opening for starters. As usual the event has been meticulously planned weeks in advance. This roughly means that everything looks good on paper, but absolutely nothing has been done.

Throw into this mix the arrival of an eminent dignitary from overseas. Yes, MM, our International Correspondent, is on a state visit. The red carpet has been carefully vacuumed around the various moth holes and the limousine has been highly polished, except for some mud around the wheel arches that is holding the rust in place.

After an extended journey, due to the inclement weather further up the line, we treated her to luncheon at the OS. Throwing caution to the winds we also dined there in the evening, our first time under the new management. We had a perfectly acceptable meal, which was a relief, although my garlic bread looked rather like chips. I refrained from making a fuss as it was all very nicely done.

We shall dine at the F&L tomorrow night and ask MM to pass her unbiased judgement on both experiences.

The shop closes early during our Christmas opening period so we have planned to take MM on a trip around the West Cornwall Winter Solstice lights. In the mean time I'd best get myself down to the shop to dust the cobwebs off the fresh produce.

*December 22nd – Wednesday* – Wind in the northeast, bitterly cold, ideal day to open the shop and stand behind the counter with icicles forming on my beard. Let's face it, it could be worse, we could have had been pawnbrokers.

Our customers were very kind and made us feel our opening was worthwhile; they both seemed very grateful.

It was good to be able to read newspapers again, to feel part of the world at large and, once read, to stuff them in quantity into my trousers to keep out the cold. After a while the stuffing preceded the reading, as there are only so many Vince Cable puns a poor boy can stand.

213

As promised we stole our American visitor away to see the Christmas illuminations but, unfortunately, we felt it prudent to shorten the tour to Newlyn and Mousehole. It was likely that ice would be a problem further out and I really couldn't risk landing our International Correspondent in a ditch for a few fairly lights – to think of the public outcry. We passed a gritter on the way out and the way back, as if to prove the point. Shame they've run out of grit but nice to see them try, nonetheless.

The lights are quite impressive and it was good to see that British International is still doing its helicopter trips around the bay. We took the parents-in-law on the excursion once. It was expensive, but well worth it to see the look on their little faces when the airborne jalopy shakes like it's about to fall apart.

Anyway, impressive as the lights were I was disappointed to note that our International Correspondent doesn't have an American accent. I was rather looking forward to a few, 'totally awesomes' and, 'do they really light each of those little candles every night?' You know the sort of thing.

We repaired to the F&L for tea and the eagerly anticipated comparative review with the new OS. I'd love to share that answer with you, but in all fairness we really ought to seek a wider sampling. What a tease I am!

As we coasted down the hill we watched the little drops of water on the end of our noses freeze and a couple of icebergs float gently into the bay. Going to be a cold night I reckon.

*December 23rd – Thursday* – I thought that it was half a degree warmer today when I first got down to the shop. After an hour of being open I modified my opinion and concluded that my feet were just as cold as yesterday, but with thicker socks.

MM was safely despatched aboard the 14:00 from PZ to a place called Totnes, wherever that is. We ensured that she was laden with a variety of Cornish produce; we understand from James Cook the importance of proffering gifts to natives. And we advised her against the sharp practices employed in such foreign parts, such as placing the jam and cream on scones in the wrong order and pasties laced along the top.

The sharp and cunning sense of humour that our Lifeboat coxswain has, had us all shivering in our boots at the bottom of the slip for this evening's exercise launch and recovery.

This sense of humour is obviously infectious. As we waited for the boat to return, the BBC weather forecast told us that this evening would be dry and cold. As he spoke we watched the snow slowly turn to sleet outside the boathouse door.

And so off to a Lifeboat evening at the OS, merrily entertained by the fabulous Bucket Boys. What a tough old life we lead.

*December 24th – Friday* – Drowsiness, affected vision, shaking, disorientation and poor reasoning; key indicators for someone suffering exposure, as my boys own book of arctic adventure tells me. Although some people may, perhaps unkindly, tell you that I display some, or most of these characteristics on a permanent basis, I didn't expect to have them all at the same time after two hours behind the counter this morning. Boy, is it ever cold.

This rather led me to the decision to take the bleddy hound out down to the, ever so big, spring tide beach. Fortunately the sea will be a yard or two closer tomorrow for the swim, else many would give up before they got there. Anyway the walk did the trick and I returned glowing and brimming with joie de vivre, and, no, that doesn't mean I tanked up at the OS on the way back, thank you; they were clean out of joie de vivre.

So 'twas the night before Christmas and I didn't stick around to find out what was happening around the house, I beggered off up the F&L. Christmas Eve is a formal dress occasion around here, though many are now letting this tradition lapse. A jolly band was playing lots of favourite tunes and everyone was in fine festive spirit. I even went to church.

Yes, you did hear right - church. Let me elucidate, and once I've done that, I'll explain that the Missus has moments of creative genius, as you'll determine if I ever get around to putting some moving pictures of our Christmas window on the website. On this occasion she fashioned a gingerbread house out of, well, gingerbread mainly. It was a wonder, with little electric lights that lit up the inside and shone through the boiled sweet windows and icing icicles hung off the icing snow covered roof.

Rather than waste this comestible delight she elected to give it to the church for the children to demolish on Christmas Day. Have no fear, this household has not suddenly got religion and you're not about to be deluged with the evangelical ramblings of a zealous Diarist, (can you have an evangelical zealot?). Anyway, no, this was more an unguarded lapse of reason; a moment of unusual, (for

215

us), unheard of, (for me), generosity. I can assure you it won't happen again.

It was a rather surreal moment as I, rather unsteadily, paraded it into the church just before the start of Midnight Mass. The looks of confusion and disbelief on the faces of the church seniors as a rather tipsy gentleman, ('gentleman' used only for effect) dressed in a sand coloured suit and boasting a floral bow tie, floated down the aisle carrying a gingerbread house.

I left brief instructions that it was to be consumed by the small children of the parish the following morning and left, narrowly avoiding the bolt of lightning that someone had carelessly thrown in my direction.

So as the Christmas fairy of time waves her starry wand in the general direction of eternity, and the Christmas tree of fate sticks a spiky finger up her drawers, its time to wish you all a very Merry Christmas.

*December 25th – Saturday* – So this was it, then; the day that we've all been told to wait for; the hours of television, radio and bill board advertising that have had us slavering to expect. A riotous day of anti-climax for many, I suspect, though the weather held in there for us, and a beach that has hardly looked more golden and beautiful.

This was the day that millions of small children were getting out of bed early for; to rip open their presents of hope, joy and disappointment when the wheels fall off. Santa, I am sure, came to the Old Boathouse, though probably only to use the toilet, which reminds me I have to check the roof for reindeer pooh.

This is also the day when over a hundred, probably quite sane souls, inexplicably take leave of their senses and run half naked into the sea. It's all done in the name of charity, and probably not half as mad as you might think. With an air temperature of around three degrees and a sea temperature of ten degrees it must have been like stepping into a warm bath. I would have found out myself, of course, but for the fact that I had to stay in to shave the rabbit.

It was the day when we all telephone our nearest and dearest that couldn't be with us, or us them. In my case I telephoned my sister instead, (yes, even moral orphans, such as myself, have families) whose message of goodwill was to berate me for a tardy posting of yesterday's Diary entry. What can I tell you? My sole Christmas present, and to myself at that, was to allow myself a little lay in on Christmas Day.

Sis, if you're reading this, believe me, I have only just removed my hair shirt, and the birch twigs, with which I castigated myself all day, lie in tatters at my feet, honest. I even forced myself to go to the OS twice in the day.

Yes, faced with the misery that is the television Christmas Day schedule, I elected to go to the OS in the evening too. C&J had laid on a quiz that was jolly good fun and surprisingly well attended. Well done to them.

Of course, I would have ended with someone famous whose birthday it was today but I couldn't think of anyone, sorry!

PS. Love you really, Sis.


*December 26th – Sunday* – So that was it then. I woke up this morning and all that Christmas stuff just seemed to have evaporated; the skies clouded over and the temperature has markedly risen, as has the wind.

Up the back of the F&L for the Boxing Day shoot it was fair howling across the fields. Fortunately someone had very kindly left a big vegetable trailer for us, and the shoot went off without a hitch. Even the trap behaved itself for the larger part of the event.

Charles Babbage, now he was a clever soul, and not just for being born on this day in 1791 and missing Christmas. Widely considered the father of computing, boy Charlie was a wiz at mathematics and mechanical engineering and also dabbled in philosophy. The latter was obviously his weak suit; if he had really thought about he would have invented something a little less frustrating.

He never actually got to build his box, the difference engine, as the cathode ray tube wasn't invented until way after he died. In 1991 The Science Museum, faithfully used his plans to build it: it worked perfectly. This was amazing as none of the subsequent models have.

And *Far from the Madding Crowd* springs to mind but not by the Thomas you're thinking of. This Thomas, born today in 1716, originally coined the phrase for his poem, *Elegy Written in a Country Churchyard*, one of only thirteen he published. Good, then, that he had another job that obviously allowed him enough time off to sit in graveyards for hours on end.

Ah, where ignorance is bliss, 'tis folly to be wise.

*December 27th – Monday* – I've been waiting for today all year. It is the day that the heavens may shine kindly on this little corner of the Internet and words will flow like honey from my fingers and onto this page. It will be like music, (but to your eyes, obviously), like a thousand symphonies of the seraphim and cherubim singing with one voice, and you will be transported high to the heavens and never wish to look at any of those poor substitute scribblings elsewhere on the World Wide Web ever again. For it is the Feast of St John the Evangelist, patron saint of Sennen Cove Diarists, amongst other jotters.

Shame there isn't a patron saint of Sennen shopkeepers, as, boy, do we ever need one at the moment. The snow seemingly stopped many visitors from attempting the trip down here for Christmas; for those that braved the journey, buckets full of rain. But at least the southerly gales seem to be abating.

I hope there's quiz on this week as I'm right up for the current affairs section; I have read every newspaper cover to cover in the last two days. I've also counted the cracks in the ceiling and given names to the 24 gulls I've spotted swirling about. Although that may have been twelve I named twice.

Tomorrow is likely to be misty, so that'll be nice for a change. And, oh joy, the first Easter egg was spotted in a shop up country today. Soon be summer.

Well judging from today's disjointed and stuttering effort I guess St John the Evangelist is putting his patronage elsewhere. I bet he's looking after that J K bleddy Rowling again.

*December 28th – Tuesday* – Black as pitch when I got up this morning. That is 6:30 for all you bank holiday, bed hugging folk out there. I thought my alarm had gone off a couple of hours early. I was sure the mornings were supposed to be getting lighter.

Although it was a glum, misty start we actually had some blue sky half way through the morning and very little in the way of rain, which was encouraging. So was the fact that we had three customers before 9 o'clock and it was reasonably steady through the day. Perhaps the patron saint of shopkeepers read yesterday's Diary and took pity.

They say a vast sum of money was spent in the last couple of days and it was nice to share in the bonanza. My arithmetic isn't up to much; I was trying to work out what percentage of one billion pounds seven shillings and sixpence is.

As you might have noticed, I cracked the technical nut of getting a little movie of the shop's Christmas lights up on the website. It originally started out in High Definition although I had to down grade it to fire it up to the Internet, else it wouldn't have got there until next Christmas. I had to ditch the music too for fear of the copyright police. The timing of the whole thing could have been better; I understand the Oscar nominations were posted yesterday.

I forced myself to go down to the OS and indulge in a little game of poker in the evening. There were only a handful of us there and I was back home before ten. Neither the Missus nor the bleddy hound were very impressed; if I go out I'm supposed to stay out to at least last knockings. It must go against the grain of life or something.

I shall make amends tomorrow night. A lively band is booked at the OS and it would be uncharitable not to support local musicians and rude to go before they finish.

*December 29th – Wednesday* – Will no one rid me of this turbulent fog! That might be an appropriate call today.

Thick as a bag, it was. We didn't see Gwenver until mid afternoon and it was the same for most of West Penwith.

I took a trip out to Helston to get a cabinet for something I fear not mention, lest I be barred from another chunk of the free world. It was foggy all the way with visibility down to less than fifty yards in some places. I wonder just how foggy it has to be for some motorists to turn on their lights – headlights that is – parking lights are as useless as having none on at all. It makes you feel as safe as a 12th century Archbishop. Yes, I know I've mentioned this before but it irks me as much now as it did then so you're getting a double dose of my ire.

There were, apparently, several surfers out there today. I know only because a few came by the shop, squelching down to the soft drinks. I half expected them to be kitted out with radar or at least a sat nav to help them find the beach while they were out there. Not surprising, there was some cracking good surf towards North Rocks when eventually we could see it.

Interestingly, perhaps, the *Sunday Express* was published for the first time in 1918 on this very day, which is odd because it's Wednesday. It is a wonder that it's still going in this neck of the woods. *The Daily Express*, whose trademark is a little knight with sword and shield, is still published today but our wholesaler,

Smiths News, seem reticent in letting me have any copies. Twice this week they've let me down.

And talking of knights, the Archbishop of Canterbury had his frightfully shortened by four of them that turned up on his doorstep in 1170. Still, it gave Chaucer a nice little earner and started the tourist business in the South East.

I'm sorry. I'm going to have to interrupt this carefully considered and well-rounded ending to this entry with a little report on this evening's proceedings.

Tonight at the OS we had a performance to take your soul, turn it inside out and spit it right back at you in the form of the Dirty Living Rhythm Band. A tall, stringy blonde, whose vocals could slice glass to match the best endeavours of Waterford Crystal engravers, and an exponent of the acoustic guitar who could have been the result of a Julian Bream, Slash and John Lee Hooker cloning experiment. Add drums and bass, it made a band greater than the sum of its parts.

Jazz, Blues and Rock with Bonnie Raitt, Fleetwood Mac, Bob Dylan and, if you listened carefully, even some Irving Berlin were delivered in perfect, melodious, in your face, certainty. Dim the lights and add some smoke and we could have been in a dingy bar in Chicago.

All that was missing was I didn't have stars to gaze at on the way home.

*December 30th – Thursday* – If we can keep our heads a minute I could tell you that it brightened up slowly today but with a nasty, chilly little easterly that crept up the trouser leg and wobbled me bloomers. By mid afternoon the channel markers were blown sideways and the bay was filled with white caps, dived upon by a large flock of gannets, shining in the sunlight out towards Brisons.

First thing this morning, a red-faced jogger put her head around the door and told me there was a seal pup at the bottom of the slip on the big beach. I have to say, I never have quite seen the point of jogging, unless the pub is about to close. I know many people in towns and cities do it, which enables them to breathe in noxious fumes at twice the rate than when they're walking. Down here there's a good mile of beach to run along, but they insist on running down the hard road with the possibility of jarring various delicate bones; and it's easier, you wooses. I don't wish to look too good in all this, or be accused of talking too wise, but I find it very odd.

Anyway, I was just in the middle of telephoning the seal sanctuary when a chap told me not to worry as he had already telephoned last night. It wasn't until after I closed the call that he told me that he was supposed to phone back, if the pup was still there this morning. I had to force my heart and nerve and sinew to hold back on that one, I can tell you. But I dare say I'll serve my turn long after he is gone.

Big excitement this evening with Rescue 193 darting around The Cove in search mode; both Penzance and Lands End Coastguard teams were out, running from Lands End to Cape looking for a lost soul. They kept their heads and waited and were not tired of waiting. Apparently this had been going on for a few hours when the call came in that the 'misper' had been found. "Where is he?" came the enquiry. "Newlyn.", the dry response.

The Shore Crew team held its own again at the OS quiz but missed the prize on a tie breaker otherwise we would have made a heap of all our winnings. So far we've met with triumph and disaster and been men enough to treat them both the same. We're going to have to find better ways to cheat.

Ah well, next time ours will be the earth and everything that's in it if the prize money stretches that far, and what's more we'll be men, my son.

Thanks Rudyard and Happy Birthday, today in 1865 wasn't it? Loved the jungle cartoon you did with Mr Disney and it's a wonder you had time to make all those cakes.

*December 31st – Friday* – Ah, here we go - the last day of the year. Just as cold and breezy as the previous day and a bit cloudy but clearing later, they said, but it didn't much.

Our friends at Smiths News, that bastion of customer service delivery, had its last shot of the year at us by reducing our most popular newspaper titles to just one each. I gave the lady on the telephone a light roasting but, of course, it was my fault for not checking the volumes each day, apparently; that and not being blessed with second sight.

Also today, the last, (hopefully), Lifeboat launch of the year. No doubt us Shore Crew will be casting lots as to who will be freezing their socks off at the end of the slip for recovery. There were certainly enough of us there.

If you thought that, in line with other publications, we'd be doing an end of the year awards job or, 'what happened in 2010', you have another think coming. There's enough of that sort of thing going on and, given this is Sennen Cove, it would make this page even shorter than it's going to be.

What do you mean? Of course this isn't sour grapes for not having my name listed in services to wild leaf foraging in the New Year honours list; just being there was reward enough. The Missus did ask why our copy of the list was ripped to shreds – must have been the bleddy hound.

She had her best mate around today, the dog, not the Missus. We had to leave them in the flat while the Lifeboat thing was going on and the Missus ran the shop. Next door's hound is a bit partial to anything vaguely edible and is a little taller than ours. Shame, as I was quite looking forward to a bit of that giant Toblerone bar we left on the table.

I think I'll be spending the last few minutes of this year up the F&L so I'll get on now. And since you'll all be reading this tomorrow –

Happy New Year!

# January 2011

*January 1st – Saturday* – Welcome to 2011.

Well I didn't see all of today as you might have guessed from the tardiness of the posting of yesterday's Diary entry. I was, after all, up well past my bedtime and I am sure that's what made me really tired.

When I did eventually surface on the day I found it a bit dull and grey, and it stayed that way until it went dark. It was cold but that nasty easterly had given up, which was a delight for static shop-keepers with a door cunningly designed to catch every breath from that direction. Despite that, we had the busiest day of the period with everyone out and about for a wander.

I was surprised to read that it wasn't until 1974 that New Year's Day became a public holiday. I'm not surprised, however, that I missed the transition as, back then, for me, every day at this time of year was a holiday as I was still just about at school. Of course things would have been different if the Government hadn't, some years earlier and much to my parents chagrin, banned children from entering the mines.

I jest, of course, there weren't any mines where we lived; it was much more likely to have been chimney sweeping.

Naturally I shall be entertaining an early night tonight unless some passing neighbour, home on leave, demands my presence up at the F&L which, incidentally, they just have. Of course, I was resolute and cast away the temptation, man of mettle such as I am.

As I expected the F&L was very quiet tonight and the band, not one of the better ones, failed to impress. My provocateurs, such as they were, turned out to be complete wimps and left the dance early. Rather than upset the Missus by turning up home prematurely, I accepted the kind offer of a lift down the hill and dropped in the OS for a quickie. The things I put myself through for that girl.

*January 2nd – Sunday* – There seems to be little sign of this spangley new year; it looks very much like the old rusty one at the moment. In fact it seemed a bit like Groundhog Day today. Yesterday felt so much like a Sunday it was only the newspapers that gave it away. Though the greyness and the Sunday feel, mainly because it was Sunday, was the same, it rained a little and there were fewer people about.

We had a decent crowd for the Lifeboat launch but this time we had the added joy of Rescue 193 in attendance, scooping our good doctor off somewhere in the distance, possibly never to be seen again.

It is our last day until the new season kicks off for us in March. With the diminishing visitors, it's probably just as well I forgot that tomorrow is a bank holiday, else I might have opened. In fact, other than Christmas Day, I do believe that's the first bank holiday that we haven't opened in six years. Frankly we're glad to be shot of it this year; it seems the snow and nasty bugs kept many people away this season.

In an otherwise unexceptional day another seal pup was found down on the big beach. As nice and cuddly as they may look, touching them is not advisable, and thankfully there were some switched on people down there keeping some small children from taking it home. The National Seal Sanctuary made a timely appearance and ushered it back into the water after weighing it.

So it will be back to walks on the beach with the bleddy hound, forays into the big city on shopping trips, all the riveting excitement that you've come to expect from this page. I know, you can hardly wait; I can almost hear the mass sucking in of expectant breath.

*January 3rd – Monday* – What else would we do on such a wonderful day, such as this, but indulge ourselves in the unsurpassable joy of doing the annual stocktaking? There is nothing more fun: short of walking over hot coals while being beaten by birch twig toting sadists, or perhaps painting myself with treacle, rolling in bird seed and lying down in a chicken coop for an hour or two. In fact there is probably an endless choice of preferable alternatives.

Just imagine the joy of opening the door and finding that the aisles seem to have grown to twice their length and the shelves twice as full. Imagine opening boxes of goodies that, on the previous occasion you opened them, you forgot to mark on the outside just how many items were in them, so you have to count them all over again.

Of course, prior to all this counting, there was the morning immersed in the preparation of spreadsheets that you can then spend the evening filling in. It is then you find that the column you set aside for the opening stock is shorter than the opening stock figures. You also note that some of the purchases you made through the year were not recorded and the paperwork is at the accountants.

It is at this point, with tufts of your remaining hair set about the keyboard, you realise that being an envelope licker in the *Reader's Digest* mail room may not have been so bad after all.

More of the same tomorrow. Perhaps we should write a book – *The Joy of Stocks*.

*January 4th – Tuesday* – Staying a bit chilly with some breaking bits of blue; unfortunately there wasn't quite enough blue to be able to make any sense of the eclipse, in fact I think we had a rain shower come through at about that time; quite apart from the fact that I'd forgotten all about it.

Slipped down to the Harbour Beach with the bleddy hound for a normal run around this morning and found that the fishing fleet had just got in. Had I known they were unloading fish I wouldn't have let her off the lead so soon. She tried her best to get her nose in some boxes of mackerel but gave up and settled for a filleted pollock discarded on the sand. I long ago learned it fruitless trying to chase her with it and rely on distraction techniques instead, which I found equally useless.

The brain numbing counting of things goes on and, surprisingly, we're still getting orders for things on the Internet, which means adjusting the count on the fly. It also meant discovering that a chrome, spring based clock in blue, ordered yesterday is no longer available. I also discovered that an alternative one I thought was green is actually silver, for which I have to thank my colour sighted Missus for pointing out.

As you may have heard VAT has gone up today. I shall not be charging you any more for this page but it does mean that it will be 2.5 per cent shorter than it

*January 5th – Wednesday* – Hello pl*ym*tes!
Only the 5th day of the new month and I've been struck by a bout of laziness. You might have noticed that yesterday's entry didn't appear until a very lamentable 10:30 am mainly because I didn't get out of my pit until a very decadent 9:30 am.

225

In my defence I'm not the only one; the promised rain didn't make an appearance at all. I replied in kind by not doing any counting today, although I did stretch myself to a little data entry.

By some miracle of self-driven determination I managed to don my walking boots and take the bleddy hound and her mate down to the big beach. I miss-timed it rather and found myself losing ground to an advancing tide. This meant walking above the tide line where the sand is soft. Very good for the quads, (thigh muscles, not the four wheel bikes), but I now know how T E Lawrence must have felt. No wonder he elected to use a camel.

After such extreme activity I repaired to the OS for a quick livener; absolutely necessary under such circumstances and I'm sure the hounds were grateful.

It has been pointed out to me, quite unkindly I felt, that all I seem to do is take the bleddy hound out and visit either the OS or the F&L at the top of the hill. What do you expect? There are, after all, only the two ale houses within walking distance.

The whole thing quite wore me out and I found myself dozing off in front of the computer on my return. I capitulated, as I needed to conserve my energy for an evening of complete inactivity.

I apologise in advance for tomorrow's entry that will, no doubt, be more dog walking and visiting the usual haunts, unless of course they open another pub in the mean time.

And since I started the whole day with an Arthur Askey catchphrase I may as well end with one. Bandwagon, of course, made its first appearance on BBC radio today in 1938. I'm sure you all remember with fondness.

Ay thang yew.

*January 6th – Thursday* – The sharp eyed amongst you will have noticed that I have censored the opening phrase from yesterday's Diary entry. I have been informed that I have once again been blocked from a certain Council's Local Education Authority web stream, on this occasion due to p\*rn\*gr\*phy, and I can only think that it's that word that triggered the wheels of oppression.

I can see that this will be a battle of wits or perhaps wills. I can understand being banned on the basis of a ludicrous lack of literary content, (apart from a cracking piece of alliteration), bad spelling and an awful sense of humour but I'm darned if I shall let them get away with banning me on the grounds of muckiness.

I have warned our whistleblower to be alert for further signs of extreme censorship, such as burning books and carting away pupils with certain surnames ending in 'nizyn' and 'enko'. I understand that the gulags of North West England are particularly harsh, and at the first signs of provocation our mole should head for the Tamar, sharpish.

Mind you they might need to bring a boat, boy, did it rain last night. It was still going a little bit when I took the bleddy hound round for her morning constitutional. The springs up by Chy Ryn were very active as usual after a downpour, but there was also a geet puddle right across Coastguard Row, which I hadn't seen before.

The wet stuff hung around until early afternoon when I went up to count the stock in Shrew House, our store. There was no sign of the little varmints, for which I was grateful, having enough to contend with after two and a half hours in the cold and damp.

In the meanwhile the Missus had packed away the Christmas window display which will also disappear from our website. We now only have the stock room to count and we're done. Yippee!

Lifeboat training tonight, where careful plans are being hatched for the SOS fund-raising day on 30th January. Despite being cold and The Cove empty, last year was surprisingly successful. So if you can't be there just send money.

Your money will go to making Lifeboats work across the country, unless you very clearly specify it is for the modest, undervalued and oft penniless Shore Crew to gain some rare respite in their hard and joyless lives down the OS. The choice, of course, is entirely yours.

*January 7th – Friday* – More rain coming down like stair rods through the night and, on and off, throughout the morning. By sheer fluke I managed to avoid the showers for the first run round of the day. Best I buy a lottery ticket.

Started on the stock room count this morning too; it's only a small stock room. Fast forward to four hours later and we're still there counting little teddy bears.

There was a little distraction. The fluorescent tube at the far end, the darkest part, obviously, is misbehaving. I had already replaced the tube and, of course, it is the starter, which won't come out. It just turns round and round in its fitting. I even had the fitting apart, gazing up at unfamiliar parts with a torch between my teeth. The best I could manage was light for five minutes, then a fit of flashing on and off, then light again for five minutes. Naturally the two electricians who have been crousting over by the Lifeboat station all week decided not to be there today. Cancel the lottery ticket.

Now here's a little nugget to make the older generation look down on the young texters of today with a smug grin. 'CQD' was introduced as the new distress signal on this day. It stood for 'seek you, danger'. It was only in place for a couple of years before SOS took over but in 1904 it certainly puts 'GR8' and 'LOL' in their place and not a mobile phone in sight.

No going off gallivanting tonight, I'm sorry to say; first of the trade shows tomorrow in sunny Newquay and there abouts. I'm rather afraid tomorrow's entry will be much delayed so you'll have to find your own entertainment, but I shall return with tales of derring-do from foreign parts in due course.

*January 8th – Saturday* – Up with the lark this morning, or more accurately the Missus was, which was sufficient a shock to send me reeling from my cosy confines.

After packing up a few basic survival rations, a clean pair of knickers, (you never know, do you?), and lodging the bleddy hound with the neighbours we headed off for the far distant heartland of hen and stag parties. The path was fraught and studded with diversions, a heinous journey if ever there was one.

No sooner had we reached Hayle than the Philps pasty diversion stepped out in front of the van and forced us into the South Quay car park. As you will know, Mr Philps makes an exceedingly good pasty and today was no exception. The East Quay may, one day, host a supermarket, cinema and untold delights but I very much doubt it. I once went to a smart exhibition that showed stunning development of the old industrial area. That was ten years ago and it still looks the same today.

We extracted ourselves and were no sooner back on the road than St Michael intervened along with his Italian mate, Costa. I for one hadn't seen this coming but the Missus was ardent in her desire to do their bidding.

I shall spare you the further details, but our entire trip appeared blighted, and left me in no doubt that the early start was indicative of some sort of cunning plan on someone's part.

We finally arrived on those north shores bathed in sunlight, which was all very pretty. Shame we had to spend the rest of the day rolled up with spreadsheets, order books and tales of the rising price of cotton and oil that will lead to shop prices being scary this season.

We spent the evening in convivial company. Yes, I know they're salesmen, but ones we've known for some seven years and we are long past the hoodwinking stage. We were also dissuaded from going to Birmingham this year. It didn't take much dissuading, for sure. We both hate the trip north and the yield has been minor in recent years.

So as happy little travellers we retired for the evening.

*January 9th – Sunday* – A very different vista to wake up to this morning - Fistral Beach in all it's square shaped glory, with the early morning sun dancing off the grand, gothic splendour of Silvanus Trevail's Headland Hotel. Poor old Silvanus obviously didn't think much of his handiwork or was not best pleased with Bodmin; he shot himself while in the lavatory of a train entering the station in 1903.

We were treated to a splendid breakfast in our hotel at a sensible hour. You are, no doubt, familiar with the usual scrum of hotel breakfasts for a wizened egg, cremated bacon, shrivelled sausage and watery tea. Well this was quite the opposite and rather welcome.

The second part of this trade show trip requires a short journey to Kingsley Village. This place was set up to showcase local foods, arts and other Cornish products and has settled in nicely in the few years that it has been there. The trade show part is held in the basement.

Now re-read the above paragraph and understand that to reach the basement one needs to traverse, what is no more than, a glorified shop. Yup, nearly two hours and many shillings later we eventually reached the basement.

It is a very small trade show and, largely, we know who will be there and what they have to offer. It therefore turns out to be a rather perfunctory visit and is knocked off in short order. The main work will be next week when we slip off to Exeter.

All said and done we headed home with the sun in our eyes. The bleddy hound showed no sign of having missed us in any respect, and everything looking pretty much like we'd never been away, despite feeling like we've been away for a week.

Those of us suffering with seasonal maladies should remember that today, in 1929, Fleming successfully treated his assistant's infection with a penicillin broth. How he managed to do all his medical research and write all those Bond books is beyond me.

And we really can't forget William Pitt the Younger for introducing income tax in 1799, to finance the Napoleonic Wars. Even after they ended in 1815, Robert Banks Jenkinson clearly felt that after sixteen years us common folk had probably forgotten why the tax was introduced in the first place and kept it going.

Even today you can hear people say, "Income tax – it's the Pitts."

*January 10th – Monday* – A right rainy day, and all day at that. A weather warning has been issued by the Met Office, warning us to expect it to be wet.

With that in mind it seemed like a good idea to drop down to the shop and count all our postcards. A lady is coming on Wednesday to take an order for the new season, so the count had to be done. You have no idea how brain-numbingly boring counting postcards is, especially when there are over 10,000 to thumb through. That is the stock at the end of the year, with many slots on the rack empty. Whoever said the written word was dead.

It was indeed given a boost on this day in 1840 when Rowland Hill introduced his Uniform Penny Post, equivalent to roughly 30p in today's money. And as today this only lasted a year before the price went up but the project, as a whole, was a financial disaster. It took thirty years before revenues returned to the pre-1840 level.

Nice to see, then, that successive governments have learnt the lessons of the past and now shy away from such loss making enterprises.

Of course sending letters didn't suit everyone. In rural areas, for example, where the average daily wage was 20d, (£5.90 today), you probably wouldn't bother, especially as you were likely hampered by the constraint of being unable to write them in the first place. Add to this that your beer allowance, (oh yes, there was a beer allowance – take heed, Cameron), wouldn't quite cover your average daily intake of 3.5 pints, every penny postage stamp counted.

Ever since we arrived here we have been constantly surprised by the volume of postcards bought each year. Having uncovered all this I doubt that I shall send a postcard ever again. I shall be too mindful of the relationship between the cost of postage and my beer allowance.

*January 11th – Tuesday* – A half decent day after a wild and stormy night and what did I do with it? Yup, buried my head in the shop for some more counting. This time I think we're near enough finished.

A charming little note through the letterbox today from the TV Licensing people; woe will betide me and geet, black, nasty things will fall on my head from the skies, if I do not buy a TV Licence for the television that I haven't got in the shop. Fair do's, they did send me another less sinister note a while back asking me that if I didn't have a TV in the shop, to let them know or else woe would betide me, and geet, black, nasty things would fall from the sky onto my head.

Unfortunately the letting them know bit would have cost me the price of a stamp, thus eating into my precious beer allowance. They assure me that if they don't hear from me an investigation will be launched. I can't help imagining some underground bunker where big, muscle-bound men in black jump suits are, at this very minute, slipping on harnesses weighed down with Uzi sub-machine guns, stun grenades and little round things that go bleep and saying 'hut' a lot.

Perhaps I ought to tell them I am out tonight. It would be rather embarrassing for them to slip down ropes from a hovering Black Hawk, smash through my windows only to find that I am at the OS losing at cards.

Apparently if I buy a TV licence for my non-existent tele I can avoid the impending re-make of *Apocalypse Now* in my front room. That is the only recourse, it seems; there is no option 'b', explaining I don't need a licence; this eventuality, apparently, hasn't occurred to them.

Maybe I should buy a TV licence for the shop just in case they plant one. I wouldn't put it past this lot.

So if these jottings should suddenly cease you may take a fair guess that woe has betided me and geet, black, nasty things have fallen from the sky onto my head. Send help at once and think twice about not having a TV Licence for a tele you haven't got.

*January 12th – Wednesday* – Rather grey and misty all day but still not half as bad as the forecast painted it.

Took advantage of the less than dramatic weather and took the bleddy hound and the Missus down to the big beach in an astounding gesture of goodwill. It's marvellous to see her gambol, chase the ball and romp all over the sand like that, but she did look quite worn out by the time we got back. We naturally strayed into the OS on the way back for her to have a drink. The bleddy hound had one too.

Amazing the difference in the beach after a bit of south westerly swell had been in there. The large drift up at the high water mark has been smoothed out considerably. It would appear much sand has been moved down to North Rocks as my favourite 'chair' is nowhere to be seen, and the wooden posts of the walkways, at the bottom of the slipway at the near end, are visible again.

Earlier we had entertained our postcard lady, whose main claim to fame was to let a recently taken order at Lands End scat to the four winds, (well one of them anyway), bits of paper never to be seen again. She then let the same process happen again with our order down in The Cove. She had some new goodies to proffer, as well. I'm sure you will be ever so excited when you see them in the shop. It's amazing what you can stick a picture on these days.

I can feel the expectant breath of the Revenue man on the back of my neck. It is the time of year for me to carve off a pound, plus inflation, of my living flesh to hand over, so that the Government can continue with its stunning good works. While employed folk have their hard earned shillings deducted from what they have been paid, for the work they have done, us self employed clowns must pay on what we might have done - a payment on account.

I do have the advantage that the money I save up for this event gathers interest at the bank, upon which I pay tax, of course. However, as I squeeze the amount due in words on the cheque page, (they really need to make cheques bigger), I can smile smugly at the 26p I have torn from the taxman's grasping hand.

*January 13th – Thursday* – Another wild and stormy night has given way to a wild and stormy morning. The sea is boiling in the bay, what you can see of it, the wind is high and the rain, although light, is whipping in.

We and our neighbours treated ourselves to a splendid little dinner up at the F&L. The place was quiet and we felt nicely secluded with our heads in the clouds up there.

I got myself dropped off at Lands End afterwards with the bleddy hound and her best mate and we walked back over the cliff path. We gave a little thanks up to Sir William Mills of Mills Munitions as we drove down, as without him it would have been difficult to see ahead. Although there is some stiff competition to the title, he is one of several accredited with inventing the windscreen wiper. We had no use for his aluminium golf clubs or his more famous bombs, (sorry, that's rather excluded today's page from schools in North West England).

It's been years since I've walked  the coast path from that direction, and boy, did it feel weird; couldn't see very far in any direction that added to the mystery of it all. The bleddy hound found some mystery of her own and smeared it liberally behind her ears, bless her.

It only takes twenty minutes to do the walk so I detoured along Maria's Lane and down over the beach for some added value. For the second day in a row we were the only souls on the sand. I was going to drop into the OS for another gratuitous beer but the rain had begun to set in and the hounds, in the state they were in, would probably not be that welcome.

I can tell you I was fair worn out. I could have had the use of another of Mr Mills' excellent inventions, the shooting stick. Gosh, could that man invent.

In the evening we practised some triage scenarios under the auspices of our good doctor. As I'm sure you are well aware, triage is the method of sorting the wheat from the chaff out of a bunch of injured French people. It's not the sort of thing any of us would like to do for real, but if we did you'd hope we would be rather good at it.

Rather better, at least, than our underhand methods of cheating at the OS Thursday quiz, which we lost again on a tie break.

*January 14th – Friday* – 'Twas quite some brillig day in the making, although the sea is still rather big and lumpy and quite wet as wet could be; I noticed some slithy toves gyring and gimbling over in the wabe too.

Just as I was about to take the bleddy hound out for her first walk round the borogroves I got a chap from our refrigeration company banging on the shop door. The matter of a faulty thermostat in one of the freezers was clearly so urgent, after three months of waiting for a part, they hadn't time to let me know it was coming. In fact it had been so long since the problem was reported, I couldn't for the life of me remember which freezer it was.

We had a little excitement with a forty gallon drum sighted over by Aire Point later in the morning. It washed in towards Gwenver

233

and the Coastguard, those beamish boys, were despatched to deal with it, vorpal blades in hand, no doubt. It will be a little while before I can report the detail, if at all, as I shall not be seeing my inside man for a week or two.

Yes, I am rather frumious to report that once again we are heading out yonder, in fact a little further beyond yonder that I'd really prefer to go. Another trade show beckons and I am in uffish thought that you, dear reader, will be Diaryless for a day or two. But I'm afraid the time has come, as a walrus might say, to think of shoes, sailing our ship east, sealing the cracks so the rain doesn't come in and taking the cabbageway to avoid the kinks, (golly, that was laboured, contrived and, some might say, utterly unnecessary).

You might have guessed by now that Charles Lutwidge Dodgson has had just a little influence today; and rightly so, I feel. Mr Lewis, as best we know him, popped off today in 1898 and left us with a wonderland of language and imaginings.

"Oh what a fabjous day! Callooh! Callay!", he might have said.

*January 15th – Saturday* – We dragged our feet this morning before setting off in entirely the wrong direction – east. The grey clouds and slightly misty air was absolutely spot on for a journey of this nature.

The Missus has been banging on for some time about a greasy spoon up near Scorrier. It's called Smokey Joe's and turns out breakfasts of various heart stopping sizes: chilli and chips, steak and kidney, etcetera along with steaming cups of tea or coffee. Just what you would expect, I'm sure.

I think I must have been oversold. So great was my expectation that, although perfectly respectable, it was rather a disappointment. Quite frankly it wasn't worth giving up my Philp's pasty for or maybe I was just too dour at the prospect of leaving the county.

It is a long and boring journey until you get to the motorway. I vaguely recall these monster roads with more than two lanes on either side and it was just as bad as I was expecting; worse still when we got to the big city. There were junctions with more than one sign that were terribly confusing, and roundabouts with more than four exits, and lanes to chose from and traffic lights to observe – in the middle of the roundabout for heaven's sake.

We could see the hotel we were staying at on the other side of the roundabout. However it was not abundantly clear which exit was the correct one to take to gain access to it. Having elected to take the wrong one, of course, there wasn't an immediate way of turning around to have another go at it. It was on the eventual second approach that I saw the pub that sits next to the hotel. Everything suddenly became clear, my finely tuned homing skills kicked in and with a couple of perfectly executed, traffic stopping, manoeuvres we were in the pub, I mean hotel, car park.

Let me tell you that the hotel is a comfortable part of a modern business park. The pub looks like a tastefully extended 18th Century minor manor house, and quite the anachronism among the concrete and brick sprawling offices and factories. In fact it is a contemporary build, made from reclaimed material, and is every part the juxtaposition that it clearly was intended to be.

Now, being in the heart of office land, you are miles away from the nearest shop or outlet likely to introduce some competition into this market. Both the pub and the hotel, more so, have leveraged this position to the hilt: my very first £5 pint! The staff of both hostelries is cunningly disguised in black skirt or trousers and white blouse or shirts . I mean for heaven's sake a mask and black and white ringed t-shirt would, at least, have given a poor chap a small clue before being set upon by thieves.

One thing's for sure, a big chair is going up against the door tonight, lest we be robbed in our sleep too.

*January 16th – Sunday –* A very lazy start to the day and a completely different view from the window; nothing quite as romantic as the previous week - a car park and the weather grey and grim.

Now there's something most peculiar about this hotel and I can't quite put my finger on what it is. It's pretty much a stripped down proper hotel, lying somewhere between that and one of those Premilodge types. With everything pretty much self-service you'd imagine hardly any staff, but there are loads of them. Perhaps that's it, the anachronism, (word of the week). In a place designed for customer self-sufficiency, there is a surfeit of happy little workers, all busying away but almost completely devoid of customer contact; just there to make all the automatic things work.

I'll spare you the details of the trade show at the Westpoint Showground. Suffice it to say we traipsed the tented corridors in the house of a thousand salesmen and emerged largely unscathed.

Did I tell you the Missus wants a new sofa? I can't really blame her, as the one we most frequently use is threadbare. We have, in our recent travels, visited nearly every furniture showroom in those towns and, remarkably, each one had a sale that ended on the day we visited. There are two such showrooms in close proximity to the hotel in which we are staying. Naturally I congratulated the Missus on her luck for coincidentally selecting such a conveniently placed hotel.

It was then a matter of small chance that, having exited the second of these establishments, empty handed, we came upon a third, right next door to the last. What exquisite joy did I feel, then, when, having entered this temple of recumbent, (she wants a recliner), delight, she happed upon the very thing – the ultimate sofa? Yes, I can feel your empathy oozing through the ether to me.

I'm not exactly sure my elaborate description of the dire consequence of pursuing such an acquisition had any impact on the Missus whatsoever. I think I might have also mentioned that I doubted the dimensions of the beast would fit through our portal. I think I will only know whether, or not, when the delivery van arrives outside our door.

I'm considering having our door narrowed; nothing whatsoever to do with fending off the purchase of a new sofa, clearly, but merely to improve the aesthetic appearance of the shop front. What do you think?

*January 17th – Monday* – TG has pointed out on the main Sennen Cove website that today is Blue Monday – the most miserable day of the year. Au contraire, I say. Never has a day, full of rain and greyness, been so joyous and full of the spirit of life, for we have arrived back home.

We packed our simple belongings and headed for the West as soon as we could gather ourselves together this morning. We even spurned the self-grabbed, plastic breakfast at the hotel, such was our haste, (and a certain natural desire to preserve our well-being), to leave behind the grim big city, its multi-laned highways, the sprawling factories and offices and the towering prices of beer.

Soon we were speeding, (a relative term), down the westward path. On the horizon you could almost see the golden light of our Valhalla, a distant welcoming glow through the teaming rain. With no furniture stores in sight our journey ran, mercifully, uninterrupted.

And, gosh, did it rain in buckets of various capacities until, on the outskirts of PZ, the buckets slowed to egg cups. Through the afternoon there was some respite before the deluge recommenced, with gusty winds, in the early evening and through the night.

The bleddy hound, returned from her stay with the bleddy hound sitter and greeted us with her usual understated enthusiasm. Never have you seen a hound with such scant regard for the presence, or else of her masters. I am sure we are mere conveniences in her life that provide the necessary trappings of existence, such as food and exercise. She was probably a cat in some previous existence.

And so we return to the unmelodramatic existence that is Cove life: the waking up, the walking and feeding of the bleddy hound, the occasional visit to the OS or F&L, the forays on the beaches and the cliffs, all as regular as a beating heart with a slight murmur.

Would we have it any other way?

*January 18th– Tuesday* – There is a fine line between the grimmest of determination and obsession, so I have observed. Me, I come nowhere near it. When determination requires even a modicum of hard labour I shall defer to the nearest store and buy one, if it's purchasable, or do without, or chose an alternative if it's not or too expensive. Shallow, perhaps, but at least I'm not obsessed, (all right, beer aside).

If you want to be determined, especially in an outdoor pursuit, today was a cracking good day for it. Last night's storm was nowhere to be seen, except for a bit of a breeze that persisted all day. The skies were blue with a smattering of scudding clouds and, in a sunny sheltered spot, it was quite warm; ideal, then, for taking the bleddy hound and her gangly mate out for a run around. The beach was out as the tide was mostly in so it was up Mayon Cliff to start with, down Maria's Lane, over Carn Olva, around Velanreath Valley on the west side and down to what was left of the beach and home. There lay the plan, at least. No bitter determination required, just follow our noses and amble along.

But it was determination bordering on obsession, or possibly determined obsessiveness, that gave my well laid plans a kick in the shin. We had almost gained the gate to Maria's Lane, no more than ten minutes into our jaunt, when the gangly one found a bone amongst the heather. There was no amount of calling or walking away that would detract her from her cause. As I walked back to get her, she saw the ruse and ran back down the path, with bone between her teeth, and settled again to feast. Thrice I went to her and thrice she fled from my menace. This was now a battle of wills, of bitter determination and what was worse, she was winning.

As I have alluded previously my experience in the determination field is thin and littered with the detritus of failure. However age and treachery are often no match for youth and, in this case, obsession.

Did I mention that I was once apprenticed as a ghillie in my youth and was celebrated for skills in stalking that would make a Navajo scout blush? Well, I wasn't, but fortunately the disobedient hound didn't know that and I was able to sneak up on her from downwind and collar her.

Once captured, I was able to tear the offending bone from her chomping maw and toss it deep into the undergrowth. I explained that future departures from 'the rules' would result in a sharp introduction of my boot to her bottom, that she clearly took note of.

Marching her smartly up the path again, tethered and repentant, I looked back to seek the location of the bleddy hound who had been remarkably attentive and compliant during this episode. I am sure, dear reader, that you are miles ahead of me, and that it will therefore be of little surprise when I report that the bleddy hound was tail up in the undergrowth, at the spot where the discarded bone had landed. There was no amount of calling or walking away that would detract her from her cause. The sense of irony slapped me across the face like a wet mackerel.

We are fortunate that the bleddy hound, while not devoid of obsessive behaviour, is somewhat more liberal with her obsessions. First she is obsessed with being in company and secondly, if you offer an alternative object of obsession, she will invariably drop the first. Thus by walking out of sight, she followed, and by offering a morsel of cheese she dropped the bone and came close enough to be hooked.

They were as good as gold for the rest of the sojourn. Let's face it; they could have been no worse.

It is a route I haven't undertaken before and the more pleasant for that alone. I knew there was a bench a little down the hill but I wasn't aware that there is an inscription upon it. It is to some beloved chap, now departed, and is of charming wit, "A place he loved after a climb he didn't."

And so to an evening of cards at the OS, (that's Old Success, LM), and a walk there and back under a near full moon, and if I had to be obsessive it would be after nights such as these – crisp and clean, everywhere tinged in bluish light. I'm quite determined about that.

*January 19th – Wednesday* – The good times continue with more blue sky and sunshine. Even that nasty little breeze has dropped. It's not the only thing, the temperature has fallen a little further today and it's a tad chilly out there.

It has to be said that I didn't spend much time outside today. I had my head buried in my computer trying to make sense of the VAT rises on all our stock and on that of the new bits, coming for the new season. Perhaps we should just sell books then we wouldn't have to bother.

Naturally it was too good outside to ignore it for long and, yes, I took the bleddy hound with me, on her own this time as her mate was out. I thought I'd have enough time to run along the beach. I did, but we were playing avoid the tide towards the end as I'd forgotten it was moving into spring tides for the next few days. It was rather pleasant down there, nevertheless, with still some big waves majestically crashing in. I might even have got a bit of a sun tan.

Talking of beaches I see the Irish airplane people are stopping their flights out to Alicante from Newquay, citing the five pound airport development charge – again. Being famed for sparkling wit and repartee, you'd think they could come up with something a bit more original; that one's wearing a bit thin, lads.

I have to say this is going to be a major impact on many people's lives who are now going to be constrained to holidaying at home this year. All right there won't be all that hanging around in airport terminals waiting on air traffic controllers going back to work; then being made to take your shoes off and having your baggage gone through and, of course, the usual language difficulties.

I think I speak for everyone here, that our hearts go out to all those poor souls who are stuck with having to holiday on their own beaches and now won't be able to fly out to the far superior Cornish ones.

*January 20th – Thursday* – It just keeps getting better and better: not a cloud to be seen today and the sunrise was a cracker.

239

Yes, the sparrow and I made a bit of a racket together this morning for the first time in a while. And what important task should drag me from my pit at such an ungodly hour? Well, two actually. First the old jalopy needed some tender love and care to help it through its annual MOT and even as I write my breath is bated awaiting the results, (and the bill). Secondly we had a Lifeboat to launch. An exercise and the first for a while as we waited for sea states to be right and planets to align, you know the sort of thing. 'Twas a little frosty on the slip but all went well and with the sea like a mill pond at low water the recovery was a breeze.

We shore crew types are to report back this evening too.

We have long been threatened with being assessed as a necessary part of our work, most probably to help us comply with health & safety requirements laid down long ago by our European overseers. We fully expect the inspectors to test us on our abilities in the areas of fag rolling, tea making and generally scratching our rears ensuring, of course, we have the appropriate protective clothing and safety procedures in place for such dangerous activities. They may even extend their scrutiny to the lesser areas of our job description such as launching and recovering the Lifeboat.

After such a stressful encounter we were forced to take remedial action by retiring to the OS to soothe our frayed nerves. Head Launcher and I have a certain reputation to uphold at the OS and despite the lure of cheap beer and light music at the F&L we demurred and stayed at the bottom.

I am sorry to report that our already miserable reputations suffered further by coming third in the quiz. We are of the opinion that the other teams were able to proffer a larger bribe than we could collectively muster. It is winter after all.

If you were there that frozen evening you would have been witness to the harrowing sight of two bowed and broken individuals as they wandered out into the night, cast out and vilified. Right too, they had better pull themselves together for next time if they want to be on our team again.

*January 21st – Friday* – My, oh my, yet another near perfect day and after the coldest night so far; I noticed a fair bit of frost and some patches of ice on the circuit this morning.

The Missus had made arrangements with her circle of ladies, to lunch today. It was either brunch, they had or it was a long, long way away - they left at ten o'clock and didn't get back till gone three, laden with bags. I have made a mental note, for future reference, that lunch is code for shopping a lot.

I consoled myself with striking forth with the bleddy hound and her mate out along the considerable expanse of beach. A conversation last night minded me to consider walking around North Rocks and heading for the far end of Gwenver. However when we got to North Rocks it was clear there is a bit of a deep gully reaching in, making it impassable without swimming.

I resolved to do the usual and sat on a rock from which I could throw the ball for said hounds. Quite by chance our neighbours from the back of us rolled up. They don't live here, but when they're down they do like to take the bleddy hound out, which is handy, especially when the shop is open.

It was while we sauntered back across the beach that my pager went off. Not the ideal spot from which to reach the Lifeboat Station in a hurry. It was fortunate that my friends were there, as I was able to leave the hounds with them and set off towards The Beach restaurant, as fast as my little legs could carry me.

It is fair to say that my little legs have seen better days, and running in walking boots and heavy warm clothes does nothing to enhance the experience. The soft sand just about finished me off, and by the time I crawled into the car park there was a high risk of there being a casualty on land, as well as at sea.

It is at times such as these, that the brain gets a little fed up with a consciousness that thinks that continuing to run to the Lifeboat Station is a good idea, and gives it a jolly good kick up the rear. In a flash it was commandeering a car to transport its pathetic container the rest of the journey. If the driver is reading this, you have my undying gratitude.

As it turned out it was the inshore boat that was required for, what was reported as, a skiff in Porthcurno in trouble, whatever one of those is. The boat was gone for less than half an hour and, having checked that all was well, returned with the 'skiff' following on a little while later. I watched it come into the harbour, it was little more than a canoe with a sail.

After such a flurry of excitement I felt it requisite to attend at the F&L in the evening. It was quiet but, in convivial company, 'twas a very pleasant session with a moonlit saunter home.

We know how to knock the socks off a jolly good day down here, you know.

*January 22nd – Saturday* – Oh how tedious; another perfect day. I'm really not sure how much more of this blue sky and sun drenched beach a poor boy can take. You could probably safely bet your last shilling, that we won't have weather like this in August, (the sunny bit, not the sub-zero temperatures).

Our visiting neighbours took the bleddy hound off quite early for a run down the beach. She came back 'some tired', so I took her out again in the afternoon. That'll teach her to go off enjoying herself with other people. It was darned cold down in the harbour, and reminded me of a mental note I made the day before, to bring gloves, which I hadn't.

It was quite busy all day with wandering souls along the road and down on the beaches; a portent of a good year to come you'd hope. We've even had the first of the year's coach party visits. Perhaps I ought to turn out a couple of postcard racks.

Cape Gig was out for much of the day too. If you ever needed a reason to row hard and fast, the freezing air will do it every time. And at least they have a purpose to their rowing; the Gig Races of the year will be upon us soon enough. Less can be said for today's prize winner for completely pointless, heroic achievement. Rebecca Ridgway, bless her, completed her row around Cape Horn in a canoe today in 1992. I mean, why?

And what with the fishing fleet out in numbers The Cove was fair buzzing with busyness; as indeed was the good old F&L in the evening. Although I have only missed two weeks worth of fun and frolic up there, including the pretty full on Help for Heroes night, it seems much, much longer. I shall have to make amends.

And since the moon was still shining forth perhaps I should leave you with this:

> *So we'll go no more a roving*
> *So late into the night,*
> *Though the heart be still as loving,*
> *And the moon be still as bright.*

While only 36 years old when he popped off, Lord Byron packed those few years full of action, mainly of the horizontal sort, it seems. A lesson of one sort or another to us all, I'm sure.

*January 23rd – Sunday* – And no guessing what the weather is like today. More bunches of good people out enjoying it, the gig out early again and the fishing fleet dotted around the bay.

Our neighbours did the dog thing for us, which left me, particularly, without anything whatsoever to do. I don't think I lifted a finger today, zilch, nadda, not one iota of effort did I expend. It was all rather nice actually.

Of course, all this doing nothing, including not doing any shopping does rather lead to a dilemma, especially when you haven't done any food shopping for the best part of a week: what to have for tea?

We resolved this issue by electing to have a Chinese take-away. This, unavoidably, did lead to some expenditure of effort in having to get off my numb behind and drive up to St Just. I was suitably tired out by the time I returned and sore in need of a hearty meal to restore my vitality, but unfortunately we only had a Chinese take-away.

I know you will be appreciating the strength of will I have demonstrated by actually raising myself up, dragging myself across the room to place finger to keyboard for this page; the blood, sweat and tears that have been wrenched from this erstwhile sedentary frame to bring a, probably, uninteresting flow of bon mots to my, certainly, saintly readers. (You'd have to be to eke the slightest satisfaction from today's drivel).

And so to bed, to quote a Diarist who actually had something interesting to write about, and continue to do nothing for a further eight hours.

Phew, I bet you're as glad as I am that that's over with.

*January 24th – Monday* – It all started out very well this morning but there were dark clouds on the horizon. No, not an allegory, there were actually dark clouds on the horizon and by mid-afternoon we had some cloud cover and, lo, wet stuff fell from the sky. I had almost forgotten what rain was.

What with my unforgivable laziness of yesterday I decided to make amends. It was into the big city of PZ after a morning of getting affairs into order. It is at this time of the year that everything automotive falls into line and comes knocking at the door for money.

The big computers at the insurance companies know it, for sure. So does my email inbox that is brimming with seasonal kind offers, alongside the usual ones casting aspersions on my reproductive performance. I don't know where these insurance companies get their information, because every company I have ever used has promised faithfully to vouchsafe my personal information, never to tell another soul. I even had an offer from an Australian sounding company that only insures young ladies. I was tempted to apply for the jape, but we all know that big computers, especially those belonging to insurance companies, don't have a sense of humour.

And neither do those of the government agency that extracts my road fund tax. It seems that if my MOT or insurance is near to expiry it will not issue a new licence online. The Post Office is less fussy and hence one of the reasons for my journey to PZ.

Being once a meticulous project manager I carefully planned to arrive at the metropolis after the lunchtime rush and thus guarantee a queueless run to the Post Office counter. I clearly failed to factor in the large number of retired project managers in PZ as the queue was practically out of the door.

Now the Post Office is run by a clever bunch of chaps. Rather than invest in the wherewithal to ensure such efficiency that there is no queue, they have invested in technology to deluge the queuing masses with advertising. There are no less than four television screens, at cleverly calculated angles, so that wherever you are in the queue you cannot escape their glare. They all run independent of each other, so at certain angles you can take in four different advertisements at the same time. Now that's smart.

Having endured twenty minutes of so of captive brainwashing I arrive at the counter, as near expiry as my van insurance. Here, after cheerily wresting the hard earned shillings from my weak-ened grip, our lady of the counter delivered the coup de grace by suggesting I try Post Office vehicle insurance. Had it been medical insurance I might well have succumbed.

I was heartened, then, when subsequently reaching the bank, that there was very little in the way of a queue. I arrived next in line to a chap who was just concluding a transaction; I queued for all of thirty seconds. You can, therefore, imagine my bemusement when the bank teller apologised for keeping me waiting.

I shall spare you the details of the trip to one of those big supermarkets, that I detest, and my stupidity of trying to acquire a television booster at an electronics chain store when I bought it with ease, and probably cheaper, at an independent store down on the promenade that I should have gone to first.

Needless to say I was fare worn out by the time I returned home. As I gazed at the plethora of emails promising to enliven my virility I did wonder if they too were privy to the fact I needed to renew my road fund licence.

*January 25th – Tuesday* – An inclement day, to say the least, and cold too, (or is that already included within the bounds of 'inclement'?).

I had to do a mercy dash into town, well more dash and not so much mercy, really. In the meanwhile the Missus took the bleddy hound and her mate out along the drenched beach for a saunter.

When I returned I found myself locked out. Now, what would you do locked out of your own home on a rainy day? Yup, I repaired to the OS for some succour and a quick libation upon which I spotted a lone soul with two hounds out on the expansive sands.

Fortunate, then, that I had remembered to pocket my boys' own semaphore flags, fashioned from glued together lolly sticks and two pairs of the Missus bloomers. I had already discounted deployment of my heliograph, made from milk bottle tops stuck to a dinner plate, on account of there being no sun.

After exhausting myself, largely through spelling mistakes and forgetting the signal for drink, I resorted to calling her on the mobile telephone. It worked a treat and we enjoyed a small refreshment while the dogs sat and smelled a bit.

Now, before I tell you that we had a marathon card session at the OS tonight and, that through some miracle of deceit and sleight of hand, I managed to come second, I must broach some grave news - the mystical Far East is calling to me, or more accurately is shouting and stamping it's foot in the manner of a petulant child. I must journey out again for a few days and thus this page will remain empty and devoid of further update until my return.

While I understand this to be a bitter blow to some, or more likely, a blessed respite for most of you, do try and contain your grief or happiness in my absence.

You may take this as a threat or a promise according to your need: I'll be back.

*January 26th – Wednesday* – And so begins our self-imposed exile to the far reaches of the peninsular – the other far reach, you know, in the other direction where lie the in-laws.

It begins in the grimmest manner – a visit to our bank manager. This is an annual event, apparently, although he was happy with a brief telephone call last year and in previous years he has visited us. I'm guessing it takes too long for him to count his bonus these days to make it to down to West Penwith. Nevertheless he is a very nice man, (let's face it, there is an outside chance he might read this), and worth every penny.

I should explain to you the seating arrangements in our van, on journeys such as these that involve carting the bleddy hound along. Before take off we have to fit the dog seat. This is an inflatable booster seat so that she can see out of the window. The covering is made from the finest Scalamandre velvet and finished by dusky maidens, (of the virginal kind, obviously), who sewed on the Maltese hand-woven lace that decorates the piece or would have if the Missus could have found one like that. Nonetheless, it almost certainly cost a fortune.

The seat takes up the majority of the bench in the front of the van, squeezing the Missus against the door and making it nigh on impossible to change gear. The bleddy hound is in such awe of this homage to her personal comfort that she prefers to sit on the Missus's lap.

There was no sign, when we left The Cove, of the high winds we had been warned of the previous evening. It was just as well, as I think we had reached Wadebridge when I remembered that I neglected to tie down our wheelie bin. The way things are going I probably didn't need to; if it's as cold back home as it is here it will be frozen to the ground.

So with my beer chilling in the garden we settled for an entire evening of the National Television Awards. For those of you that would deem such an evening as the devilish offspring of terror and tedium and would prefer to pull out your fingernails with a curling tong, all I can say is you have not experienced the alternative: three hours of back to back *Last of the Summer Wine*.

*January 27th – Thursday* – There are some things that are just so unexpected that they can turn your whole day upside down.

Things to do in a North Devon county town on a cold, grey day in January – yup, you go shopping. Actually this was my idea. I needed to buy a book. Just because I have yet to be subject to hours of repeats of a certain long running TV series there's no need to be complacent and tempt providence.

I had planned to go alone, to amble around at my leisure and take my time selecting a suitable read. As it happened the Missus and her Mum tagged along. No problem I thought, they both have previous for full on shopping marathons, and was comforted with this certain knowledge that I had plenty of time to buy a book and settle down with a pie and a pint in a local hostelry and wait for the shopaholics to return.

Er, no! Despite tricking me with a three hour parking ticket they were done and dusted inside an hour and I hadn't even reached the bookstore. I was so upset I bought a pair of wellies and some walking boot socks and then left one of the socks in the welly boot shop. Oh, and I did buy a book!

Women doing all their shopping in less than an hour! We'll see chip shops selling Vietnamese catfish next, for heavens sake.

Well, as it happens, I was going to share this with you last night but I deferred, to ensure there was no lasting damage before commending it to you.

There is a chip shop around the corner with, yes, Vietnamese catfish on the menu, I jest not, except they call it basa just in case you might be put off. Surely not!

Given that I am still preparing Diary pages the following day, consumption of this exotic beast did me no harm at all. In fact I can heartily recommend it. No doubt when this news breaks the boys at Newlyn will be packing their sandwiches for a bit of a longer run than usual.

*January 28th – Friday* – The day started out blue and sunny but darned cold. The Missus had planned a trip down to Exeter for a craft fair, which was exactly where I didn't want to be. It did mean, however I was left without transport of an automotive kind.

I have mentioned before that the area in which we are situated is sadly short of places to exercise dogs. However, since our last visit I have re-examined the locale with the aid of a satellite, which showed that a wooded valley runs up behind the house for nearly a mile with what, suspiciously, looked like a path running into it.

With few alternatives I donned my walking boots with my recovered second sock and set out to explore with bleddy hound in tow. Sure enough a path led into the, mainly larch, wood and all started out well until .. it just stopped. Or more accurately it crossed a bridge and headed back in the direction we had just come.

It had taken less than ten minutes to traverse this small section of the valley. It was as if the work persons who had fashioned the path, probably by stamping up and down a lot, had got fed up of stamping up and down a lot by tea-break on the first morning and not come back.

So short was this walk I dragged the poor girl around again. She was less than impressed the first time and the second was simply a chore. I would have gone around a third time but she was having none of it and made it clear by heading for home.

There was some benefit derived from this minor stroll – when we arrived home the closing credits of a certain old television series was playing.

*January 29th – Saturday* – My Missus has a little weakness. No really, there is a flaw in that porcelain veneer of perfection. She likes railway journeys.

Well, there was me looking for something different to do today. In the back of my mind I remembered hearing that there was a bit of a walk along the river towards Instow, from Barnstable railway station. It is the old railway track that has been made into a path, from Barnstable all the way through to Bideford and now forms part of the Tarka Trail.

Why not, thought my fit and active brain. I'd take the dog and wherever I'd got to by the time the others had finished whatever it was they were doing, they'd give me a call and collect my well exercised bones from whatever point I'd reached by that time.

This was a well thought through and infallible plan until the Missus saw that a train was waiting in Barnstable station after she had packed me off on my way and, unbeknown to me, decided that it would be top hole to take the parents-in-law on a trip down to Exmouth.

I'd estimated that Instow, some seven miles hence, would be a laughable target and, in the worst case if I actually managed to get there, I'd find a suitable pub there to rest my stretched sinews until I was recovered.

Ho, ho! The call I received a mile into my journey said that the little train journey my adopted family had embarked on would take them until 4:30 pm to complete. It was now only noon. I'm sure you can see where this is going.

With no hope of recovery until at least five o'clock, I simply had to keep going or souse myself in a pub for three hours: a happy thought, but not with the bleddy hound in tow.

Five miles in I noticed the typical signs of a blister arriving on my right heel. The boots I have are excellent, they have served me well for twenty years, but are not designed for a metalled path. So at the next rest point I took the opportunity to tie them up tight, such that the likelihood of blood passing my ankle was negligible. Randolph Fiennes would have been proud. A foot going black. Oops there goes a toe. Never mind, another nine left.

By the time we reached Instow the bleddy hound and I had formed a strong bond, I had dragged her the first five miles and now she was dragging me the back five to our revised destination, Bideford. Such was our camaraderie we shared a roll-up and told each other dirty jokes before we drew our aching, (she will contend that), frames to the west and to the end of the cut path.

I have travelled better paths, seen better views, walked longer and less wearied, but this was a sojourn to be savoured. Ten miles, she and I trod and ten miles we conquered desperation, pain and suffering and she still wanted to play bleddy chase the chicken when we got back home.

Have you ever seen *Ice Cold in Alex*? You should, just for the scene where after miles of desert they arrive in a bar and get served an ice cold beer. That was us, her and I, although she demurred on the beer.

A gritty sort of pub, and the last place you would want to take out a copy of *The Times* to read, despite having used the last ounces of your being to acquire a copy, and a pair of reading glasses, (I forgot my real ones), because you thought it would be quiet and you'd need something to read.

Never mind, that John Mills moment will never leave me. In fact, next time I'm here, I might do it again. Although I might start a bit closer and leave the bleddy hound at home.

*January 30th – Sunday* – I have returned and just to prove it I am here. Fresh home from foreign parts as the rocket scientists among you will have divined by noticing four Diary entries dumped, unceremoniously upon you, en bloc.

It appears I missed a Lifeboat shout on Friday, which was irritating, and I was not there for the Lifeboat SOS Day on Sunday either, details of which, no doubt, I will be appraised of in the fullness of time. Without a launch in 1790 neither of these events is likely to have happened. The original, the first purpose built Lifeboat, was launched on the Tyne today in that year, the brainchild of William Wouldhave and built by Henry Greathead.

The return journey was uneventful, though I spent most of it with a dipping sun in my eyes. However tortuous the travelling may be from time to time, at least it is heading in the right direction.

It happens sometimes, that when researching items and ideas for these hugely informative and educational pages, one haps upon matters of such interest the Diarist is oft carried away, and perhaps should be. Such a thing happened when I went to look up the background to a memorial I saw on the east side of Bideford Bridge, at the end of my walk on Saturday.

The memorial is that of John Richard Pine-Coffin, a name that had some potential for a rib or two among the words of this Diary. However, when I looked up some references, what I found was a military family whose combined exploits read like a boys' own book of derring-do.

I offer you one example, for fear of boring those less interested and for turning these pages into something that they are not, not to mention copyright theft. If you want to read more the Internet is littered with this family's ripping yarns. This comes from an obituary of Lt Col John Pine-Coffin from the *Telegraph* newspaper – I have paraphrased pending permission from the newspaper:

Pine-Coffin was sent to Nassau in 1963 to investigate Cuban exiles infiltrating one of the Bahamas off-islands. He was mis-landed in thick mud and deciding that his only chance of progression was to strip off, did so.

Wearing only his red Para' hat and a pair of flippers and covered with mud he was confronted by a band of armed Cubans. Being the British sort of chap he was he told them that they were trespassing on British soil and should surrender.

The following morning the Royal Marines came in to rescue him and were somewhat astounded to find Pine-Coffin and his radio operator in a clearing with the Cubans, disarmed and surrendered. An OBE followed.

He was, of course, laid to rest in an oak casket.

Now where was I? Ah, yes, The Sennen Cove Diary.

11:30pm: took bleddy hound out for last walk, wickedly cold, fear of bits falling off, returned home, sharpish.

*January 31st – Monday* – As you probably will have read there was a bit of plundering in the harbour last night with three outboard motors being taken. It has happened before but thankfully not a usual event for this neck of the woods.

It was still darned cold first thing but the sky was blue in between the clouds and a fair bit of sun shining through. So good in fact the Missus took to her heels led on by the bleddy hound and her mate down the big beach.

After fixing a light on the van I followed her down in my new wellies. Half way across the beach it felt like a summer's day, or perhaps rather better than some of the summer days we've had recently. We sat for some time, sunning ourselves on the rocks at the far end. How lovely it was.

Best I tell you about how lovely it is down there because you won't hear from anyone else this year. The powers in Westminster have told the slowly dissolving South West Regional Development Agency not to spend any money on tourist advertising this year, so they haven't.

On the other hand you might hear quite a bit about Yorkshire this year. The same Westminster chaps have sent Yorkshire Welcome, the SWRDA equivalent, a nice big £10 million cheque to extol the virtues of going up t' North.

Now I'm not going to be childish and say something like you'd need money like that to put Yorkshire in a good light. That would indeed be petty and unnecessary and I'm sure the nice chaps up there are worth every penny.

I don't know what we've done to upset them, up there in the big city. Surely they can't still be harbouring resentment over that little misunderstanding we had in 1497.

Penniless or not we'd hope our good reputation will stand up without further advertisement. My only sincere hope in all this is that Yorkshire Welcome don't fritter this princely sum away on clever television leverage. The last thing the world needs is another series of *Last of the Summer Wine*.

# February

*February 1st – Tuesday* – Heck, that's a bit scary isn't it? February already, which roughly means another six weeks before the shop opens again. We do try not to count off the days because they seem to go a bit faster, which is a paradox, as when we count them off until we close, they go slower.

Still, we can still enjoy every day as it comes, even one that started out as misty as this one did. There seemed to be a lot of brightness shining through the cloud and by early afternoon it had blossomed into a mild, blue sky day.

You can't not go down to the beach on a day like this so, with hounds in hand, I did. The tides are all wrong this week so we only went as far as Carn Keys, the black huts just above the beach, and sat on the rocks. Well I did anyway and watched the crashing waves crash, which I've found crashing waves often do, while the hounds ran around and dug holes.

It must sound idyllic if you're sitting in a stuffy office somewhere reading this. I could tell you there is a price to pay for all this nice stuff to make you feel better, but I really can't think of one at the moment, sorry.

Cards, of course, in the evening down at the OS; I've found myself in the play offs for third place next week. This is only by dint of the fact that not all the players are signed up members of the league, not that I'm any sort of riverboat card sharp. Naturally I do keep a Derringer in my sock just in case.

On late arrivals back home the bleddy hound brooks no argument that I should take her out for a run. I normally try to get her to drag me towards the beach, which is quicker and requires no torch. She was having none of it tonight and ran off in the other direction up through the RNLI car park and through Coastguard Row, which generally does require a torch, which I didn't have.

It's also not easy keeping up with a sock full of Derringer.

*February 2nd – Wednesday* – I slept in the manner of a felled tree trunk last night. In fact it was only the trilling of the Missus's alarm clock that roused me sufficiently to notice that it hadn't roused her. Why she had set it in the first place is beyond me as it performs little service to her.

It would seem that we had missed the threatened rain and it was merely grey and damp when I took the bleddy hound around for her morning constitutional.

Not long after I returned, and still early in the day, I received a telephone call from the chaps that insured my parents-in-law's oven saying they had reconsidered their position and would now replace the broken item.

It was only yesterday that I despatched a letter to them after they had refused to pay up on some grounds buried in the small print of their contract. I could not possibly reveal the methods employed within the letter, the subtle but keen turns of phrase, eliciting such a speedy and effective response.

Needless to say my pen is for hire, at very reasonable rates, for all manner of contractual difficulty whether the contract be written or implied. Errant suppliers that don't supply, service providers that fail to provide and spouses/partners/girl-boyfriends, (delete as appropriate), who, perhaps, may need encouragement or retirement are all within the remit.

Letters may be handwritten, typed or, for a small premium, crafted from the cuttings of newspapers and magazines as required. I might have suggested no win, no fee but I find that so cheap and tacky for a superior service such as mine.

Needless to say if I am not successful there will be some nuance in the small print that means I will most certainly keep your cash.

*February 3rd – Thursday* – Up to a rather sparkly sort of day today but with a stealthy little breeze that crept up in force throughout the day.

It was kind of hard to notice it really, it was more the things it was doing. Down on the beach, with the bleddy hound, obviously, (as if I could get away with going there without her) the thrown ball was going miles with little effort. It did give me a little moment, though.

Amidst a stormy sea there was something of a quiet patch into which I threw the ball. The bleddy hound duly followed. I had thrown it a tad further than I intended and she was soon swimming. The ball, however, was veering into a much more volatile patch, so much so that I lost sight of her at one point. Thankfully she is a strong little swimmer and, aided by a thumping wave up her rear she was soon storming ashore.

I, of course, had utter faith in her ability but for gawd's sake don't tell the Missus. She'd have apoplexy followed swiftly by some sort of bloody retribution upon my good person.

And, talking of retribution, we won the quiz tonight, HL and us, beating the best brains in The Cove and some visitors.

Whaddya mean, hollow victory, then?

*February 4th – Friday* – What a grey day again. The sea is fair boiling and banging over the lower parts of Pedn-men-du and up the cliffs at Aire Point: a lovely sight from a distance.

The bleddy hound and I cut lonely figures on the beach again. It's difficult not to be drawn down there, especially when the tides are being kind, although we did keep a respectful distance from the water today. We even avoided being sucked into the OS for a livener on the way home – it's a big and long one tonight up the F&L so I thought I'd better keep my powder dry.

Yes, today is the start of the Six Nations Rugby Union Championship and England are kicking off by beating, I mean playing, a bunch of chaps with amusing sing-songy voices and a long tradition for working underground; no, not the seven dwarves – Wales.

We thought we'd celebrate the event with a meal up there first with our neighbours, which vouchsafes me a lift up there, always a bonus, and some soakage, essential.

During the dark days of winter the F&L do something called Fiver Friday: a choice of steak & chips or fish & chips for five pounds. Now, the F&L have elected to follow the lead of that diminutive television cooking chap, Huge Brackenly Wherewithall, and replace the traditional cod with pollock, a favourite of mine, so I had it. I was not disappointed, in fact I was very much appointed as it was knee tremblingly good; an 'ansum' sized coupled of lumps with crisp batter and not a drip of excess oil in sight.

All this and the England rugby team kicked bottom, in the most satisfying manner.

What more could a poor boy ask for on a breezy winter's day?

*February 5th – Saturday* – The sea is still being big and brash and the sky is still being dull and grey and the wind is still being high and mighty. The waves were fair thumping over the harbour wall and half way across the beach such was their ferocity.

You'd think the harbour would be pretty much sheltered from a beefy south westerly wouldn't you? By some quirk of nature it was whipping from top to bottom at low water. The poor bleddy hound, being a tad closer to the ground that most of us, wasn't entirely amused with the sand blasting in her face.

Later in the afternoon we were treated to some mizzle mixed up with the wind blown surf already in the air. All in all a grand day for the high stool, so that's what I did and shuffled off down to the OS to watch some more rugby.

It seems the OS has jumped on the 'fish fight' bandwagon, that of Large Leafy Witlessness alluded to yesterday, with posters in the window. It wasn't immediately apparent how this support is manifested, as there was haddock on the specials' board. I did ask the bar staff and one of the kitchen porters but they didn't know either. Anyway, the poster looks very nice in the window.

After all that rugby watching and intellectual debate at the bar I was quite worn out and returned home for a bit of a rest and some tea before striking out again for the usual F&L bash.

What tenacity, what faithfulness to the cause. There will, no doubt, be a blue plaque on the wall after I'm gone.

Another g&t please, landlord!

*February 6th – Sunday* – Dragged my sorry frame from bed late this morning as you might have guessed from the tardy posting of yesterday's Diary entry. Can't imagine why I felt a little on the listless side, maybe they're putting something in the water these days.

It was the Missus who suggested it. I was all for being the epitome of temperance today; after all I had single-handedly vouchsafed the financial well being of both local alehouses for the foreseeable future in one afternoon. So you might well imagine my heavy head, I mean heart, when she proposed a Sunday lunch at the F&L.

Being the soul of romantic indulgence that I am, I had no choice but to cede to her gastronomic whim. And darned fine it was too and for around a fiver you really couldn't knock it.

After dinner the Missus reckoned it would be a very fine idea to walk the bleddy hound back down to The Cove. That is for me to walk the bleddy hound back down The Cove while she drove the van back. A kind of retribution for me enjoying myself so much yesterday, perhaps.

The weather had brightened up considerably and that punchy breeze had much diminished. It really was quite a pleasant wander along the coastpath from Land's End with a bit of a bouncy sea on my left and the bright moors on the right. It was also a fitting test of my legs after last week's punishing trip. Things went well, but at three miles per hour there was a bit of knee wobble. It could have been a balancing problem, through, an ill placed roast potato, perhaps. Hard to tell, really.

And last today an empty room. It seems Mr Gary Moore has left the planet.

*February 7th – Monday* – Although starting out grey and misty, bits of blue started showing through by late morning, turning an otherwise ordinary day, into and ordinary day with a bit of sunshine.

It was the sort of day you'd take two dogs and run them up through Vellandreath, along the coast path and into Gwenver.

In an amazing conspiracy with Nature I looked out across the bay and thought: it's the sort of day you'd take two dogs and run them up through Vellandreath, along the coast path and into Gwenver. So I turned to the Missus and enquired, "Missus, cast your good eye out hence and tell me is this not the sort of day to take the bleddy hound and her mate next door and, for a change, run up through Vellandreath, along the coast path and into Gwenver?"

She looked out across the bay and replied, "Husband, you speak with good and sound heart, for a change, (she never said 'for a change' but I could see it in her bad eye). It is an excellent sort of day to take my 'ansum dog and her equally loving mate next door and run them up through Vellandreath, along the coast path and into Gwenver. And what is more, good spouse, I shall don my stout walking boots and accompany thee hence."

It will come as no surprise to the more astute reader that, on a complete whim, we decided to take the two dogs and run them up through Vellandreath, along the coast path and into Gwenver.

Somewhat spoiling the light mood it was a disappointment to see the amount of dog's doo along the footpath. If your dog heads off into the rough ground, fair do's, so to speak, but how can you justify not picking up from the path itself. If we dog owners and hounds are barred, wholesale, from the beach this summer it will be of little wonder, with owners of scant regard to good sense.

So with hop, skip and several jumps we descended the rocky

drop into Gwenver. It has been some while since we've been there. Its peace and solitude at this time of year are to be savoured.

Now, if you're not keen on retracing your steps up the rocky incline, as the Missus wasn't, then there are only two ways out of Gwenver. One is up the cliff behind which is steep and laboursome. Even Edmund Hilary wouldn't argue with that, largely, I imagine, because he is deceased. The other is round North Rocks and only then at low spring tide, unless you have some mountain goat in your ancestry and fancy climbing over the boulders.

Nevertheless, the Missus was keen to explore in that direction.

We had timed our visit to coincide, roughly, with low water but were a tad late. As we worked our way around the rocks the tide pushed in an exploratory finger cutting off our retreat for a moment.

It was not so much the fear of being trapped by the incoming tide but the ignominy and embarrassment and, in no small measure, the light-hearted ribbing for the rest of one's days, of living down a rescue by Lifeboat and/or Coastguard that drove us back.

Safely back on Gwenver we took time to admire the tranquillity of our condition before heading back up the rocky climb, along the footpath and across the beach.

For a second time today the Missus caused me to be surprised, for it was she that suggested a detour via the bar of the OS. It was a very fitting end to a ripping little adventure and most welcome refreshment.

They are offering some inducement to dine there by handing out vouchers. We may well take up the kind offer tomorrow evening, after all, how could we in sincerity recommend, (or not), a meal down there to our visitors without having tried it first.

You will now, no doubt, be in a state of fascinated suspension, with abated taste buds at the ready for my detailed critique. I urge you now to go read some Gill, Coren or venerable Winner as after tomorrow they shall be mere jetsam in my wake.

*February 8th – Tuesday* – Such is the popularity of the Diary in the pervasive ether that is the Internet these days, that I am constantly bombarded by requests by other website owners to link to them, well at least their websites.

The latest is a rather coy little purveyor of ladies undergarments situated in Scottsdale, Arizona. It is not so much the geographic separation, or that the goods are somewhat diverse from our own that makes a potential link incongruous, but more that the garments in question are not designed for ladies, at least not in the anatomical sense of the definition.

This puts me in mind of another request from a week or two ago. It was a young lady, (an anatomical one, as far as I could discern), who runs a website all about Cornwall and places where you might stay here. The site is based in Yorkshire. It is full of interesting facts, useful if you wish to visit here, such as The Round House Gallery is at Land's End and that the Curio Shop, (now only web based), is a toy shop in Penzance alongside Lamorna's Farmers Market.

The Old Boathouse, now thankfully de-listed, was a fine shop in Penzance selling local produce, gifts and home to the Sennen Cove Dairy where you can get delicious local ice cream!

I look forward to visiting Yorkshire again one day. The view from the top of Snowdon is awe inspiring, I believe and Isambard Kingdom Stephenson's steam suspension bridge over the Tyne should not be missed.

Having looked out of the window I established that only a complete fool would take a dog on the beach in that wind blown rain. As the bleddy hound, her mate and I reached the far end we also established that I must be the only one in the village.

Well I did promise you that I would emulate a superior food critic today apropos of our meal at the OS tonight. So here it is.

Vanessa couldn't make it, so I took the Blonde. I had prearranged to land our helicopter on the lawn but as luck would have it, they haven't got one. I was suitably put out, as an establishment in this price bracket should surely have one, or at the very least a landing pad on the roof.

As I always prefer to have my back to the bar and those awful working type people, I instructed the maitre d' to find us a suitable table. Unfortunately it was made of brown wood and faced a rather irritating print of some other working type people pulling fish out of basket, or some other rather tiresome task.

I chose the sweet & sour chicken with a side of whitebait and the Blonde had the steak. I fancy the chicken was rather dowsed in something Uncle Benjamin had a hand in, and the whitebait almost certainly came to find us from Iceland. It was wholesome and edible but would have been much better had the chef rolled the fish in seasoned flour and egg himself, and used the time opening the jar to create a simple sauce for the chicken instead. The Blonde said the steak was very nice.

And I would add a little Giles Coren but I simply don't have the space.

So there you have it. I'm expecting a call from the Guardian/Telegraph/Times at any moment. I just hope they send me somewhere nice to eat, with a helipad, naturally.

*February 9th – Wednesday* – Grey and damp out there again. Just the day for a picnic, we reasoned.

We have, for a long time, wanted to wander around Drift Reservoir as it looks like a rather good place to wander and, for once, nowhere near the sea. There is not much information on the Internet or anywhere else about the path that is quite visible from satellite. Not surprising really as the sign that says "No Unauthorised Access" isn't visible from a few miles up.

We only found it having packed our sumptuous lunch and the two hounds and ventured out there. Apparently, we found out later, there is a little bit of woodland at the western shore that is accessible, but the path is quite difficult to follow.

So, packing our disappointment alongside our comestibles we headed back west and regrouped in the car park at Land's End. The weather was clearing a bit and as the dogs chased a few rabbits we took luncheon, of course, with lashings of ginger beer.

Not 'zackly the high adventure we had anticipated. I let the Missus drag the bleddy hound and mate back home via the cycle path while I drove back.

I had developed a hankering for a bit of beef pie while up at LE, quite why will forever remain a mystery. A chance conversation in the shop at the top extended this to a hankering for a bit of beef and stilton pie, homemade, naturally.

Having found a recipe I despatched myself to St Just for provisions including flour for the pastry. The greengrocers had flour that was labelled as 'ethical'. It would have been much more fun to use unethical flour but unfortunately they didn't have any.

Have you ever tried to make your own puff pastry? Don't. Especially using a recipe that is clearly wrong. You would have thought that an ethical flour would have refused to join in on such a travesty, otherwise what's the point?

There is lots of marinating and waiting for pastry to rest, (rest? It hasn't done anything), so this culinary delight, (possibly), is for tomorrow evening. I shall let you know if we end up with beans on toast.

So as the struggling chef of eternity, watches his mix stick hopelessly to the pastry board of time, and the rolling pin of fate clocks him round the back of the head, it's time to say goodnight.

*February 10th – Thursday* – Elements of life can be a disappointment at times.

The aging gunslinger of the old West would naturally expect a procession of young guns queuing up to test his mettle. Did he still have his edge?

Head Launcher and I rolled into Dodge Sennen Cove and settled at the bar of the OS Saloon well aware we may be hunted men. After our definitive quiz win last week, we were tense. Our fingers floated dangerously over our ball point holsters; our senses primed for the slightest sound of hoof on tarmac in the car park.

It was early yet, we agreed. High nine o'clock was still a little way off but we could hear the whistle of the PZ express in the distance. A single bead of sweat hung daringly on HL's eyebrow. He flicked it off into the furthest spittoon; you could hardly see his hand move.

The barman nervously polished his whisky glass. Unusual, we thought, this is the OS after all.

HL and I looked at each other, our eyes narrow as slits in a pasty. Wordlessly we tossed back another red-eye and slammed our glasses on the bar. The barman refilled them instantly, well instantly after twenty minutes of recording his last five minutes of inactivity on Facepage.

The air hung heavy from the smoke of cheroot, or would have done if smoking in Dodge hadn't been outlawed some years back. Sheriff Brown had a lot to answer for, that's for sure, and maybe he was since Marshall Cameron put him up in Boot Hill, who's to know.

We eyed the clock. The interminable tick tock of the old wall clock was missing. The landlord had replaced it with a battery operated one and completely ruined a perfectly good cliché.

The door to the top bar swung open. HL and I spun around, every sinew singing, every muscle tense and quivering. Ah, an old timer so close to an untimely end. He had been one of the lucky ones back then; narrowly missed a music round sizzler and had hidden behind a bar stool for the sudden death playoff, that had seen HL and I nail a bunch of high rollers from Tombstone St Just.

That was it; the time had come and gone. Nothing. No one had showed to challenge the best quizsters in the West. Time to make a break for it.

Butch HL: Ready? OK. When we get out there and we get to the horses, whatever happens, remember one thing . . . hey, wait a minute!

Sundance Me: What?

Butch HL: You didn't see Coxswain out there did you?

Sundance Me: Coxswain? No!

Butch HL: Oh good. For a moment there I thought we were in trouble.

[Both run out of the building, only to be met with the sound of quick-fire unanswerable questions.]

*February 11th – Friday* – A grey and misty day but bright in parts and mild too.

Things were all set for a laid back and lazy day when the neighbour phoned to get the Missus out for one of their lunches. I'm sure I have explained before that these are the longest lunches ever and involve the loss of pounds – and we're not talking slimming.

That left me with two dogs, a bright mild day and miles of empty beach. No prizes, therefore, for guessing where I found myself for a couple of hours of fun and frolic.

Flicking through my emails I noticed that I had been invited, by the St Just Chamber of Commerce to a free training day. This is to enhance my committee skills and is delivered by a body called the Cornwall Voluntary Sector Forum who are doing it on behalf of the PCDT, (whoever that might be – ah, found it, Penwith Communities Development Trust, possibly).

They are funded by Take Part Cornwall that is managed by the Cornwall Voluntary Sector Forum. Take Part Cornwall is part of the wider Take Part Pathfinder Programme, which is funded by the Department for Communities and Local Government and managed by the Community Development Foundation.

So that looks like five quango type bodies; so nice to see all that fat being cut out of the public sector. Trying to be positive, I'd say these guys are probably the ultimate experts in delivering a course on committees; heck, I'm impressed that they delivered anything at all.

I'm not sure that I'll be attending. It was a bit short notice for me to get my committee together to decide which one of me will go.

*February 12th – Saturday* – Bright white fluffy clouds, bit of blue sky and a big surfy sea and what do we have here? Breakers Café open for a bit of a trial run ahead of half term. Ah, the season is almost upon us and we must gird our fridge magnets, dust off our nick nacks and buff up our balls: open four weeks hence.

It will be, once again, safe to bring unruly children into the shop this year. You have Ramsay McDonald to thank for that. In 1932 he introduced a bill to raise the age of criminal responsibility and ban the whipping of the under 14s; a sad day in history.

I spent this afternoon indulging in sport. It is little wonder that I am the epitome of health and fitness; it is, after all, a fair walk down to the OS to watch the rugby. I demurred on watching the second game as I was fair worn out after nine tries. I need to reserve some energy for the bun fight up at the F&L tonight too.

Some bands seem to gather a following beyond their not inconsiderable talent. It appears that SKA groups tend to have more than their fair share of this phenomenon, for example Pond Life and, the band playing tonight, Rudie's Message.

We were pinned to the bar for much of the evening, (not necessarily a bad thing), by the assembled crowd vying for mosh pit supremacy. The joint was fair jumping, even after a well attended quiz night the previous evening.

Then a nice little wet walk home. Ideal.

*February 13th – Sunday* – They would have had us believe that today was piddling down with rain, grim and nasty. Not so. The rain belted through overnight and is currently sitting over those heathen parts north of Launceston.

Still we've been left with a breezy and bright day and a rather big sea running; the waves are fair 85 p'ing in, (they would have been pounding in but cut-backs, you know).

It would be unkind to say I'm a creature of habit, but Pavlov, had he been around today, probably would have written another theory if he'd met me. Anyway, I do like to watch selected matches of the Six Nations propped up against the bar of a friendly ale house. This time Ireland put up a rather ferocious battle against the French, but unfortunately lost by a whisker in a rather exciting game.

I met a very pleasant chap and his Missus during the game. They hail from the far South Coast where he is a Lifeboat man and a presenter for a BBC radio station there. I didn't think he was that bad looking.

Having had conversations with my chum about Lifeboat shouts we duly had one at around 6:00 pm this evening. A fishing boat in trouble off Tol Pedn, anchored in this rather foul sea. The launch had to be carefully timed to hit the water between large swells and the boat bounced off into heavy seas. She won't be back tonight, that's for sure. In fact it's not looking that good for recovery for the next couple of days.

Time to settle down with my zip up slippers and a nice mug of cocoa.

Goodnight.

*February 14th – Monday* – St Valentine's day; or rather just plain old Valentine, perhaps. There were several martyrs of the same name but very little is known about the one whose feast day this probably is. Likely a Christian priest in the early days when Rome hadn't quite grasped that religion could be a more effective a tool in the furtherance of world domination than a big army; not to mention the commercial benefits; did the poor begger in. Bits of him can be found in Rome and Dublin, strangely.

Initially there was no notion of romance unless you count Claudius II's love of knocking off vicars. No, it is very likely Mr Chaucer concocted the connection with, "For this was on Seynt Valentynes day, Whan every foul cometh theere to chese his make ..". Apart from being the first dyslexic poet he was also quite influential and the association of Valentine's Day with romance stuck.

So who am I to buck such a long established trend? I took myself off for a romantic shopping trip, by myself obviously, to the metropolis. Why romantic? Because I spurned the advances of the big chains and shopped locally, well locally if you live in PZ, which seems quite a romantic notion these days.

I know I've said it before and am in grave danger of being ranked among the long haired, sandal wearing, tree huggers, (without the long hair, any hair actually), but there is much to commend the little shop. Chief among these is service, by and large, with good products coming a close second. Regardless of the hype there isn't a great deal of difference in price either and in many cases, it's cheaper. So there, I've said it, with apologies to long haired, sandal wearing, tree huggers everywhere but you've really got to work on that image.

More romance again later, this time down on the beach with the hounds. That sea was  still pretty tremendous and even an hour after high water it was still doing a passable impression of coming in. There was the odd shower about but largely bright and beautiful. See, desperately romantic.

I did, at last, capitulate and indulged in some sort of social intercourse with the Missus. Soft, I know, I just hope that it's not habit forming.

There is a momentary drop in the swell early tomorrow morning, a small enough window to perhaps recover the Lifeboat.

So it's early to bed tonight. Good job too. I am quite wore out after a day advancing the cause of little shops everywhere and saving the planet to boot and wringing the last gossamer threads of romance from my dark and cynical being.

Oh, I almost forgot. Congratulations to Jess and Tim who got engaged yesterday. You see, that's what all that romantic nonsense leads to, the darned young fools.

*February 15th – Tuesday* – An early start this morning to catch that dip in the sea state so that we could recovery the Lifeboat; worked a treat and she's sitting ready.

Some heavy showers passing through today but brightening up some in the afternoon. The sea came back with a vengeance; climbing half way up Aire Point and crashing around Pedn-men-du it attracted quite a few watchers.

Another big adventure today as I forayed out beyond the comfort zone and into Hayle. Our counter top collection needed to be delivered to St Julia's Hospice which  I discovered was the worst sign-posted hospice in the country. Still, got there in the end and afterwards revived myself with a Philps pasty. As the rain hammered against the van panels I tuned into Radio Pasty.

They have a bit where they tell you what's on around Cornwall. For your delectation I can inform you that Quintrell Downs Old Mining Society are holding a talk tonight on mining development. It is to be held in the ground floor meeting room of the Town Hall; if all goes well the meeting will conclude in the cellar of the Tinners Arms next door!

Short lived cards night tonight, mainly because I lost but also because I am getting up at silly o'clock to take the Missus to catch the early train. She is going on a retreat for a few days in the big, big city with her mate.

I will, of course, endeavour to hide my pitiful demeanour and maintain the Diary with good heart. It won't be easy, I can tell you. The all night partying and the attentive dancing girls can be very distracting, so I've been told.

*February 15th – Wednesday* – It was up before dawn even had a hairline fracture to take the Missus to the station. Rather cleverly she had sent all her packing on so she didn't have to drag her luggage around Harrods, Fortnum & Mason and to high tea at Claridge's. It just wouldn't do you know. At the latter establishment she shunned the offerings from China and India and supped on Cornish tea; quite right too.

She had spent the night awake for fear of oversleeping, or somesuch idea and the hound kept the vigil with her. In consequence I was left with a bleddy hound with use for nothing all day.

When dawn did break it was followed by a fairly miserable affair, gloomy and grim, in fact quite horrid, with heavy showers until late morning. The sea is still fairly large and was forecast to be bigger than yesterday, but it wasn't.

I managed to drag a drowsy bleddy hound out to the beach with her mate while we still had a little beach to play on. High water was just after 3 pm today but at noon there wasn't much sand on show. It was, however, bright and sunny in the afternoon, not that the hound would have noticed – she slept 'til evening.

I had just served up my lonely tea, a very fine repast made from my own head, when the pager went off again; a fishing vessel leaking oil, I believe, in the vicinity of Sevenstones. The Lifeboat will spend another evening in Newlyn, but recovery should be a formality for low water tomorrow morning.

Oh, and I've been asked how much you gave for the Hospice collection so clearly spending time updating the Special Notices section of this website was wasted effort. So for those of you that find it difficult pointing your mouse to other areas of the home page, (including the shopping bit where exciting and quality purchases may be made for very reasonable prices), you raised £760. Thank you.

*February 17th – Thursday* – An earlyish start again but this time for Lifeboat recovery; at low water the sea calmed down and allowed the boat to be recovered without a hitch, well, apart from the hitch it was supposed to have. But I can tell you it was a tad

265

cold hanging around on the slipway despite a rather bright and, in places, sunny day.

Due to the tides it was an early run down to the beach for the bleddy hound. Her mate was out so we were on our own today. I know it might seem rather boring continually taking her down the beach day after day, but what can you do? She loves it and there's less risk of her coming home covered in her favourite perfume.

It has been a quite day other than that, with a bit of time on my hands; time indeed to make some tomato chutney ahead of a long overdue curry and cards night tomorrow. I suspect that it may have some unexpected qualities; the saucepan I used to cook it in has never looked cleaner. If it doesn't go down well I could always bottle it and sell it as kitchen cleaner.

Time then to settle down and watch the goggle box; I always thought that our nice big television was quite the modern addition to contemporary living. That is until I read that a demonstration of colour television was performed at the Dominion Theatre in London. It was shown on a screen 12 feet by 9 feet. All very ordinary I'm sure you will agree until you realise that this was in 1938.

So with these wondrous contemplations bouncing around my capacious mind, where indeed they have room to cavort, I felt it best to retire.

*February 18th – Friday* – Well it wasn't so bad before the rain started. Then it did and it was.

Before we were deluged I managed to get a beach walk in and a run up to the Post Office where I forgot to buy a Cornishman. Fortunately it wasn't the primary reason for going, or I would have felt very silly.

Talking of silly, we had a team from the Highways Department here this morning with a couple of trucks and several burly workmen. They were here for less than an hour and it wasn't immediately apparent what they had been up to. It was when I went up to the Post Office that I noticed that they had tarmaced a patch at the top of the slip about four feet long so that they could put around six feet of double yellow line down with a termination point.

The yellow lines used to stretch around by the Roundhouse all the way to the entrance to the Harbour Car Park. However this belongs to the Harbour Trust and the council parking restriction has, for years, been a bit of an anomaly. So that has cleared that up then and a line has been drawn under it, well two actually.

So as alluded to yesterday it's off for curry and cards night, conveniently upstairs at the F&L. My tomato chutney has matured nicely and I added to the jollity with a rather smart ginger chutney. If the tomato one has bite, this one taught it how but held back on most of the lessons. It is a veritable monster, that should be in chains in a dungeon somewhere. Having unleashed this, I should very likely win the card game.

PS. My compatriots loved both chutneys and I lost.

*February 19th – Saturday* – Right, go to the loo, grab a cup of cocoa and a sandwich on the way back and make yourself comfy. This is a long one.

I might have mentioned before Christmas that I bid in a local charity auction for a trip down a tin mine. Well, if I didn't this will come as a complete surprise to you all, and if I did, you'd probably have forgotten it was so long ago.

Today is the day that the carefully nurtured acquisition came to fruition. I shall endeavour to convey my experience in so few words as not to put off the disinterested, but enough to entertain those that have always wondered what it would be like, or moreover what it was like to carve your living out of granite. (I lied here, it goes on forever.)

The entrance we used on this occasion was halfway down the zawn under the old Levant dressing areas. It was the one part of the experience I hadn't been looking forward to – I have a small aversion to heights, or rather falling from them to a sudden stop.

In the days running up to this event I had imagined the worst of conditions, the longest of ladders and the most precipitous of cliffs. On the day, however, the slope, though steep, was pretty much terraced with plenty of foot and hand holds, although there was a waterfall running down it for added effect. I made it to the adit entrance without so much as a nod in the direction of a coronary.

I had imagined the involvement of some water, indeed I had been warned that even wearing wellies I would get wet feet. A raging torrent, disgorging itself from the gaping maw before me, was not in this preconceived picture. Wet feet would be the least of it, for sure.

Our guide used to work at Geevor in the 70s and 80s and knows every inch of the mine, which was comforting. He is also a veritable font on geology and the history of how the mine was worked through the years. Being an expert he also provided torches and hard hats without which, judging from the number of clangs of toughened plastic on granite, my head would have resembled a half eaten toffee apple.

The first section was low, very low, hewn out by hand at the early part of the 19th century. I know that it is common belief that our forebears were of smaller stature than ourselves, (certain Cornish stalwarts of the F&L excluded), but they weren't that small. No, the miners who fashioned this tunnel only put pick to granite that realised a return or impeded their progress.

In those days miners would bid for sections of the mine in which they worked. There was a pecking order and they were paid for what they brought out. Out of this they paid for their candles, from the mine stores, and all their other tools and facilities.

As we advanced, we advanced through the years. The next section bore scars in the rock walls where hand drills bored holes for gunpowder, dynamite then gelignite as technology developed. Progress was in the region of eighteen inches a day. This section was noticeably taller and perhaps slightly wider too.

Regardless of the age of the section we were constantly tramping through a flood of water of varying depths. We were shown features in the rock, the early formation of stalactites, shafts to other levels and dead rock, (if I remember the term correctly, meaning waste rock devoid of value), that had been piled up into dry stone walls in every spare inch of space.

Eventually we arrived in a small chamber where we sat and had our croust. Here was situated a small water pump, maybe the size of large chest freezer of the type you see in supermarkets. We were told that on other levels these pumps would fill a twelve feet high chamber. Our guide told us that once it would have been painted and polished.

A little further on, we came to Victory Shaft. This is the main shaft descending from Geevor, the one whose top gear you can see from the St Just to St Ives road. We were approximately 280 feet below the surface here. Down this shaft miners would descend to their work, dropping in cages at 28 feet per second, as rock ore would be pulled to the surface in the adjacent shaft. There is, if you so wished to indulge, a series of ladders that run up an adjacent third shaft. There is a platform at the end of each ladder and another and another zigzagging all the way to the top. Our guide told us that when he was younger and fitter he went up this way. It took him thirty minutes without a break.

We returned to the pump chamber and made our way behind it, through a narrow gap into another set of adits running away up to Pendeen, well under it, at least. After a while the adit narrowed and lowered to a crawling section. My travelling companion at this point demurred, and I'm not in the least ashamed to say I readily agreed. While I have no particular concerns in the claustrophobia department, my aching bones and particularly my knees would not have thanked me for some extended punishment.

We returned to grass, as they used to say, well satisfied with our little excursion underground. In fact, as you may have guessed from the interminable length of this essay, I was completely bowled over.

Our guide, to whom I shall forever be indebted, is a trustee of Geevor Mine. His actions, along with those of his fellow dedicated souls, keep the remaining unflooded levels maintained with funding from Cornwall Council, Lottery and Geevor ticket sales.

I had naively assumed that all the water that had filled my boots on its way out of the mine had found its own level and exit courses. It is actually the Geevor Trust's work that allows this and staves off the flooding of the remaining levels. While currently the water exits to the sea from the cliff, from a flooded mine, it would almost certainly course out from further up, where lie Pendeen, Trewellard, Botallack and St Just.

My overalls bear testament, after their fifth rinse, that this is not just water. Hap I could make a small trinket from the tin deposits in my sink. It wasn't that long ago I remember the Red River at Gwithian still being red and a great ruddy bloom in St Ives Bay.

I urge you visit Geevor Mine and drop a few coppers in the collection tin too. It's not just Cornwall's mining heritage you're protecting, it's Mrs Trembath of Calartha Road, Pendeen who'd rather not have a toxic river running through her turnip patch.

For all you girls out there who couldn't give a tuppenny darn for a bunch of old mine workings, I apologise profusely for ruining your day with this drivel. For all you boys out there who love a bit of boys own adventure, good wussn't it?

Got to dash now. The Missus is home tonight and I have to vacuum the dog and polish the goldfish. Anyone know how to get a nasty bit of dancing girl out of a sofa?

*February 20th – Sunday* – Well, not surprisingly I can't top yesterday for eventfulness.

We do however have a visitor to add a little excitement to our otherwise undramatic lives. She is one of the young ladies that visit during the summer and provides some, ahem, assistance in the shop. She is here for a week.

She was very concerned for my well-being after yesterday's exertions, and felt rather aggrieved for me that I had been attacked by grannies. I had jocularly explained to her that my shoulder was somewhat bruised after I had been attacked by granite in the mine. I suspect that this will be the tenor of communications for the week.

Naturally there was some beach walking involving the bleddy hound and her mate today. Walking boots being order of the day, as my wellies are still soggy. Those acres of deserted sand are no more, the solitary contemplation on rocks at the north end, seemingly a thing now lost. It was like a day at Crufts down there; breeds of every description running around and cavorting gaily and there was just as many dogs too.

Yes, it is the half term holiday and we are transformed from sleepy hollow to school playground at break time. Breakers Café attracted a few in the morning but right on cue the rain started and cleared The Cove but for a handful of hardly souls.

I understand that there is more rain pencilled in for tomorrow. I feel a St Ives trip coming on. It is after all what you do on a rainy day with a frisky teenager in tow, I believe. I can't wait.

*February 21st – Monday* – Currently our bathroom, when available, is maintained in the manner of a Turkish steam room where the mirror, should you wish to use it, for example to shave, is in a constant state of opaqueness. The toilet tissue in this environment has become diaphanous, to the point usage requires some dexterity to avoid whatever the term for an inverted pitfall is. The sweet odours that pervade the room are so numerous and diverse they would, were they sounds, be subject to a noise abatement notice. Such is the tragedy of a lone male in a house full of girls. Yes, I know there are only two of them but, in some cases, the whole is greater than the sum of its parts.

I pointed out yesterday that since it was due to rain, which it duly did, a trip to St Ives was on the cards. I haven't been to St Ives since the last time I was there, so it was high time to remedy that great omission in my life and go again. It was exactly as I remembered it, wet, busy and full of shops geared to accommodate the every whim of a visiting tourist.

The Missus had entertained the girls there on previous occasions and knew where a half decent meal was to be had. I can heartily recommend it. The place was simple and clean, the service friendly and efficient, and the menu happily leveraged our local produce. It is called The Beach Restaurant and although I wouldn't recommend you go out of your way to visit, if you are there it is a more than satisfactory place to repast.

After our lunch the girls set about the task of investigating the plethora of emporia with particular regard to the more expensive looking ones. I wandered about the narrow streets and looked damp.

I had asked in the restaurant whether they could recommend a butcher in town, as we needed some meat for tea. My enquiry was met with a look you might expect to receive if you asked directions to the nearest gay brothel, at the door of a Benedictine Abbey – ok, perhaps not the best analogy. What I am trying to say is that St Ives isn't exactly blessed with what you might call shops of substance; ones selling the accoutrements of basic life.

I did find the town's sole butcher. He had the haunted look of a Horseshoe Bat hanging in an unconverted Cotswold barn. I was expecting a bit of a cheery welcome, something that said thanks for supporting this local business. What I got was a surly grunt from a man as grumpy as a convention of North African dictators. I understand his burden but I wasn't encouraged to return.

Naturally the sun broke out as we headed out of town. I didn't dare look back lest I be turned to a pillar of salted pilchards. This is a fishing village, after all. It's not that it's such a bad place, it has done what it needed to survive and has ended up, to quote Mr Allen, a travesty of a mockery of a sham, a pastiche of what it once was.

It wasn't long after we got back that someone left a small muddy bundle of rags outside our door, that turned out to be the bleddy hound we'd left with our neighbour. They had taken her up Land's End for a run around you see, which clearly she did.

Tomorrow it is set to rain again. I don't think I shall be tempted to go to St Ives.

*February 22nd – Tuesday* – Largely a grey day today with the sort of rain that soaks you through without you noticing, initially at least.

We had the neighbour's hound for the day so staying in was not an option; best then that we scout out for some excitement down on the expanse of beach that the remaining spring tide offers us.

It took us a while to get going as the Teenager needed to attire correctly for the conditions, and on the off chance that she might bump into Marvin Humes. Oh, do you not keep up with modern popular culture? He is a singer with the pop sensation JLS, for heavens sake – all right, I had to look it up too.

The bleddy hound could not care less, nor did her companion, and both cavorted like cubs, with gay abandon - Nothing like a good woggle on the beach if you're a young hound.

When we reached the far end of the beach, which, on a spring tide is further than normal, we did so have such a whale of a time. When another neighbour and her dogs joined our pack it verily turned into a jamboree. I'm surprised we didn't do our best to light a camp-fire around which we might sing songs of rousing cheer such as, *Ging-gang-gooly* or, *A Life on an Ocean Wave*, such was our happy demeanour.

Despite the weather there were many other walkers and dogs on the beach and we thought it a good turn to let their hounds play with ours, though many demurred.

And try though I might I could not think of a sentence into which I could crowbar the word, Akela.

It is after all the anniversary of the 1857 birth of Sir Robert (Stephenson Smyth) Baden-Powell, founder of the Boy Scout movement. He was also a brilliant military strategist and held Mafeking against a superior Boer army for 217 days, a feat often overshadowed by his later exploits.

War hero or not, in a society where we have allowed ourselves to be governed and manipulated by fear, it is unlikely that the movement would ever have got off the ground if he had tried to start it today.

"So Mr Powell. What's that? Lieutenant-General Baden-Powell. I see."

"So Lt-Gen Baden-Powell you saw nothing wrong with taking a group of young boys away on a camping trip by yourself?"

"You wanted to promote in them, moral strength and character, good citizenship and develop their physical, mental and emotional fitness. Highly commendable, I'm sure, Sir."

"Our team of experts from Child Services are interviewing the boys now, Sir, so we'll see just how you, ahem, instilled that in them, eh?"

"Oh, and we found a number of the boys were armed with knives, Sir. They said you were teaching them how to use the knives. You don't deny that, Sir? You are aware that it is an offence under the Violent Crimes Reduction Act 2006 to supply persons under the age of 18 years with a knife. Of course you weren't, Sir."

"And in this book of yours, Scouting for Boys, you seem to be inciting others to take young boys away from their homes and teach them similar, ahem, skills."

"So let's just summarise shall we? You want to take young boys away 'camping', dress them up in shorts, long socks and a scarf tied with something you call a 'woggle'. You want to arm them and teach them how to use knives and have an ultimate aim to start a world-wide cult called 'Scouting'."

"Do you have a solicitor, Sir?"

We wouldn't part on such a sour note. I leave you with the Cub Scout promise:

*"Aklea, we will do our best to do our  duty to God and the Queen to help other people and keep the Cub Scout Law."*

Whomsoever your God and your queen might be.

Goodnight all.


*February 23rd – Wednesday –* It was supposed to be a bit better today but we're still being mizzled upon. There's still a bit of swell around , not as large as last week but apparently not bad for surfing out the back. Swell still comes over the wall near high water for the few, very few, watchers in the Harbour Car Park.

'Tis the season for boat maintenance as there's no chance of getting afloat at the moment. There are punts lined up in the car park and Brisons, the gig, is getting a shiny new coat of paint.

Must also be the season for shopping, as if the Missus didn't get enough in London last week. She and Teenager disappeared off to the big city, leaving me and the bleddy hound to our own devices. Cue a run down to the big beach, although we did go around the coast path to get there today.

It wasn't too bad down there, although there were noticeably fewer visitors around. Odd really, as the Beach Car Park was busy enough. They can't all have been in the pub, surely?

And since I've deluged you with long and winding tales over the past few days I shall leave you with a few lines from a chap that managed to knock out over 200 published poems, including at least a couple of epics, before his untimely death today, in 1821, at the age of 25 years. Although not generally appreciated in his lifetime, John Keats also managed to enter a phrase into common usage, *'A thing of beauty is a joy forever.'*

> *Oh soft embalmer of the still midnight!*
> *Closing with careful fingers and benign,*
> *Our gloom-pleas'd eyes, . . .*
> *Turn the key deftly in the oiled wards,*
> *And seal the hushed casket to my soul.*

And if that hasn't managed to get you to drop off, read the whole thing that almost certainly will.

*February 24th – Thursday* – I wasn't going to mention this as it seems a little pointless scrabbling around after crumbs from the national press table. But then our International Correspondent, MM, who I haven't mentioned for some time, sent me a link to a British national broadsheet that required some attention.

The article concerns the recent news that the Cornish pasty has been awarded European Protected Geographical Indication, (PGI), meaning it can't be manufactured elsewhere. I suspect that MM is stirring the pot in the safe knowledge that her local man, from Cheshire, can still turn out 'genuine' Cornish pasties on that side of the Atlantic without fear of retribution. (That is until a few of the boys from the Cornish Liberation Front form a radical splinter group and head off to the Eastern Seaboard.)

The article was entitled, "What's the point of protecting the pasty?" and from a purely personal point of view I tend to agree. When I lived out of county it never occurred to me to eat a Cornish pasty, even if I could find one, (a certain well known and universally derided version naturally excluded), for broadly the same reasons you wouldn't eat escargot, grenouilles or cheval outside France or Jack Russell outside Vietnam. It just isn't right, somehow. I can, however, see the point of hamstringing the competition if you are a Cornish pasty maker trying to extend your market.

No, what irked in this article, (written by William Sitwell by the way, if anyone from the CLF is reading this), is that it was written with the benefit of utter ignorance. By his own admission, the only pasty he has ever eaten was at a service station when he was, 'worse for wear'. It's like saying, "I don't like fish", after having the half eaten 'fillet o' fish' retrieved from the bin outside McD's on the High Street, after fifteen pints of Bishop's XXX at the Dog and Duck, or, "I don't like kebab", because of the stain it leaves down my shirt front on Sunday morning.

He goes on to say that the pasty sits too heavily on his tender constitution but that it may well have been good after a day's tin mining. Perhaps if Mr Sitwell had been bothered to get up off his reposed backside and make the trip to Cornwall to try a genuine pasty, he might well have expended sufficient energy to actually enjoy it.

He is also editor of *Waitrose Food Illustrated*. I rest my case.

Teenager's Dad turned up today which has evened the balance a little. We're now only slightly outnumbered.

Unfortunately I had to leave him to fend for himself this evening as Lifeboat training beckoned. He was a tad too weary to give us a hand at the quiz down the OS too, which was a shame. Our miserable reputation, that has taken years to blacken, took a bit of a beating tonight as we couldn't even cheat our way to a decent position.

If this carries on we'll have to apply for a PGI to vouchsafe our worthless behinds.


*February 25th – Friday –* It started out a grey and dismal day then slowly got worse. Ideal, then, for a picnic!

Missus cooked some sausage rolls, chicken thighs and made some sandwiches and packed them all up in a hamper with lashings of ginger beer. Teenager loaded Timmy, I mean, bleddy hound, into the back of the van and we all went off for a jolly adventure. We foiled spy plots, got kidnapped, escaped, uncovered major crime rings and spoke with plummy accents all day long. Ripping!

After all that, we headed down to Praa Sands, which down here is pronounced Prey Sands. A smart lady in the shop once berated me for the dialectic quirk and said, "It isn't spelt like that", to which I replied, "Neither is Norwich."

It is a place I'd never been, strangely, and so much more welcome a trip for that. Only grey and mizzly when we arrived, it was a pleasant walk along the entire length of the beach with bleddy hound and her mate in tow. Couldn't help but notice the amount of detritus thrown up along the high water mark, which I imagine is a result of being in close proximity to busy Mounts Bay and the Channel shipping lanes. There was even a large, (three feet), conger eel washed up, which was an education for Teenager who thought fish came in packets.

If you are geologically minded there are features here that will captivate your interest. If you are not, there is an earthy cliff full of pebbles, a fossilised peat outcrop, rocks and sand. At the far end of the beach is a wartime pillbox half filled with sand that somehow managed to descend from the cliff above, the right way up.

It had just started to mizzle heavily when we arrived back at the van for our picnic. And a very fine picnic it was too. In the time taken to consume it, the van became so steamed up, it took half an hour before we could move off.

The mist was as thick as a bag, along the Helston road, either that or the windows had steamed up again, and we nearly missed the turning off to Prussia Cove. The small and unkempt car park is at the end of a long and winding road. When we got there no one wanted to decamp, for a second time, into the wet and clingy air. Since you can see nothing from the car park we turned around and went back. The diversion was not entirely wasted as I had not seen Porth-en-Alls House before and it looked rather enigmatic in the swirling mist.

The rest of the day was rather dull by comparison so I shall not tell you about it. Suffice to say we had tea at the F&L, which was very appropriate, since it is the last evening for Teenager here. and the first day for the new inhabitants of Horizon Fields, who were up there in force to celebrate.

*February 26th – Saturday* – I thought I'd gone deaf this morning, until I realised that Teenager had gone home. The continual chirrup is not the only thing that we miss. It is the broad beam first thing in the morning and the smile too: the unconditional optimism of youth.

We'll have to make our own entertainment now for the two weeks we have left until the shop opens. I suspect this will mainly be spent downstairs getting things ready. So until Monday we shall do what we do best: nothing.

Naturally, at the end of half term the sun shone through and it rather looks like next week will be wholly better than this one. It is a bit breezy, though, and the temperature has dipped a little; still, a cracking day to witness a little rugby, with the main game of the day being in the late afternoon.

This dovetailed nicely with a curry night up at the F&L followed by the usual music filled free for all. 'Twas busy too, with all in high spirits, dancing and making merry.

All this and a clear, starry night to walk home in; it doesn't get much better really.

*February 27th – Sunday* – It looked rather sunny and pleasant out of the window at lunchtime today. I couldn't possibly divulge the state of this morning's weather as I took, what is known colloquially, as a long lay in.

These, for me, are few and far between and are to be savoured. It is a day when I am not roused from my innocent slumber by a wet and rough length of slippery flesh embedded in my ear. For that is the bleddy hound's conventional method of getting me out of bed, with her tongue.

For all its seeming charm, the day had a vicious sting in its tail. There is an icy wind blowing in from somewhere in the north east quarter. At some point during the evening it had gathered sufficient ferocity to dislodge our newspaper bin, that has several hefty rocks in it to ward against such eventuality.

The majority of visitors have now departed and The Cove is once again a place of quiet solitude. This is infectious and as I pointed out yesterday it is a time to do very little.

A rugby match beckoned from the OS I and answered the call for a couple of hours. I was fortunate in my timing, as I believe there was a football match playing at roughly the same time. I had to fend off several would be watchers, who would have had the channel changed and completely ruined my selfish little day.

Time now to gird my loins and prepare for the frightful time we have ahead: work!

*February 28th – Monday* – You may be pleased to hear that I did see morning tide today, the last one in February, no less. And a very fine morning it was too if you don't count the cold bits.

We were supposed to start work in the shop today, but the Missus reckons that the three hours a day we promised ourselves, only applies to the morning, and since she didn't get up until nearly afternoon, the opportunity was lost. This has a very familiar ring about it. Last year, and I think the previous two before that, we were scurrying around the night before opening getting things ready. You might have noticed.

I can say, with a certain smugness, that I did do something business orientated today. We had our postcard rep arrive, the first time he has done so for two years and only then after we had complained. This is the chap that purveys our 15p postcards, or at least used to. It is with gravity and regret that I must inform you all, that after seven seasons, the 15p postcard is no more. Pension-

277

ers the world over will have every right to shake their badge bedecked walking sticks, (the walking stick badges have also gone up by the way), in angst and despair, but I'm afraid it will be to no avail. Just let it be known that for every card sold henceforth, we shall smart with empathetic affront and share your pain.

On a brighter note Cornwall has been voted best place in the UK for food. I can say this only on the basis that, a) from personal experience it is likely to be true, and b) some maid on Radio Pasty said it. Unfortunately I can find no shred of documentary evidence littered about the Internet or in the newspapers that supports the claim. However, I can tell you with certainty, that in the *Western Morning News* 'Business Farm Awards', the chap that supplies our Cornish Early potatoes won 'Best Commercial Farmer', and top awards also went to a dairy, (or was that diary?), farmer in St Buryan, and another also for milk production up at Trengwainton.

Take heed and enjoy while you may the sight of cows grazing in our fields, for they are very likely to be short lived. Our farming correspondent tells me that one highly respected dairy farmer in St Levan, has chucked it in, following a great number of other artisans of the dairy world. You would too, if you were being paid 1p less per litre than the cost of production.

The big supermarkets are crushing quality dairy production in this country. The only way that milk can be produced, at the price they have decided to pay, is through intensive farming methods. Think battery hens, but with cows instead that never leave the shed; never see a field.

Oh, crikey, he's ranting again. Yes I am, and this time I don't care. I am livid that some faceless, corporate body has decided that I don't want to pay a few more pence a litre for my milk to sustain a failing industry; where the taste and colour of the food on my plate has had to be added as the original intensely farmed product has none of its own.

I'm off now to enjoy some milk that came from a cow in a field; to have some meat that has been locally reared, properly processed and has not a drop of water in it; with some vegetables that grew in a field close to here and hasn't been half way up country and back before I bought it; and a can of cider that probably hasn't ever seen an apple. Well you can't be good all the time, can you?

I also promise I shall not be half as grumpy tomorrow, honest.

# March

In the news: *The Windsor report published yesterday into police force salaries highlights a culture of large bonuses, expense payments and massive amounts of overtime.*

*March 1st - Tuesday* – A grey, overcast day today, so no temptation to go wandering off instead of working in the shop and working in the shop we did.

It was the Missus's turn to entertain today's rep, this one for biscuits and fudge. This chap also supplies rock, and this year we are having rock with Sennen Cove written through it. I bet you can hardly wait. We have shied away from personalised rock previously, as you have to order a lot of rock before they will make it for you. So when you descend upon us this year, as we very much hope that you will, be prepared to eat rock, lots of it. We will frown upon any shopper that leaves without at least a stick. Next year's star buy - false teeth.

I was in the kitchen for the back half of the afternoon, cooking a bovine creature that I had known calf and heifer, so I didn't see this develop. Out in the bay a lone surfer had found himself a little rip to get stuck in. By the time his mate had tried to raise the alarm at the Lifeboat Station, he was pretty much ashore. He looked a tad fatigued but was back out again in the gloom of early evening. What tenacity.

The weatherman had promised us a nice warm blanket of cloud to sit under this evening. Imagine my surprise when, walking home from coming second in the regular cards game at the OS, (yes, second I'll have you know), I look up to a spangled sky. One of those rare occasions that I don't mind the weatherman getting it wrong, although I imagine if you hadn't covered your bulbs, you would have been a mite upset.

*March 2nd - Wednesday* – The cloud cover that we were promised last night had arrived by morning and happily broke up again in the afternoon. Not that it really matters to us since it was another day of shop preparation, interrupted by yet another rep visit.

I noticed that some work had commenced to repair the driveway up to Chy Ryn, at the end of The Cove. It must be a couple of years ago now that the earth bank that supports it collapsed, leaving a rather delicate top layer in one place. They have now filled the hole with cages loaded with foreign rocks. Let's hope the rest of the bank stays put or The Cove will have a small replica of the Old Man of Hoy to wonder at.

Watching workmen fill a hole was, I'm afraid to say, the highlight of a very mundane day. There is not much excitement you can glean from cleaning shelves and floors, clearing empty boxes and repositioning stock to try and make it look attractive. I know because I spent several hours watching the Missus do it.

What you can take pleasure in, perhaps, is that this is the second day that I have completely avoided spilling grumpy words onto this page. It can't possibly last.

*March 3rd – Thursday* – Up with the lark this morning, assuming that there are one or two lazy larks about; although any lark, worthy of the name, would have been up shrieking the arrival of a morning as dapper as this one. Not a cloud to be seen, a nice big golden beach and crisp as a student's bed sheet.

No slaving in the shop for us today. There is an exhibition held every year up at the Royal Cornwall Showground that panders to the good folk that have anything to do with the catering industry. It is a veritable cornucopia of food suppliers, financiers, equipment suppliers, brewers, vintners, growers, merchants and other thieves. We have not been for a few years as the turnover of companies tends to be quite slow. Nevertheless, it is not too far to travel and there is always the chance we might find something interesting and worthwhile.

Unfortunately this was not to be one of those times. It is, however, rather nice hopping from stand to stand and trying out the delectable delicacies on offer. You could quite easily indulge in a three course meal sullo zoccolo, (come on, the Italians must have a phrase for eating on the hoof as well as outside, surely), including a different wine with each course if so you chose. If you really pushed your luck you could probably get away with having it at a properly set table.

We even met our Cornish tea man, which gave me the chance of trying out the brew that the Missus had up in the big city, albeit not quite in the heady surroundings of Claridge's tea rooms. It is quite the elixir that the Missus described and I would venture that perhaps milk would rather spoil it. Anyway you will get your chance to try some by greasing our palms with pieces of gold when you visit the shop, if we ever open.

We arrived home laden with goodies of all descriptions with enough time to rest our weary bones ahead of a Lifeboat exercise this evening. The boat was fair outnumbered by crew of both shore and boat variety. I'd wager we will not be so well endowed come Sunday's morning splash.

Time to wrap up warm now with even colder weather on the way. It wouldn't be right to open the shop without a freezing easterly blowing through the door.

*March 4th – Friday* – Another right on, smashing day to have to contend with. What a shame. But more work is required downstairs so I waved the Missus off at the door and wished her well. I, on the other hand, had weighty matters to consider. We are on the cusp of St Piran's Day and pasties need to be made and refined.

If you recall, and I'm sure you do, back in September I reported to you that Cornwall Council had made a loss in their department that issues Penalty Charge Notices (PCNs), you know, parking tickets. I think I might have even been a little derisory too and was not alone. The newspaper that I took the article from seemed also to be pointing an accusatory finger.

Well, Cornwall Council certainly woke up and smelt the Cornish tea, I can tell you. The gritty team of Civil Enforcement Officers, (what we used to call Traffic Wardens), that serve the Penzance, Newlyn, Mousehole and Marazion areas notched up 245 tickets in the first two weeks of February against 28 for a similarly quiet period last year. I think both of them should be congratulated. Yes, that's right, there are two of them, approximately one ticket per hour each. Hardly flat out, you'd say.

So our local paper obviously heaped its praise on our noteworthy little department for turning a tax draining loss into a profit in a little less than five months. Well, no actually. The stalwart crew, or rather the Council as a whole has been lambasted for squeezing the poor innocent motorist.

Now, I have to agree that the Council could have made itself look a whole lot better, by perhaps using the money to encourage cheaper town centre parking. I know there are problems with resident parking etcetera but I feel it is, perhaps, a tad unfair to give out wholesale for doing a job badly one minute and too well the next. After all, if we all parked legally they'd find it hard to issue a ticket in the first place.

I have to dash now. I just remembered where I left the van.

*March 5th – Saturday* – St Piran's Day indeed, patron to tinners, and such a de facto saint for Cornwall he has all but knocked poor old St Michael off his perch. This is probably just as well, since tinning is pretty much scat, he wouldn't have much patronage to provide else. Anyway St Michael probably has enough to do looking after men's underwear.

And, on this special day, the sun came blasting through, although there was a fair old haze all around and a bit of cloud that moved in later in the afternoon. With the wind dropped it was quite a temperate day and the run down the beach with the bleddy hound was something of a heated event, given I had dressed up for winter.

In case you missed the hype, it is World Book Night tonight. A million books are being given away throughout the world on the premise that you read them and then pass them on. In the UK this event will take on increasing importance, as it will be the only place you can get a book for free when they close down all the libraries.

The lady, who is doing her bit in this part of the world, has elected to stand at the Lands End signpost. I imagine she may well be going home with most of her stock, as most of us were up at the F&L watching the very excellent Devil's Creek.

So, as the author of eternity, turns over another page of time, only to find out that the binding of fate has glued together the pages that explain the plot, it's time to say goodnight.

*March 6th – Sunday* – Grey, cold and overcast just the sort of day for a Lifeboat launch. Not just any old launch today; we are hosting visitors from Lizard Lifeboat Station. Now that their new boathouse is well on the way to completion, it was a chance for the crew to get some hands on time with the Tamar class Lifeboat that they will be using by the end of the year.

The timing of the recovery was somewhat acute, as I needed to bake my pasties for the F&L pasty competition in the afternoon. There is a category for traditional pasties and another for novelties. The judging panel was a fine selection of gentlemen, (mostly), pillars of the community, sober, (possibly), paragons of virtue whose wisdom, tasting skills and honesty are beyond reproach. Incorruptible (for anything less than a fiver), the word of these demi-gods is universally accepted as law and each judgement is final and irreversible.

You will already know that SN won the novelty section with a fine crab pasty. It pains a sensitive chap, such as myself, whose reputation for modesty and humility are legend in these parts, to have to reveal that I won the traditional pasty making category. Oh yes, it was me, I triumphed over seemingly insurmountable odds. A pasty maker of the highest quality, I beat the opposition into a cocked hat, numero uno, the big cheese, top of the heap, top dog, king of the hill, pasty supremo and head honcho. Ahem, excuse me, might have got a little carried away there. Yup, I came first.

I suppose I better reveal, before someone else tells you, that there were only around half a dozen entries in the traditional category. Further, many of these added carrot to the filling in what I can only assume to be some sort of satirical joke, leaving just two entries unadulterated. Still, it was fun celebrating, nonetheless.

So, after such an action packed and exhausting day I must hang up my rolling pin and retire.

*March 7th – Monday* – Another spanking day of clarity and sunshine with a huge golden beach spread out before us. Appealing, certainly, but it was more time in the shop for both of us this time.

Many thanks to the hundreds of people who have offered their congratulations on my little pasty success, and a special thanks to the two people that offered their congratulations so that I was actually aware that they had. I haven't heard from Mr Michelin yet, but I guess it will take a few days for the news to leak out.

In the mean time, pasty protection status news has reached the shores of South Australia where, in the Yorke Peninsula they are quivering in their boots. Cornish miners populated this area in the 19th and early 20th centuries, attracted by copper mining, so much so it became known as 'Little Cornwall'. Each year since 1973, the 50th anniversary of the demise of the industry, they have a little shindig known as the Copper Coast Cornish Festival, whereupon they make and consume vast quantities of Cornish pasties.

In a town, Wallaroo, named after wallabies urine, you'd think they had worse things to contemplate. Our head pasty honcho has assured them that the spindly tentacles of the European Union are unlikely to reach that far. In fact they can wash down their pastry delights with Aussie Champagne, grate Aussie Parmesan over them and sit them alongside an Aussie Arbroath Smokie and no one would give a stuff.

After all we make their beer over here and you don't hear them complaining. No surprise really, it's not exactly what you'd call a fair trade.

*March 8th – Tuesday* – I think this is a better run of weather than we had in August last year. If it would like to transpose itself to August this year I would be more than grateful. And still we are not out in it, choosing instead to buff the shop into a shiny icon in this lost corner or the world.

So lost were we in our buffing and restocking, that we quite forgot that we left our entrance mat hanging off the rails across the road. I suspect that it would have been quite safe and, if it wasn't, we need only look for the ruffian with several kilos of sand in the boot of his car.

The poor bleddy hound has suffered greatly these last few days, the big beach being beyond reach of the little time we have to commit to her. She has had to suffice with a minor run around on the Harbour Beach for exercise. Nevertheless, she is getting used to sitting in the shop and gazing out the window, as she will have to endure for the next eight months.

I am also trying to work out if I am possessed of skills of a prescient nature or just a Jonah after our little chat about traffic wardens, or whatever they're called now. A chap, resembling such an epithet, was spotted in The Cove a couple of days ago and nailed a few unfortunates. I shall be mindful of my language in future.

With all the fuss over university fees that is hitting the headlines recently, it is comforting to note that the students won't be wasting their money. Sheffield Hallam University has undertaken a study that revealed small seaside towns, such as Padstow and Bude, are more reliant on tourism than larger seaside resorts and rural communities. This results in low wages, seasonal unemployment and a proliferation of small businesses.

Stunning, isn't it? I have no doubt that next term they will learn that big cities have more people living in them than smaller ones, and that nine grand for a year at uni might have been better spent on beer and skittles.

Kerr-ching! Ay thang yew.

*March 9th – Wednesday* – The wind picked up a little today but the weather front that passed through brought us no rain at all. The sea has churned up somewhat, giving a bit of a chance for the thrill seeking kayaks, charging through the surf mid-morning.

The Missus had some errands to run, (often spelt s-h-o-p-p-i-n-g), in the big city today, so work in the shop almost ground to a halt. I did manage to do a little bit down there, but without the Director of Operations I was a bit nervous about doing anything major. I do so get told off, you know. That just leaves two days to do what looks like a week's worth of work. Situation normal, then.

As pressed as we may be, at least our little world doesn't have to cope with a culture of high salaries, big bonuses and outrageous expenses. That isn't a complaint; it was our decision to run a shop in a backwater little seaside village. I suspect big money like that will only come with a lottery win, which is about as likely as the alternative, but I'm probably too old now to join the police force.

I did manage to get some time on the Harbour Beach with the bleddy hound and her mate. They were joined later with some more buddies, and a right good time was had by all. Strange news from a neighbour, though, that a familiar local hound went missing last night; it seems a suspicious van went off at the same time and the dog has not been seen since – all very queer.

Relief, then, this evening when JP happed upon the unfortunate mutt at the bottom of the bank the other side of the Harbour Car Park, with a broken leg. Must have been chasing gulls and forgotten he couldn't fly.

*March 10th – Thursday* – Not such nice going out weather today, so working in the shop was not quite so irritating. We are getting together slowly but have raised our game from, 'slight concern' to, 'mild panic'. Clearly if things haven't been fully completed by midnight tomorrow night, we'll invest in, 'sod it, no one will notice that'.

Miraculously, our favourite newspaper supplier has remembered that we are opening this weekend. Unfortunately, they had entirely forgotten to populate their computer system with any stock to be delivered to us. After eight years of dealing with them, I know that it is today that I need to call them and arrange things, as it is the last day that volumes can be settled for our opening and instils in them some feeling of urgency. When you have to play psychological games with your supplier it should be time to say goodbye. Alas there is nowhere else to go.

I had to run into town this afternoon for a couple of quick errands, (often spelt e-r-r-a-n-d-s when I do it). One of which was a visit to my accountants, to pick up some files. This is usually a short operation and often necessitates parking on double yellow lines. Today, however, I caught sight of a traffic warden in view of where I would normally park. That's three in almost as many days. Since there are only two of them, I'm beginning to wonder if they've undertaken a course in omnipresence, as part of their training.

After two weeks or more of seasonally sparkling weather, I note that there is some rain on the way, even snow up north; must be nearly time to open the shop.

## March 11th – Friday – 'O-Day' minus one, and at last the deep clean of the shop is complete, or at least has had as much done to it as it's going to. I'm sure we will have forgotten something, but hopefully nothing crucial.

The Missus had a good clean up behind the counter too. This pretty much guarantees that I won't be able to find a thing tomorrow, so don't come in asking. Each year is pretty much a new learning hair-pin bend, as a few months is a long time in shop keeping.

Pasties have been ordered and so have the bread and other fresh goodies that will, no doubt, be finding their way to the bin by the end of the weekend. I can, of course, now honestly state, that the pasties are supplied by an award winning pasty maker!

I couldn't tell you much about the outside world today, as I didn't see much of it. It was a bit grey all day, but the wind had dropped quite a bit and there was a fair few people milling about, although if it rains tomorrow you can bet they will all disappear.

I can't tell you just how much I'm looking forward to getting to grips with the weekend newspapers tomorrow, (if they turn up). So much so, I better get to my bed early so I'm bright as a new pin in the morning to enjoy it all the more.

At least you early birds will be able to read this page over your tea and toast of a morning. Oh what joy!

## March 12th – Saturday – Yawn!

Yup, up well before any self-respecting lark or sparrow with digestive issues.

All the relevant newspapers had been delivered but naturally it couldn't be that simple. We also had another large lump of magazines dropped on the doorstep. It took me a while to realise it but these had a delivery date of 2nd March, long before we were open, and had already been invoiced to us. It made sense of the recall note that I had received yesterday asking for the unsolds of this delivery to be returned. Following so far?

Of all the low down, dirty, double-crossing tricks; if I'd had a brother the dirty rats would have killed him already. If this carries on I'll have to make them an offer they can't refuse. In this game of double bluff and dirty tricks, that has to be the lowest bowl so far.

Still, a nice enough morning for it, with a fair few people still out and about. I reckon the crew of Ben My Chree is quite happy about seeing this morning too. This was the boat picked up by Sennen Cove Lifeboat last month with a leaky oil pipe and towed into Newlyn. I suppose this wasn't going to be their year; the gill netter is now several fathoms down, a mile off Gwennap Head.

She was taking on water in the early hours of Friday morning, north east of Scilly. Scilly Lifeboat and Rescue 193 both attended and between them took all five crew members off the boat. The Lifeboat shadowed the vessel until first light, as its mizzen sail was set and driving the netter on an erratic course. Rather looked like it was trying to get back to Newlyn by itself.

Although I garner detail for these reports from the Internet and, now we're open again, the newspapers, very often I am alerted by interesting sound bites on Radio Pasty. Now it seems, this very valuable and venerable resource is under threat. The BBC, in the extremity of its need, has decided it a spiffing plan to rob local communities of their voice.

I couldn't call the BBC in Cornwall faultless, or without bias in its dissemination of local news, but none of the commercial stations come close in either depth or breadth of information provided. Think, The Daily Mail verses the Beano, and you wouldn't be far off the mark. Knocking Radio Pasty off the air would leave something of a yawning gap in all sorts of ways down here and, I imagine, in your communities too.

The Diary is ready, at a moment's notice, to step into the breach. I can just imagine the puzzled looks and consternation when we take to the air.

*March 13th – Sunday –* What a sparkling little day we're having today; bit fresh perhaps but clear as a bell and wall to wall sunshine. And with the sunshine came a healthy number of people, probably as opposed to a number of healthy people; I didn't enquire about their well-being.

The Missus rolled her sleeves up again to get to grips with the spring clean of the store room. She must love the smell of polish in the morning.

It doesn't take long to get back into the groove, (rut, possibly?), what with familiar faces coming in for a little chat, the, 'have you gots', the warming of pasties and the ordering of more goodies. It's as if we've never been closed.

The scrubbing in the store didn't have much chance to get going as I had negotiated a little Six Nations watching in the afternoon. And what a knicker-gripping little session that was, I can tell you. I've wangled an even better result for next week but you'll have to wait for the excitement that will bring.

If it stays like this all year it will be a cracker. Fingers and toes crossed.

*March 14th – Monday* – A bit of a weather mix today, bits of grey, bits of blue and by the end of the afternoon, a gathering breeze. The heavy rain promised us, slipped by to the west just leaving us a little misty, however another heavy load made contact over night, just the way we like it.

Talking of heavy loads, our friend at the Laurel and Hardy Newspaper Company responded to our dilemma first thing. She gaily told me that no money had been taken from my account for the magazines they arranged to send us when we were shut, that I never got until they were due to be returned. No, not at all as we pay by cheque, don't we?

"Well, no", I told her in soft and garlanded tones, "We pay by direct debit as we have for the last eight years", I soothed. She told me not to have such a soft and garlanded tone with her, as it was the accounts department that was to blame. I replied in a quiet and unassuming voice that my soft and garlanded tones were on account of suffering abuse from L&H News Co for eight years and perhaps she would like to get her boss, whose message she was careful to point out she was relaying, to speak to me directly, thus avoiding any upset derived from my soft and garlanded soothing.

I still await the call with soft and garlanded tone carefully husbanded. Never in the field of human news agenting has anyone had to deal with a company so inept and incompetent that it would put Frank Spencer to shame.

Then, half way through the morning a little Lifeboat shout: an upturned life raft out towards Wolf Rock, spotted by a fishing boat that was standing by. The assumed likelihood is that it was from the Ben My Chree, sunk on Saturday off Gwennap Head, but it had no obvious identification marks on it. The Lifeboat collected it up and stuffed it in the boot of the Tamar. This requires emptying the boot of the Y-boat that normally occupies the space, which made its own way back alongside the big boat.

When you arrive anywhere  you unload the boot, which is exactly what happened here. The life raft was duly drawn up on the Harbour Beach and the Lifeboat recovered on the long slip. The excellent and devoted Shore Crew made light work of a little swell at the end of the slip and the boat was recovered in short order. Oh, and the Boat Crew were there too.

After a morning like that the only thing to do was a little honest shop keeping and, failing that, we just stood behind the counter and served a few people. It is also the time of year when, having just flattened the last cardboard delivery box, another dozen turn up at the door. It won't be long now before the sound of a van pulling up outside will strike a deep, irrational fear in our hearts.

Ah, the joys of shop keeping in early season.

*March 15th – Tuesday* – I had a very nice chap waiting for me to open the shop this morning. He introduced himself as a senior territory manager from the Laurel and Hardy Newspaper Company. Politely, and with soothing tones, I asked him how long he had nurtured his death wish, which was apparent by turning up in Indian country at the start of the season.

He was, unfortunately, unaware of my predicament with the company that he works for. He announced that he likes to visit opening newsagents, which only confirmed my suspicions regarding his suicidal tendencies. He asked if I was aware of the L&H Co.'s systems and procedures so I felt it only polite to ask if it was.

Moving on swiftly, I am sure you are aware that it is Spam appreciation week, that's the pink meaty, (allegedly), foodstuff, not the stuff that arrives in your email inbox. I'm not sure it deserves a whole week, or more than a short paragraph. Time's precious and I'm not sure I'd want to just fritter it away!

Today had so much potential to be bright and spangly. Sadly the mist clung on all day and the nasty little cooling north easterly kept most folks in the pub. Still, there was no rain and it was bright in parts. How we long for more hardy visitors.

After Cornwall's undoubted successes in the food sector of late, it's nice to see that beer is pulling up its shirt sleeves to get in on the act. A micro, (presumably), brewery in Crowlas just won best beer at Tewkesbury Beer Festival; St Austell has formed a deal with the 'boy' band, Fisherman's Friends, that will see the brewery broke by year end – free beer for the boys – and the nettle beer dispute with the Revenue men will catapult it to international notoriety.

The British Beer & Pub Association is throwing in their tuppence worth as well, asking the Government to hold off taxing beer at the next budget. Apparently there are around a million people that depend on beer for work; I know what they mean; I can't work without it either.

*March 17th – Thursday* – Another corking morning with the beach looking resplendent in all that clear sunshine. And despite it coming to rain in the afternoon it seems we are very much on the cusp of spring.

And being on the cusp of spring, we have daffs blossoming in the hedgerows, gorse flowers starting to show through and the spring-like sounds of dumper trucks running up the hill and drilling in the harbour.

Yes, this is the time of year when anyone who wants to do any building does so, either to be ready for the season or to avoid the seasonal crush. One such project has started at the foot of Stonechair Lane. A big hole is being dug and the Diary, being the interested organ that it is, is looking into it. The narrow access means only a small dumper truck can be used to cart away the large rocks and soil being excavated. There will, no doubt, be a groove worn in the road up the hill by the time they've finished.

The doughty lads from The Cove also are hard at work in the harbour, repointing the wall between tides and pouring concrete into the potholes in the western slip. We shall all be looking bright and shiny for the new season when it gets here.

There will be a short hiatus in production for the next few days, I'm afraid. The Diary is sending its top, (often spelt o-n-l-y), respondent on a tax payer funded fact finding mission overseas. Facts such as, 'is Guinness still black' and, 'are there still lots of bars in Dublin', will be fully researched using our reporter's finely honed investigative skills? Before you all go rushing off to complain to your MP about waste of taxpayers' money I should point out that it is this taxpayer who is footing the bill for this essential probe, more's the pity.

And just remember that begorrah is probably something created by an Irish Frankenstein.

*March 16th – Wednesday –* An absolutely beautiful start to the day, although still misty in The Cove, the sun breaking into a lovely big blue sky; certainly the best looking day of the year so far.

Nevertheless, a sombre day as it is the funeral of Martin who was, for many years, manager and landlord of the OS. He suffered a debilitating condition that saw him off rather earlier than is natural: a sorry loss of a first class chap.

We shall leave it to that for today, I think.

*March 18th – Friday –* It has  been some years since this correspondent has taken to the air, at least in powered flight. I recall the old Flanders and Swann gag that if God had intended us to fly, he would never have given us the railways.

Since they haven't built an Irish Sea tunnel yet I was left with little choice. I have to say the new aeroplanes these days are quite something: one set of wings and enclosed cabin. This one still had propellers, though, which was comforting.

Having been so long grounded the veritable joys of passing through an airport have thankfully eluded me. The last thing I expected was the controls placed upon fluids. This requires the passenger to ensure all liquids are carried in containers of less than 100 millilitres. When was the last time you saw a bottle of shampoo that small. Even then all these small containers must be put in a clear bag. Yup, I didn't have one of those either.

It was fortunate indeed that I was the last one through the security channel, as those behind me would have been huffing and puffing at my ineptness. They, no doubt, would have been doubly irritated by my ignorance of the sharp pointy things rules too.

My bag was minutely inspected, as the x-ray machine revealed to the watcher some more hidden contraband. It wasn't until the third time of scanning, that I felt it might be helpful to ask what it was they were looking for.

The small pair of beard trimming scissors has resided in my wash bag for almost as long as I can remember, except that I had forgotten they were there. Even had I remembered, it would not have occurred to me that they posed any sort of threat to anything more robust that thick stubble.

I was let off the hook and allowed to keep my scissors and my toothbrush on the condition that I didn't clean my teeth in a threatening manner. On the upside, my wash bag now glows in the dark.

Dublin was bathed in sunshine, we found, after an uneventful flight. The fast bus into town dropped me off around a mile from the hotel, so I managed a little sight-seeing, and a quick drop into Toners bar for a bit of a pit stop on the way. When I got there, the hotel looked a little posh, a converted Dublin town house and would have been ideal if my travel agent hadn't cancelled my room. So while the travel agent blamed the booking agent, and the booking agent blamed the hotel, I stood and considered which park bench would be most comfortable.

Two and a half hours later, with my patience lying in the gutter alongside my will to live, I was bustled off to another hotel. Having already walked some distance I was utterly delighted to understand that the new place was more than a mile away and far, far away from anything that vaguely resembled a shop, eatery or, heaven forefend, a drinking establishment. Oh, but it was right beside the new Lansdowne Road stadium, The Aviva.

I am sure that one day I'll look back with amusement at this little misadventure. Right now however, I am teetering on the brink. The slightest infringement of excellence in customer service will tonight, be met with retribution on a biblical scale – providing the infringer is a good bit smaller than me.

So far from civilisation am I, that a train trip is required to get me back into the city. I shall spare you the gruesome detail, but it involved the visitation of many of Dublin's landmark buildings, all of them bars.

*March 19th – Saturday* – Let me tell you something about Dublin bars since I have already spent so much time in them.

First if you are under five feet six inches you will find it very hard to get served. In most of the bars the counter top will be above your head. The stools, of which there will be many, will require a ladder to mount. Hence on a rainy day you might hear the phrase, 'a grand day for the high stool'.

Most of the famous bars are maintained in the condition that you might have found them over 100 years ago or so; years of nicotine staining on the ceilings and the walls, (which, presumably, now has to be manufactured), dark wood, mirrors and gas lamps. They ooze atmosphere.

The service is also exemplary. Before deregulation, a few years ago, you could only be a Dublin barman after a seven year apprenticeship. This ethic still clings on in most of the bars and even in the busiest, where you have to fight your way through the door, you are never kept waiting more than a few seconds.

As if to underline my point I trekked out to Dalkey this morning, on the train they call the Dart, hereabouts. Here there is a gem of a bar, more of which later.

Dalkey is a seaside town and I need a seaside fix on a frequent basis having moved to The Cove. Strangely it was not as I remembered it, and the town was not exactly by the sea, and there was no sign saying, 'to the beach'.

A hunger pang had commenced on the train to Dalkey, so the need for some solids had come upon me. The first choice, a bakery on the main street, (see I can do non-bars too), was small and full so I elected a side street café that was also busy but had a free table. I settled for eggs on toast with additional bacon. This arrived as hard fried eggs on toast, whose relationship with the toaster was sadly brief and unrequited. The dry rashers faired no better in exciting my appetite. I hadn't tried the coffee yet; can you muck up black coffee?

So, with tummy suitably lined it would have been rude not to sample the local culture. Down a side street there is a bar with a very unassuming, single storey frontage. It is called The Club and if here, you really must.

I shall try and be brief here as there is much yet to tell you. My hand written notes, (yes, I can write too) run to a page and a half on this bar; it really was that stunning.

Through the doors the bar opens to a cathedral of a place, with vaulting ceiling panelled in painted glass with large decorated beams. The walls alternate with ornate mirrors and wood columns, and the bar area floor is a mosaic. The bar itself is substantial and is ranged with big heavy high chairs. From the ceiling hang immense lamps, and a gallery leans out over the bar area, walled with wrought iron. The lounge, with parquet floor, of course, is

293

sumptuous and there is a member's bar off to the side, slightly raised and screened.

The toilets, I'm sorry but I have to mention the toilets, match the ornateness of the bar, with Victorian wall tiles and big chunky porcelain. Everything, from the front door to here, is immaculately clean.

Ok, so it's back to Lansdowne Road to try and do something about getting a ticket for the game. Someone said that there were some likely bars in Ballsbridge, (no snickering at the back, there), but 'twas a wild goose chase.

I had resigned myself to watch the game from the hotel bar, from where I could hear the roar of the crowd in the stadium. Just as the national anthems were being played, a chap ran into the bar clutching a handful of tickets, 20 euros each, if you please.

Were they real, I asked? Of course, said he. Only one way to find out methinks and charged off in the direction of the appointed gate with my hot ticket in hand.

Now the appointed gate just so happens to be on the other side of the stadium, twenty minutes' walk I was told. This is where all those hikes with the bleddy hound come into play – fit as a fiddle, me. It is unfortunate that fiddles aren't known for three quarter mile dashes so at this end of it I was fair near on my knees. Having a tense few moments, while the genuineness of my ticket was checked, gave me sufficient time to establish that the seat was at the top of the stadium. Worth every gasp as I was right on the half way line with a bird's eye view – priceless – and only 20 euros for a 90 euros ticket.

Ok, so we lost the game. But that wasn't the point of travelling here. It was to be here, and in the stadium, to watch an Ireland versus England Rugby Football match. Been there, done that.

I shall not bore you with the after match scrum, the endless replaying every mistake and error. Suffice it to say, it was everything I expected it to be, and more. The city was alive with throngs and thronging voices in happy song, whichever side you supported.

*March 20th – Sunday* – A late awakening, unsurprisingly. The rain, that inconveniently fell last night, had  long gone and it was another bright and spangly day.  It was time to head off to Malahide for some more seaside; so that is why I am  writing this in Howth, which is where the train was going instead.

Think St Ives with lots of open space and trawlers, rather than under 10's.

Down on the little quay there is a line of fancy fish restaurants and fishmongers, with fancy menus and fancy prices. Good luck to them they were busy enough. On the opposite side, all the trawlers were tied up alongside, and groups of people were looking down into the water between the boats. Just had to go and see what they were looking at - seals. Four or five spaced out between the boats just sitting in the water looking up, and the people looking down. It was hard to tell who had come to look at whom. "It's a quiet Sunday, let's go and look at the daft people lined up on the quay".

I walked all along the sea front and not a bar in sight. This can't be the only place in Ireland that doesn't have a bar, surely? No, up the hill a little way and the bar I chose had an empty seat beside me. This is the empty bar stool that is clearly reserved for the looney that wants to talk to you. Now, sitting next to the looney in the bar, in a strange place is one thing, sitting next to the looney in the bar who has a thick Dub accent is quite another.

The usual defence is to nod a lot and try and say yes in the right places. This strategy tends to lose its effectiveness when you constantly have to ask the looney to repeat himself several times first.

Exit stage left to another establishment, and hope the looney doesn't follow you. The Cock Tavern was definitely the place to be, and with steep steps leading up to the door, that you'd hope would deter any half cut looney from attempting the climb.

I'd been harbouring dark thoughts since my little wander up the quay. They had been brooding all the while, or is that breeding? Either way they were increasing in volume.

Oysters! I believe I've mentioned my little penchant for the slippery little bi-valves before. As time progressed the desire grew and the shop down on the front selling them drew me to it. And a very fine experience it was too with half a dozen West Coast natives, dowsed in a little lemon and Tabasco. Bleddy lovely!

I ended up missing the train I had intended to get, so popped into the very touristy, Bloody Stream bar and turned my ear to a bit of live music that was being offered. And why you may ask, as indeed did I, is the bar named the Bloody Stream? Because that is the name of the river over which the bar was built, of course, and over its door is this sparkling bit of advice, *"When money is tight and hard to get, and your horse is also ran, .. a pint of plain is your only man.*" Thank you, Mr O'Brien, for that.

And as a finalish note for this page, a trip into town and into the very fine Shelbourne Hotel for a splendid little g&t. Sure, the English masters have gone now but this establishment persists, its mix of art deco and Victorian splendour just about holding out against the backdrop of the genteel St Stephen's Green. And they let me in.

*March 21st – Monday* – Now, if you've been waiting for four days for this page to appear on your screen go immediately to March the 18th and start reading from there.

It is, at last, home time. An earlyish start and a bus trip back up to the airport and wave goodbye to the old town and its famous bars.

The Missus tells me that the earlier flights of the day had been delayed, due to fog at Newquay. Fortunately mine left on time.

You may, if your memory is keen, remember that this little jaunt was not a frivolous venture. You may have received the opinion that all I did was frequent the famous bars of Dublin and enjoy myself. Au contraire, this finely tuned reporting brain was never for a second off duty, no, not for a moment.

I can confirm that I did indeed seek out the facts that I so earnestly sought. Guinness is still black, and Dublin certainly sports a fair number of excellent drinking establishments. I'm sure there was a longer list of facts I had to report but for the life of me I can't remember a single one. How very odd.

No odder though than getting home and finding a cuckoo in our little nest. We are playing host to a wanderer from out of town and another two bleddy hounds.

I wonder when the next flight back to Dublin is.

*March 22nd – Tuesday* – Spring! And a sublime start to it as well, with the mist hanging off on the horizon and a nice big beach for most of the day.

The Missus took off with the dogs and the squatter down to the big beach and left me with the shop. My penance for four days in Dublin will be long and hard I imagine.

Then into the afternoon I started to feel unwell, with influenza type symptoms and other unsavoury aspects that I will, of course, spare you. Suffice it to say it has cured my cough.

It could have been a bug I picked up on the aeroplane; I've heard that happens, you know. Or it could be my body reacting to the sudden cessation of Guinness and other imbibements being poured into it. I think this very unlikely, since I was quite conservative with my consumption throughout the weekend, honest; although there has been a black elephant with a white head perched on the end of my bed the past few nights. If he's still there tomorrow morning I'm going to have to find out who he belongs to.

I've no doubt it will be short lived, my illness, that is, not the elephant as I believe they have an extended longevity, and I shall feel chipper again by morning.

If you are reading this at a reasonably hour this morning, it was and I am.

*March 23rd – Wednesday* – A little hazy this morning but when you have a morning this good what's a little haze. And what's more it stayed that way all day and even a stiff easterly couldn't put the dampers on it.

The first basking sharks of the season have been spotted off Newlyn by a few divers mucking around off the beach down there. This is a good two months prior to their usual arrival time and, no doubt, an indicator that the world is coming to and end.

And to reinforce this portent of doom, the supplier of the software that makes my website work has gone bust. Since I bought this software the world has moved on, to the brink it would appear, and the products that are available to replace it are far more complex, probably beyond my meagre capabilities.

It's not so much the selling of goods, it is production of The Diary that is at stake here. I am fortunate that I have much experience in the selection of commercial software, even then it is a labyrinth that I could well do without getting into.

So if one day you wake up and reach for your laptop, iPad, smart phone, or whatever web enabled device you employ and find and empty space where these jabberings normally reside, you will know why; presumably after breathing a sigh of relief that I have been silenced forever.

*March 24th – Thursday* – Another sparkling day in paradise only mildly tarnished by that stiff easterly. If you could find a bit of shelter from it, warmth and sunshine were all yours.

Bit of a shocker to hear that the Pandora Inn in Mylor has gone on fire. Sounds like half of Cornwall's fire brigade were there and the RNLI even got in on the act, transporting firemen up the river to help out. Looks like it fair near finished the place off.

In the meanwhile, the Finding Sanctuary project moves on apace, drawing up Marine Conservation Zones around the peninsula coast; there's a nice little map in the Cornishman this week. The problems rather appears to be that the areas they seem to be recommending for conservation are all fishing areas, and the fishing communities are concerned that their voices are not being heard. You have to say they seem to have a point when you see Mounts Bay, Lands End and St Ives Bay all pencilled in as no go zones, of one severity or another.

Talking of no go zones it seems many of the public toilets are under consideration for closure, as the local council cut backs bite. There is some hope, though. Some bright spark in Cornwall Council has suggested that 'SatLav' will provide some relief so to speak. For a small consideration you can have the location of the nearest convenience sent to your mobile telephone. Very useful, I'm sure, when, in the extremity of your need, you are informed the nearest lav', sat or not, is several miles away. No doubt there are commercial opportunities here too, such as including in the message the location of the nearest underwear shop.

And to finish off our day a little Lifeboat launch and a recovery up the short slip for a change. Now we haven't done that for a while.

*March 25th – Friday* – Woke with a start this morning; I thought someone had fitted me with a toupee over night, until I realised the bleddy hound was lying on my head.

Bit of cloud around this morning but still bright and that nasty easterly has died away. Later the clouds scuttled off and we had a right rip-snorter of a day, best of the year so far, very probably.

More signs of spring about such as the Scillonian starting regular trips from this Saturday, and the little man from our refrigeration company coming in to service our collection of fridges and freezers.

And you will be delighted to know the first fish order of the year and from The Cove at that. This, of course, heralds a fish reference in every Diary entry from now to the end of the season. Don't fret now; I'm only softening you up for when the axe falls and my web software keels over and dies.

For a footnote today, the very excellent Bucket Boys down at the OS tonight. The joint was jumping, I can tell you, together with a bunch of very disgruntled locals who are used to having the bar to themselves.

*March 26th – Saturday* – I don't know how much more of this good weather we can take. I mean it's just not natural. I thought we might be in for some normal weather first thing as the clouds were all over us but they soon cleared away and showed us a nice big blue sky. Even the mist that tried to come in mid-morning was hurriedly shown the door. It's just downright outrageous.

Had a hard job getting rid of the squatter this morning; she promised faithfully to begger off before 10.00 am but then there was the St Buryan farmers' market that she just had to visit and I'm sure the dogs just need one more run down on the beach. Must have been nigh on midday when we finally saw the back of her. Only kidding DG, mainly.

Our hearts took a little leap of excitement this morning at the sight of MT steaming out of the harbour with a boat full of pots. We understand that Big J will be following suit tomorrow, although it's likely to be another month before the crab and lobster start rolling in.

What with the pots going out, the Ice Cream Parlour opening today and a steady trickle of people down the road, The Cove is really coming alive. It would be nice to imagine this is the foothills of a stupendously fabulous season. Can but dream, can't we?

And so to the F&L again for a Welsh band, called the Navigators, (must have been lost), that travelled so far and gave us some good cheer this evening. They were fine and full of humour, as was the very camp hairdresser chap, who entertained us after the ball was over.

So let's drink to the spirit of gallantry and courage that made a strange heaven out of unbelievable hell, and let's drink that one day that this country of ours, that we love so much, will find dignity and greatness and peace again.

Great words, but sadly not mine. We salute Mr Noel Coward who shuffled off this day in 1973. Difficult to believe he was Cornish, isn't it?

*March 27th – Sunday* – That's more like it – some proper seasonal fog for a change; thick as a bag too, first thing – a real proper job. Met Office reckoned it would burn off by lunchtime, but it had other ideas and hung around all day, despite the sun making a brave attempt to break through a couple of times.

And it was first thing this morning too with this, 'clocks going forward' lark. The early morning Lifeboat exercise drew a few people in, but I imagine most were still languishing in bed. It was just as well my well-tuned, internal clock came up to scratch, as the one on my mobile telephone that says that it will change automatically, didn't.

Anyway that's the third person today who's been in the shop and said the bleddy hound's so cute they want to take her home. I wish they wouldn't tease so.

On the subject of taunts, there has been a regular line of people gleefully telling us that the weather in PZ is fabulous. Even a visitor from the top said it was two or three degrees warmer up there too. The final straw was when a lady, who I told it would be fine by lunchtime, scowled and told me it had been fine in Porthcurno all day, as well.

I'd quite forgotten the MO's track record in this area. I'm going to have to hone my weather forecasting skills; they've obviously gone off over the winter.

*March 28th – Monday* – Still a bit misty this morning but a far better proposition than yesterday; nice day for a picnic, perhaps.

Not that we'd want you to disappear elsewhere, but Kynance has been voted the UK's number one spot for having a picnic. However, it is unlikely that many people will turn up. Some idle party with plenty of money, and clearly nothing better to do with it, has polled a group of potential al fresco eaters by asking  if they fancied a picnic. Apparently sixty per cent said that they would love to, but are put off by wasps and the like, and a bit afraid of getting dirt and sand in their sandwiches. Fussy beggers, ain't we?

Cornwall has put its hand up to become a 'living laboratory' for natural energy, so Tim German the Council's energy boss tells us. He reckons we have the best resources for it: solar, we have the best sun in the country; hot rock, we have the hottest rocks; wave energy, we have the biggest waves and wind. Yes, we have more wind than anyone else too.

It seems Cornwall will soon have a sustainable energy probe stuck in every part of it, including where the wind comes from. Someone should have a word in Tim's ear – never volunteer.

Experts fear the adder population is in decline, with development breaking up their traditional breeding grounds. They obviously haven't been down here. An adder was spotted down Stonechair this month, and we're overrun with the blighters during summer time.

I actually got my act together today and put some effort in getting our little boat ready for sale. I'd quite forgotten how heavy it and its engine were, so I was grateful to be able to rest my aching back when we closed. Just got settled when next door rang to ask if I could help take a chest of drawers up the top.

Went to print my advertisement for the boat after tea and my printer broke down. Does life get any better than this?

*March 29th – Tuesday* – We had some rain overnight, and we seemed to be threatened with some more for most of the day. It wasn't until late afternoon that it brightened up.

As a result we were much quieter than of late, which was really just as well, since the few people who did turn up looked rather askance at my blackened fingers.

I mentioned I had a problem with my printer last night. It stems from the fact that all the ink that doesn't find its way on to the paper, ends up at the bottom of the printer in a big sponge. When the sponge is full that's the end of your printer, unless you recourse to clever instructions on the Internet that tell you how to remove and clean the sponge.

The particular instructions I found were very good. Although, as recommended, I wore gloves, by the time I had removed the sharp metal mechanism of the printer my gloves had been subtly punctured, and sucked up ink into the fingers. Not only that, but the sponge was so old it fell to pieces while being washed.

I have spent the morning looking for a new printer.

Had a visit by two lovely ladies from the Indian sub-continent today. This in itself was not unusual; we have visitors from all over the globe here throughout the year, (cosmopolitan us, I told you). What was unusual, was that one of them was very interested in our pillboxes. I had to ask twice in case I'd misheard her heavy accent. She was only a young thing too, and said she'd seen a reference on the Internet.

I took her outside to show her the two you can see from the shop. She was singularly unimpressed. Perhaps pillbox means designer clothes shop in Hindustani.

Despite our brightening up we didn't see a surge in customers so I repaired to the OS, where I lost at cards. My championship run apparently over, I best do some work for a living.

*March 30th – Wednesday* – Tempus fugit! Or, as literally translated from the Welsh: time flies like an arrow; fruit flies like a banana.

It is a letter day, so red, you could make post boxes out of it, a day so momentous I'm surprised they haven't written a folk song about it. Nothing will be quite the same ever again, although what is written about it may well be very much the same.

It's not that it rained this morning, or that the sun came out briefly in the afternoon, or even that the mist descended upon us before evening drew in. Nor is it that Goya and Van Gogh shared a birthday today, albeit 107 years apart. These things are mere passing instances, hardly memorable at all.

In the words of the great Rolf Harris, 'can you see what it is yet?'

Okay, I'll stop teasing now. The Diary is one year old today. Although there were a few entries prior, this day marks 365 consecutive entries, in fact this will be the 366th, I think. Well you count them, then.

This was supposed to be an experiment. Whether I continue will have to be seen. I suspect since little changes here the entries will look rather similar to their previous year counterparts.

Now for the book, and the film of the book; I can't wait to see Claudia Winkleberry slapping her forehead over this one. What a girl!

*March 31st – Thursday* – Oh, all right then, I'll carry on for a bit.

Naturally we were all a bit jaded this morning. The anniversary party did go on a bit, well at least until 10.00 pm when it was bed time.

Woke up to a bit of a gale going on and a bit of rain in the air; fortunately it was pushing in from the south west or thereabouts and was much worse on top and the other side. First time in a while that we have had a bit of sea running too; I tell you, that's a lot of bits.

All this inclementness hasn't done much for the business. We were much busier last week, but at least we've had some time to finish the storeroom cleaning and make ready for the first big rush of the year - we sincerely hope.

There might be an even bigger storm brewing too. I have just heard that the Government has thrown out Cornwall Council's £62 million proposal to upgrade the Isles of Scilly link. Apparently it is a tad too ambitious and should be scaled back. On the face of it the decision looks a little naughty, as both the last Government and the current gave the plan the ok in principle. Although a little past the ides of March, I do suspect a little Julius moment in there somewhere – allegedly.

Fortunately a plan B has been held back against such an eventuality – trippers visiting Scilly next year, will be able to experience the natural environmental features such as seals, dolphins and basking sharks, at a much slower pace, as they row their gig across.

I see that St Austell wasted no time at all in putting up their already exorbitant beer prices in the OS. It has resolved the question over where to go tonight after Lifeboat practice, though; up the top for a pound a pint.

Skinners, in their indomitable style, have prepared a special brew for the forthcoming Royal nuptials. They've named it *Kate Loves Willy* and at 62p a pint, (1982 prices), who can blame her.

# The Last Word

In the big city, a smoke filled lounge in St James' all green leather and cut crystal tumblers. Two gentlemen sit opposite each other in wing-backed chairs. One casts a booklet down on the highly polished mahogany table in a derisory fashion.

"That's it then, Caruthers."

"What, what. Finished, what."

"Yes, Caruthers, all that writing finished. Seems like the chap just ran out of days."

"Utter poppycock, what."

"Yes, Caruthers. Someone once said everyone has at least one book in them. It's just that for some people that's where it ought to stay, eh, eh."

"Yes, very droll, Smithers, what. Let's hope it's just one, eh."

"Bad news, Caruthers. Just been looking at this world wide web jobby. The blighter has a web place called world wide web dot old boathouse dot com or somesuch. Already started on the next one, old chap."

"Gadzooks, Smithers. Someone's got to stop him.

"What do you recommend, Caruthers? Letter to the PM?"

"No use, old chap. Eton boy, you know. Churchill, different kettle of kedgeree altogether. Harrow, you know."

"Nothing for it then, Caruthers. Simpson. Bring the brandy."